JOY OF LIFE ...

A MODERN Odyssey

About the Author

Jean-Christian de Mons was born 1941 in Breslau, former Germany, now Wroclaw, Poland. After the escape from the Russians he spent his early period in Lower Saxony/West Germany. The military service at the Air Force followed the attendance of the Hotel Academy and then the practical formation in the hotel business.

He joined the merchant navy working as steward on cruise ships followed by receptionist jobs in several renowned European hotels before being called to Mozambique/Portuguese S/E Africa by his granduncle to become a citrus farmer. The agitated situation that ended in the civil war induced him to return to Europe.

For over three decades he served as chief steward for Lufthansa German Airlines. He invested much time to learn some additional exotic languages besides English and French and completed a management course and learned flying. As counsellor he joined the production of two documentary movies in China. With his Korean wife he is living now near Weilburg/Lahn in Germany.

Jean-Christian de Mons

JOY OF LIFE ...
A MODERN Odyssey

Bibliografische Information der Deutschen Nationalbibliothek

Die Deutsche Nationalbibliothek verzeichnet diese Publikation in der Deutschen Nationalbibliografie; detaillierte bibliografische Daten sind im Internet über http://dnb.d-nb.de abrufbar.

Satz, Umschlaggestaltung und Verlag: BoD · Books on Demand GmbH, Überseering 33, 22297 Hamburg, bod@bod.de
Druck: Libri Plureos GmbH, Friedensallee 273, 22763 Hamburg

ISBN: 978-3-7693-7460-5

This title is dedicated to Jeffrey J. Osbun, Los Angeles and Christopher E. Vale, Cook Islands, New Zealand.

All my friends urged me to write a second book following my first title/autobiography * ON THE RUN ... childhood memories from 1944 – 55 *, because they thought it to have been so exciting and extraordinary circumstances that I'll mention later on gave me a lot of time to oblige and start writing again. I wish you much pleasure while reading it!

***

What kind of headaches are involved for young people when presented with the question of what to do after having left high school.

I decided to start an apprenticeship with a Public Relation Company, but allowed me some time to consider the matter while doing my voluntary 18month's military service at the German Air Force. If my test had been satisfactory I would have extended my service time to 7 years to be trained as a Jet pilot, but my right eye did not pass the check.

As alternative I decided to take a course of medical orderly after the obligatory basic infantry training. That was mostly done by hard drilling sergeants who had still served in WWII. Unforgettable were the so called *fancy-dress-balls*, when we at some unpredicted time were suddenly woken up with an alarm whistle and ordered to get dressed and assemble outside with ready assault luggage within 10 minutes!!! Officially it was called *NATO ALARM*. Often that was followed by an orientation march that lasted into the late morning.

The digging of trenches was an easy matter, because the area near the North Sea was sandy. There was also an historical relic from WWII, a rocket launcher for the V2 that had destroyed so much in London.

1960 was for farmers a very bad year. So our commanders decided to assist the farmers in harvesting especially wheat and rye. Soldiers all over Germany were sent to the countryside to do their best.

The same happened when the Elbe river endangered by inundation Hamburg and its surrounding got assistance by the soldiers especially for piling up sandbags.

After the basic training I was called for a longer lasting medical course of instruction. After I had successfully passed the test I was sent to Fürstenfeldbruck Air Base near Munich. It had just been taken over from the US-Air force with all its amenities. I was assigned to the troops physician's assistant responsible for the patients files.

In that time exercises followed that we fully equipped trained battle like situations. In one case I happened upon a team of medical orderlies to participate in a flight with a DC3 Dacota air plane. Later I experienced a mission of several weeks in the NATO-headquarter in Fontainebleau near Paris. After my return to Fürstenfeldbruck I was sent to another medical course to Munich. When having completed it successfully I was allocated to the Air Force Medical Institute in Fürstenfeldbruck Air Base.

It was equipped with a low pressure chamber to test the ability of jet-pilots to endure attitudes of over 30.000 feet = 10.000 meters. At this time a longer lasting NATO-alarm was announced. The reason were the tensions between the western powers and the Warsaw Pact nations especially the Soviet Union. It was triggered by the stationing of middle range rockets by the Soviets in Cuba. By the coming around of the Soviet leader N. Krushchev a WWIII could be avoided. In this situation an extension of my service time was ordered.

In the meantime I had changed my professional plans and booked a course at the Hotel Academy at Bad Reichenhall/Bavaria. Theory and practise were exacting but presented much fun and mediated the flair of the international world. One of my best colleagues Christine Prager was the daughter of the manager of the at that time very fashionable Swiss *Mövenpick* Restaurant chain. My professional course was followed by a regular formation at the distinguished 5-Star *Ritters Park Hotel* in the famous Spa Bad Homburg v.d.H. near Frankfurt/Main. By coincidence my aunt and later my grandparents came to live there.

Having finished my formation I applied for a job as steward in the First Class of the Cruise ship *MS Hanseatic* of the Hamburg-America-Line.

This ship had the size of the tragically sunken *Titanic* and had served before WWII as *Empress of Japan* on the Pacific route between Vacouver, Yokohama and Shanghai and as a troop carrier during the war. After a general overhaul the new baptized *Hanseatic* was put in service as cruise ship mainly in the Caribbeans, Madeira and in the Eastern Mediterranean Sea.

On my first trip I went to New York with many prominent people in the First Class. Then we continued our voyage along the Eastern coastline of the United States to Fort Lauderdale/Florida. From there we started our cruise through the magic archipelago of the Caribbeans. As there were no passport controls anywhere I got the idea to go to the post offices to get the necessary stamps into my passport to prove that I have been there. In addition to my regular passport I had a seaman's book that served me as document for ship crew in all harbours of the world.

Haiti had once been a prosperous black kingdom of free former slaves. At the time of our visit at Port-au-Prince it was still an exotic pearl compared with the presently impoverished country.

***

Haïti.

Roi Henri Christophe de Haïti

Henri Christophe was born as a slave on the British Caribbean island Grenada. He was a participant at a massacre under the sugar Barons and escaped unharmed finding a new home in Haiti at that time a florishing French colony. He started his career as an equerry and later restaurant owner. A friendship with an American lawyer from Boston was very helpful who improved his general knowledge. When the ideas of the French revolution expanded and finally also reached the slave quarters of the island an insurrection spread like an conflagration over Haiti. The ownwers of the sugar and cocoa plantations were killed or expelled and the garrisons were systematically wiped out. Henri joined the black army and became soon a respected leader and organizer.

1802 he was promoted to a Brigade-General. When Napoleon declared the independence of the colony Henry decided with his partner Petion to eliminate the dictatorship of Dessalines at

Port au Prince and claimed the Northern part of the Island for himself. With strict measures and established law and order in the chaotic land. The agriculture flourished under his guiding hands and most of the export was going to the Northern states of America that admired him for his ability. 1811 Henri established a hereditary monarchy but never forgot his humble origin. For many decisions King Frederick II. of Prussia in Europe served as his ideal. The "Code Henri" was an adaption of the Prussian law. For public works like streets, schools, public buildings and the fortifications the whole population was brought into action. The gold currency "Gourd" was a symbol for a sound economy. With strict measures his Majesty carries through his plans. The return of the French colonial power, a second enslavement or a rebellion of his subjects tormented him. At the zenith of his achievements and esteem he got very sick and lapsed into depression. At the end he committed suicide with a silver bullet from a pistol near his castle he had named "Sanssouci".

***

When the German cartographer Waldseemüller, who gave the new continent after the reports of the Genovese sailor, explorer and merchant Amerigo Vespucci the name AMERICA. He was also busy drawing a map of the Caribbean islands. That one besides Hispaniola was named after San Juan and the port-city Puerto Rico. When the maps were printed the worker in charge exchanged by mistake both names and from that time the island's name became Puerto Rico and its capital city San Juan. The most Southern wards islands of the Antilles are Trinidad and Tobago. Their ownership changed frequently but remained finally an English colony. The cultivation of the sugar cane plantations required many good workers. Instead of importing slaves from West-Africa the governor decided to hire reliable and experienced workers from Bengal in East-India. Because of the better living conditions and the pleasant climate most of them remained there after their working contract had been fulfilled. As a consequence Hindi was taught besides English and Spanish at the schools. Like in Rio de Janeiro they celebrate carnival in a colourful and turbulent manner.

St. Martin/San Marten had often changed ownership until one day two ships with religious refugees landed at the same time on the island. In spite of starting to fight against each other with weapons the leaders found a clever solution. The two groups choose from their midst two runners. The lot decided that the French one was sent to the North and the Dutch one to the South to run along the coastline. From where both met on the other side of the island a straight line was drawn to the starting point.

The French got the northern part and the Dutch the Southern one and everybody was happy. Together they celebrate the French national day on the 14th of July and the Dutch the birthday of King William-Alexander on April 27th.

The Super-Powers, the UNO and the many conflict parties on that tormented globe should take an example at this human way of solving political problems.

The existence of countless Spanish treasure galleons carrying gold and silver to Spain, made the Caribbeans a paradise for pirates, corsairs and filibusters. There was a time when the pirates choose the island of St. Croix to create their own state. One of the most prominent and notorious pirates was captain Morgan who plundered Spanish treasure galleons by order of the english Queen Elizabeth I. the *Virgin Beth*, who participated fairly at the booty. As reward for his faithful services for the crown he was appointed governor of the island Jamaica.

Half of the Virgin Island group was formerly a Danish colony. The capital of the central island still bears the Danish name "Charlotte Amalie". Now it is US-American territory. 1917 the US congress acquired this islands for strategic reasons for the ridiculous price of 25 Million US $ from Denmark. The Eastern part remained however in the British Empire.

The largest island Cuba remained most of the time in Spanish hands, until it came in its younger colonial time into US-American influence. A pseudo Republic was established that developed into an US-dependent military dictatorship. After many political disasters the mass of the people rose 1959 under the leadership of

Fidel Castro, a former lawyer. After a lasting civil war a socialist system was established that still exists today 2024. As the only island in the Caribbeans Cuba has an extended railway system that serves mainly to transport sugar cane, tobacco and other agricultural products. Because of the continuous embargo and import stop the cars in Cuba are still well maintained museum pieces from the early 50th and preponderant American brands.

A very strange Antilles island is Saba. It consists of a huge volcano that rises straight from the sea. The other volcano island is Montserrat. The Southern part with its capital city Plymouth was covered by ashes during a tremendous eruption in 1990. It is considered as the Caribbean Pompei. Not only in Jamaica but also here you can enjoy the warm hearted calypso music and the sound of the ingenious steel pans.

Especially I liked both French overseas departments Martinique and the butterfly shaped Guadeloupe with French ambience, flair and culture.

From here came originally the Empress Josephine Beauharnaise, the first wife of Napoleon Bonaparte. Like in the Dutch colony of Aruba near the coast of Colombia the € is the local currency. It might be interesting to find out how often all those islands have changed their languages and their ownership.

Apart from the exotic nature and endless fine beaches the Caribbeans have something for level-headed investors. South of Western Cuba are the small Cayman islands. They are still a British colony like Nassau Bahamas, but are a *Tax Heaven*. Revenue tax on income, savings, profits, inheritances, wages and sales do not exist. The authorities are happy with taxes on imports, licenses and tourist hotels. The island is a place for countless international anonymous post office box companies and banks, to hide money from the greedy governments at home.

Rather bothersome are the frequent hurricanes from July on which hit often the Southern regions of the United States and the archipelagos Nassau Bahamas and the Bermudas.

On our trip from New York back to Germany there was again some prominence on board that preferred the several days lasting exciting and comfortable voyage with the glamorous "Hanseatic" from the flight with the Lufthansa "Super Constellation". Back home I changed my shipping company and applied for a job as steward on the "MS Schwabenstein" of The North German Lloyd, Bremen. This semi First class & mixed cargo ship served some regular ports on its final destination Yokohama/Japan. Other ports were served on special demand. The 80 First Class guests were boarding the ship in Southampton and Antwerp. Most were owners of land holdings in Malaysia and Batavia for rubber and cocos plantations. The "MS Schwabenstein" always served the ports of Penang/Malaysia, Hong Kong and Yokohama. All others like Pusan/South Korea, Shanghai, Kaosiung/Taiwan, Manila/Philippines, Singapore, Colombo/Ceylon were only served on special order. Shanghai was still hermetically closed for foreigners except seamen.

At one occasion we were on the road of Bugo/Mindanao/Philippines to pick up the whole production of a local pineapple factory. Since there did not exist a harbor the packed canned pineapples were sent by rafts and flatboats to the ship and hoisted on board with our own derricks.

Just for fun we asked our cook for some pork meat and happened to get with the help of a hook some smaller sharks and let them rot at the hot side of the vessel to get some skeletons to sell to passengers or tradesmen.

When we passed home bound the Suez Canal the ships were invaded by merchants during their waiting time in the Bitter Sea. The traders accepted all kinds of currency, even coins for their touristic goods and exchanged the coins on other ships into banknotes ... very clever dealers.

Once I experienced a heavy storm in the Gulf of Vizcaya and was nearly swallowed by the ocean while trying to reach the chinese laundry at the stern of the ship. On one occasion we landed in Kaohsiung/Southern Taiwan where we got some cargo to load. All work at the port came to a stand still for 3 days because the nation celebrated the "Double Ten Day"(10th of Oct. 1911) when the Manchu Dynasty was abolished and the modern Chinese Republic was inaugurated by Dr. Sun, Yat Sen from Canton. Even the President Marshall Chiang Kai-Chek was present and made a speech at the city hall, promising the refugees from mainland China, who were still living in shacks, to provide them with decent living quarters.

In spite of the masses of people I loved Hongkong. There was always such incomparable vitality of the people who wanted to achieve something in life under the protection of the British crown and government. After we had docked a tailor came on board to collect orders from the crew that were executed overnight or in 2 days. From that time nearly 60 years ago I have owned silk shirts with my Chinese name/logo on the breast pocket and a lovely stitched silken dressing-gown.

After some Far Eastern turns I decided to return to the international Hotel business. But before starting to work again I took some holidays in Berlin where I stayed with my mother, who was taking care of the household of her sister who accompanied her husband on a lecture trip through some Universities of the USA. He was the dean of the Free University. Everyday I took the dachshund "Rody" to leisurely explore the fascinating city. I always started my excursions at the distinguished Café Kranzler and the begin of the Kurfürstendamm, the prominent leisure promenade of Western Berlin. One day, while taking a walk with dachshund "Rody" along the wall I was approached by an unsuspected person that asked me for an address of an American intelligence service. After some phone calls I got the correct address and accompanied him after having treated him with a beer and potato salad. He seemed to trust me and revealed to me, that he was the driver of the feared and dreadful Minister of Justice Hilde Benjamin just escaped through a secret tunnel to the West. At his connection with her had collected some informations that might interest the Americans. At the reception we were separated and never met him again. A well educated officer asked me how I had met that person and interrogated me about my professional and familiar background and checked everything through the authorities. I was proved to be clean. When I told him about my relatives who had been hanged in 1944 as members of the German resistance he became very interested. He knew the names of my relative, the Counts of Schulenburg. One had been the last German ambassador in Moscow. He asked me if I had any interest in working for the American CIA. They were always looking for experienced young people for this pretentious job. I explained to him that I detested spending my future life mostly in hiding. That was my only encounter with the CIA. We wished each other "Good Luck" and said goodbye leaving behind a file of myself in the archives.

Then I decided to improve my French and to study at the Alliance Francaise in Paris. In my spare time I worked as a receptionist at the Grand Hotel Opera, to which belonged the famous "Café de la Paix".

In streaming rain and bad sight I arrived in the city and stuck tight in "Les Halle's" the former night market and "stomach" of Paris. After having safely parked my "Healy" between cases with cauliflower and other vegetables I took my umbrella and went in search of a cheap accommodation. The owner of a bistro informed me that he had a room but just for about four weeks. In this time I would have enough time to look for something convenient. I accepted the offer.

The room was a surprise for me: wallpaper, curtains and bedcover … everything was in pink colour and mirrors were everywhere even at the ceiling. The best was the spacious bathroom and an iron wrought balcony from where I could observe the milling crowds especially at the lively night market. A very funny situation. My room belonged to an hourly hotel where the nightly butterflies were residing. The owner of my room was away for some weeks in the countryside to expect and arrange the care of her baby. In the following weeks I happened to meet all the other Ladies when coming home from the Grand Hotel Opera taking my "Coup de Rouge or my Calva" in the bistro. All were very nice helping me to improve my colloquial French and exchanging views.

"Les Halle's" were at that time the eccentric playground for night revelers.

There existed two Restaurants where workers in blue garb mixed with Opera guests in smoking, traders and members of the haute volée. They had funny names:*Le chien qui fume* (the smoking dog) and *Le pied de couchon* (the leg of the pork).

Even when I had found a simple but expensive room on the "Ile Saint Louis" I passed my bistro in "Les Halle's" when coming from or going to my working place when it was not raining. I was always greeted by some of my former "guardian angels" who were not busy with a happy hello.

My distinguished "Stresemann" receptionist outfit was specially noticed by the customers of the Ladies who were curious to know who I was and found it extremely funny when they heard that I formerly used to reside there. The nice occupant of my pink room had given birth to a healthy boy and ceded it to an appreciative childless couple in the countryside.

After some time I gave up my expensive room on the Île Saint Louis and moved to the Seine gauche at the Quartier Latin where also many students of the Sorbonne and the École Polytechnic were living. The "Jardin des Plantes" (Botanical Garden) and the

"Pantheon", where all famous French people are honoured, are nearby my new lodgement.

My Institute, the "Alliance Francaise", was not far away. My simple "Hotel Normandy" was paid monthly in advance. The single window was a little bit oblique but closed firmly. I fitted my room to my requirements: The upper side of the wall was crossed by a water pipeline. There I installed two hooks and hung there an always blown up air mattress "for any case". There was no table! I improvised and got a fitting board to cover the wash-basin. So I could place my utensils there to prepare myself some hot water for tea and write on my knees. My suitcase was placed on top of the wardrobe. Outside was a combined Turkish WC with a shower. The oriental WC had to be used in a hovering position. To use the shower one simply folded down a wooden grill and pulled the chain to operate the shower. French luxury.

Nearby my habitation were plenty of cheap student bistros/restaurants. With my student card I could use the mensa of the Sorbonne. In the Grand Hotel was a staff canteen. So provision was no problem. In any case I had a delicious round hard-cheese from "Les Halle's" in a cotton bag placed on the window sill. A bakery was just around the corner where I could get a fresh crispy baguette. Those, who knew Paris well were acquainted with the run down area at the Rive Gauche, where the Tunisians, Algerians, Marocains and other Arabs used to live. There I dined frequently and enjoyed fritters of lamb meat with hummus, tahina and couscous. Next there were the many Vietnamese eating joints which offered some delicious surprises.

Nearby was also a coin washing and drying place where one often had a chat with others waiting for their laundry to be ready. At the Place de Contrescarpe/Rue Moufftard was my favourite Coffee house where I could smoke my pipe, read the "Le Monde" or "Le Figaro" newspaper, watch the passers-by and chat with the patron or other customers, mostly students. In a small lane in a souterrain Marika Kowatc, a Hungarian brocanteuse (flea market trader) had her exotic store. For over 30 years she lived in Paris and was completely happy with her job and income. Clochards supplied her with articles they had rescued from the rubbish containers during the night. Marika had originally studied art at the Sorbonne and ended up somehow in this milieu.

She lived in the Arab quarter. Just for fun I helped her equipped with a chisel, hammer, napkin and goggles to restore her living quarters. Some years later this quartier was discovered by housing speculators and ended as a fashionable place in the hands of the "upper ten". My metro station was "Gobelin". Directly beside it were the barracks of the "Garde Republicainé". Thanks to my student card I could use the Metro and Busse's on easy terms. That is the reason that I rarely used my old Austin Healey sports car. Another privilege as a student was that I became a member of the Cinematheque, a famous institution that collects worldwide rare and sometimes forgotten preciousnesses and pearls of the international film industry that are not shown in regular cinemas. So I became an "aficionado" of classic movies.

I persuaded my mother to visit me for a couple of weeks. At my night shifts she warmed my bed, and left me when I came home to sleep equipped with Francs, a 10er Metro ticket, city- & metro maps and directions for museums and sights. She managed to never get lost.

When it was convenient with my school and working schedule we met at the lobby of the Grand Hotel Opera or at a well known Coffee-House or at home. Sometimes I left her my bed and slept on the air-mattress.

On free weekends I took her to Versailles, Bois de Boulogne, Fontainebleau or took her on a trip on the Seine with a "Bateau Mouche". I showed her also the roof terraces of the noble department stores like "Les Galleries Lafayette" and "Printemps" from where you got a marvellous view over the city and Montparnasse. As my mother spoke fairly French I booked a funny play with J.C. Brialy and J.P. Cassel in a theater near the Champs Élissées. She enjoyed very much the "Marche de Puces" (flea market). During a shopping spree I discovered a fashionable red hat for her. The search for fitting shoes "Prussian size 42" was in vain. We did not miss to take a walk along the Seine with its book stalls near the Pont Marie. Down, underneath the arcs of the bridges, the clochards assembled holding tight their bottles of red wine.

Compared with those creatures I was living like a prince.

The time had passed like a flight and now I was standing on the platform of the Gare d'Est waving my white handkerchief at the leaving train to bid farewell to my mother. I had been lucky to experience Paris in a friendly atmosphere. Just one year later a student revolt took place that was directed against the conservative Government of President General Charles de Gaulle. The eloquent leader of the revolt was the French-German Cohn Bendit who was later on deported from France and made a political career in Germany.

When back in Germany a message from my aged granduncle from Mozambique/Portuguese South/East Africa reached me. He proposed to me to introduce me with the management of his citrus plantation. His son had a good job in the Australian government in Canberra and was not interested. I was thrilled and followed his invitation. That was a unique chance to enjoy a peaceful, interesting life far away from the crowded and noisy Western world. I took a plane to Lisbon and then to Luanda/Angola and Beira/Mozambique with the Boeing 707 of the TAP. The crew distributed certificates to those passengers like me, who had crossed the Equator by plane for the first time. I took my chance and talked to the crew and passengers.

I was expected by my Grand Uncle with his Landrover, and after he had made a tour around the busy port town he took the way home. On the long trip to the plantation we met many trucks coming from Rhodesia. My GU told me that this street was passing the farm. Many of those truck drivers were customers buying fruit and vegetables at his stand at the side of the street. On the railway track beside the street a long cargo train pulled by two locomotives were hauling copper ore from Katanga/Congo to Beira's port.

On half way home we left the road to pick up Emanuel the houseboy who had been treated with his right broken leg by the missionaries. Finally we arrived at Maforga, where aunt Rosemarie was expecting us with the "Sundowners". After I had given a report about the family happenings at home, Schulz the cook sounded the gong for dinner. Because of my arrival he had taken care to prepare something special. To celebrate the day a first class cape wine from South Africa was offered. The houseboy who served the menu was dressed all in white but was barefooted. At 08.00 p.m. came the moment to listen to the news of the world like every day by BBC London. The radio was battery operated because the farm had no public power supply yet. Good light was delivered by so-called effective brass "petromax" petroleum lamps like they still use on night markets all over the world. From time to time they had to be pumped up to deliver the necessary pressure for dusting the petroleum. For shorter use candle lights with matches were in every room of the bungalow. The library was equipped with professional subtropical agricultural and world literature in English and Portuguese. Hunting guns, ammunition and documents were stored in a padlocked steel locker. After dinner we enjoyed sitting in the dark on the front porch enjoying the fabulous star littered firmament with its strange star constellations, the prominent Southern cross and the moon rarely seen so clearly on the Northern polluted hemisphere.

From the jungle behind the plantation we listened to the chattering of the monkeys and the crawling of the toucans. Far out in the savanna in the front of the farm we listened to the occasional roaring of the lions and the sound of the nearby passing trains carrying copper ore to the port of Beira at the Indian Ocean. At this railway line U.G. had its own short side track with a loading ramp for its agricultural products. U.G. gave me an example how he had adapted to the local unreliable mentality: When he needed two waggons from the railway authorities at about 03.30 p.m. in the afternoon he ordered them already at 09.30 a.m. in the morning, Usually the waggons were delivered with the usual delay some time in the afternoon, That saved UG many headaches and chagrin. On Monday morning many of his farm-hands arrived late or not at all at the intended working time. The reason was that they had consumed too much of their home made alcohol "Pombe" made of fermented bananas and some tropical fruit. The signal for the beginning of work was given by beating the triangle of iron pipes hanging from the branch of the avocado tree beside the bungalow. All bigger duties were shifted to Tuesday to avoid vexation. U.G. was a good actor and pretended to be very angry. Behind his back the farm-hands were giggling and shouting in the local Matebe language "Baas kuleketa maningi!" … "The patron is very angry!".

Not just of the climate, the clocks are moving more slowly in Mozambique. Later when I was fully integrated into the working issues of the farm I happened to perplex U. G. When harvest of oranges and grapefruit was due, our tractor drove the loaded trailer with the plastic cases to the loading ramp in front of the railway waggons and took the empty trailers back to the plantation. The few workers in charge of loading the boxes with fruit into the waggons formed a chain. I was at the front in the wagon piling up the boxes and gave the command to speed up the procedure. The workers considered it a great fun to see the "Peceino baas" = "little chief" working so hard. The unloading of the boxes in the gremio/agricultural society in Gondola happened in the same speedy manner. As the owners of the farms/plantations were mostly elderly persons they could of course not actively integrate into the course of work, but were busy supervising that the work was done properly according to the rules. The most important was the proper care of the backbone of the plantation, the orange- and grapefruit trees. Without chemical means it did unfortunately not work. They were already applied before the blooming period of the trees. That was done manually sparingly with spraying canisters belted to the back of the sprayer whose face was protected by a mask. The experienced sprayer did not use too little or too much of the poisonous liquid from Monsanto or Bayer. At last it was done shortly before the fruit ripened to avoid vermin drilling holes into the fruit and mould fungus spread. The ground around the trees had to be kept free of weeds and had to be fertilized from time to time. Much work but it paid off. The old type of oranges originally from Spain "Valencia Late" stood the test. Besides grapefruit and oranges that were the crop for export there was some other income destined for the domestic market like beans, peanuts, sweet potatoes, corn cob, avocados, mangoes, maracujas, bananas, melons and limes. A gardener took care of the kitchen garden under the supervision of aunt Rosemary. The surplus products were sold at the nearby roadside stall to the passing truck drivers from South Rhodesia. My aunt had planted some tea-bushes and spices and got a lot of suggestions from neighbouring farm-ladies concerning keeping roses and other flowers.

UG had taken care of irrigating water for the dry season by creating big round concrete containers. Adjoining the bungalow existed an iron stand with a zinc water container on its top for kitchen and household use. Its water was replenished by means of a vintage English Lister diesel engine that pumped water up from a deep well. A round African style of guest house adorned with Bougainvillea was situated at the left hand side of the front of the bungalow. Inside the main building were two ground level bathtubs and three flush WC's. In the spacious living room was an old piano where my aunt enjoyed playing from time to time. All sleeping rooms were equipped with mosquito nets. The windows and outside doors were fit with mesh wire frames to let the air in and keep mosquitoes and night roaming insects out. I was very interested in all those exotic bugs and spiders and asked for a big glass jar with a cover to trap some of those species. With the help of a "petromax" that I positioned behind the meshwire-frame I caught some of those fascinating mini monsters and inspected them by means of UG's big magnifying glass. Both were also interested in my mini zoological collection. Magnified some of the spiders looked like animals from prehistoric times. The following weekend in the afternoon I went, accompanied by our faithful dog and equipped with my micro zoo, through the bush to the homestead of the farm-hands. I was reverentially greeted by the eldest and chief of the community. I told him in broken Portuguese that I had something extraordinary to show him. I explained to him the simple use of UG's magnifying glass. I guessed right, nobody in the village had ever used one. It took some time until everybody, including women and children, had taken a glance. To make it more interesting I explained to them that in times long ago, before human beings appeared, those spiders and bugs were of giant size like elephants, rhinos and hippos. I told them also about animals from other parts of the world like kangaroos, camels, wales and bears and showed them pictures in a book from our library. Then I started to collect vocabularies of their local tribe language "Matebe". On my next visit to the village I gave the eldest some coins of German currency as a souvenir. On another occasion I surprised him with the multi-functional use of my Swiss officer's knife that even had a tiny saw for wood and a magnifying glass. One day I was bitten in my right leg by a relatively harmless snake. Instead of consulting the far away mission I went to my friend, the experienced village chief and he treated me perfectly with extracts from officinal herbs and leaf dressings. On one of my inspection tours I came to notice an alley of trees which had visibly been planted intentionally a long time ago. My aunt told me that they were "Kapok-trees", which produced a silk like fibre that was once fashionable in the high society for filling cushions and light bed covers because the fibre was stronger, lighter and softer than silk. It is still used in Thailand to fill silk pillows. Since the invention of foam-rubber by the western chemical industry this unique natural product has sunk into oblivion. One day I asked UG if there existed a place where one could take a bath without attracting a tropical disease like "Schistosomiasis"?

He told me that when he was younger, he walked through the jungle behind the farm to a small river where he used to swim. But when he became old, the wilderness had taken over and the path had been overgrown. With his permission I got two skilful farmhands and started to clear the former path by means of machetes. After only two days the job was done and we could enjoy a bath in the rock encircled pool. The only surprise during our work was a lazy poisonous black mamba snake that crossed our way and disappeared in the thicket. On hot days I often enjoyed swimming there, sometimes accompanied by aunt Rosemary who was younger than UG and still very sporty.

Our farmhands got wages of course, but in addition they received by law an extra allowance of elementary subsidiaries and working outfit. Other support was given voluntarily by the patron like medical and birth aid.

On one occasion I became an obstetrician when a black farmhand who was in labor got her baby prematurely on the Land-rover's loading area while we were driving to the mission. That is not a great affair when everything works smoothly and when it concerns healthy African women.

In most cases they got a midwife and medicine man in their village to take care of the matter. They used to be well acquainted with the application of effective natural medicine.

I always enjoyed it when UG drove to Salisbury, the capital city of South Rhodesia, where we always stayed in the imposing "Meikles", the typical luxurious colonial Hotel for the upper class. It still exists! UG did some shopping and then we went to the country club where we met all renown people including the sympathetic Ian Smith, a Scotsman, who was the Prime Minister and leader of the white minority government. In spite of the fact that the UNO had announced an embargo over South Rhodesia the economy boomed. Articles that had formerly been imported were produced in the country. In the club area's parking lot you did not see the latest models. The cars were maintained in excellent technical shape. For me as aficionado of especially vintage English cars it was a wonderful experience to see this cars that since long time disappeared elsewhere. The main former export crop tobacco went after the embargo via the South African Union to China. There was no unemployment and all shops were fully stored with goods from South Africa and friendly nations. At this time South Rhodesia was the healthiest national economy in Africa. In spite of the terrorists who acted from abroad the Rhodesian National Forces managed to maintain law and order. The country was self-sufficient and did not need to import provisions. It was a tourist paradise for adventurers who crossed Africa by truck. Everywhere, not only at the Victoria Falls foreigners had the feeling to be heartily welcome. Black citizens offered well maintained, comfortable and cheap "Bed & Breakfast" accommodations. The South Rhodesian currency was stable: 3 SIM$ = 1 US$ = a can of coffée in the five 5-star "Meikles Hotel". Some conversation with well informed personalities in the Country Club cooled however my former enthusiasm. Further reports from the Northern Regions of Mozambique about murders of farmers and businessmen and the destruction of farms and the infrastructure by terrorists supported by the Soviet Union were hushed up by the Portuguese authorities and media to avoid a panic. They enforced my decision to reconsider my plans to stay in Mozambique. Finally I discussed the matter with UG and my aunt, who were of course very disappointed, but understood my motives. Finally I booked a return flight with TAP back to Europe. I had just one last wish, to use the passenger train to Beira that originated from Salisbury. I said goodbye to all the farmhands and the folks in the settlement. My friend the village elder, presented me with a tooth of a beast of prey as mascot and the hunter of UG gave me the skin of a snake as an adornment of my safari hat. I promised them all to send some interesting picture postcards from Europe to the eldest via my granduncle.

All were visibly sad to see the *Pecorino Baas* (Little Patron) leaving. What would the future keep in store for all those pleasant people?

In nearby Gondola I boarded the steam-train and stored my luggage in a First Class compartment carriage. Then I waved

Goodbye/Adios to my relatives and all the other well wishers. At this train the tender was placed in front of the steam engine. On top of the tender two soldiers were positioned behind a machine gun protected by sand sacks. I went to the second class carriage where a battalion of soldiers with their officers were seated. The captain informed me that terrorists had the day before assaulted a train in the North near Nampula that had cost the lives of some civilists and railway employees. They had gotten the order from their superiors to protect this vital railway line as precaution.

The conductor told me that part of the line was enclosed in the flatlands by an inundation of the Rio Pungwe, but Beira was dry. Everybody could afford the train. The 3rd Class had just wooden benches and the 4th was for black farmers with their pigs, sheep's, goats, chicken and turkeys.

The first class was impressive. There existed two foldable leather benches on one side with lockers for bed-linen on night trips. The walls were covered with mahogany. Opposite was a foldable mahogany table. A brass bowl at the corner of the window side provided hot and cold water and a little compartment offered towels, soap and aftershave. Over the table was a locker with Rhodesian Railway Company's own stationary with an old fashioned ink pot, a writing pen and blotting paper. The window and glass door to the corridor could be closed by means of jalousies. At the end of the corridor was a common shower. If service was required for cocktails, tea, coffee or shoe shine one pulled a chain beside the door and the servant clad all in spotless white appeared to ask for the wishes. That was traveling in style like in the time of Cecil Rhodes the "Empire Builder".

The flat areas before Beira were under water. The people had for the time being taken refuge on the side of the railway embankment and erected some reed huts.

Beira was dry and I spent some time in a coffee house and became absorbed in reading one South African newspaper after listening to BBC London all the month. The whole political situation puzzled me: The Soviet Union had tried to infiltrate and undermine the strategically and economically immense important white dominated South African Union and had failed. Next they had looked for an easier target and concentrated their subversive activity on the peaceful Portuguese colonies of Mozambique and Angola and incited the population to revolt against the Portuguese authorities with terrorist acts. Later in future the "clove" revolution in Portugal made the way free to release the Portuguese colonies into the independence and they became an easy victim for the Russians. Long lasting civil wars in Mozambique and Angola devastated the once prospering countries and left a chaos. Even Fidel Castro sent troops from Cuba to support the communist fractions in both counties. It was a shame that the UN did not send "Blue Helmets" to end the conflict. The Soviet supported leaders won and since that time both countries became "Socialist States". Then it was time to take a taxi to the airport. I was really set at rest when I finally took my seat in the Boeing 707 of the TAP to Lisboa via Luanda. During the flight I had a lot of time to exchange views with the cabin staff and acquaint myself with their professional life. In spite of the "glamour" that surrounded their job I had the impression that one was in need of a thick skin and a solid character to accept all disadvantages of that profession. When we crossed the Equator for the second time I felt already like an old hand on the international parquet. I felt very sorry especially for the older people, who spent their lives in the colonies and were now losing their seemingly secure existence were not really welcomed in the tiny homeland Portugal and considered as a burden for the local society. There were problems in progress.

Already at Lisbon airport I was shocked about the masses of ill-humored people and the sunless gray sky after coming from my peaceful subtropical paradise. In Frankfurt and Munich I had to get used to the first night frosts.

At the apartment of my mother I sat down at my travel-writing machine to prepare three job applications. One was going to the Savoy Hotel in London, the second to an international import & export company in Bremen and the third one to Lufthansa German Airlines in Frankfurt. It was destiny that Lufthansa was the first one that answered and asked me for documents and professional certificates concerning my past. I had already provided them with a "Curriculum Vitae/Live record" together with my application. After a few days I received an invitation for an interview.

First of all I was asked why I had the desire to become a steward. To know the world, to widen the horizon and meet interesting people and colleagues was accepted. To get a comfortable job with a good income was ridiculous because it was a hard job with low wages for the first few years. The job was sometimes drudgery in narrow cabins, at impossible times and fast changing climate zones, agitated flights and medical and other problems with passengers. The young female applicants were warned from light minded sexual relations and taught pregnancy protection. The much fewer male aspirants were warned of frivolity. Homosexuals were not discriminated to hide their inborn inclination. Their demeanour should however just not offend the passengers. The cabin management had discovered that those stewards were much more devoted towards the passengers than the "normal" colleagues. It was well known in airline circles that over 50% of the stewards of VARIG/Brazilian Airways were queer.

During the psychological test LH tried to find out if the applicant was suited for this job and if they were disciplined and ready to subordinate themselves. Those who were unable to do so were rejected. Others who manage to deceive the psychologist were soon exposed on one of their first flights. Very important was the behaviour under duress especially in emergency situations like engine trouble, fire on board, difficult medical cases, terrorists on board and the search and treatment of bombs.

Good appearance and faultless bearing especially when in uniform were a matter of course. Just good polished dark leather shoes were accepted. The young Ladies where taught to apply a decent unobtrusive makeup. Conspicuous jewelry was strictly forbidden. At this period the stewardesses were all without exception good looking.

A further challenge was the intelligence test of quick response and activity. From the head of the commission everyone got a catchword and had to compose with that one a short story within a twenty minute period. If required it was given to the graphologist for a judgment. Later I was asked why I had such delicate handwriting. I explained it as follows: On my many foreign trips I used a lot of picture postcards to send to my relatives and friends. In telegram style I added the latest news and saved an aerogram for communication. Another fun were the exotic stamps.

Next followed the language test in conversation and writing. The knowledge of perfect German was the rule for all foreign applicants. Germans were not allowed to speak a dialect in contact with the passengers except for Bavarian traveling groups who invaded the plane with expressions like; "Jo mei, dos is a gaudi …!" I often imitated the way French, English, Americans and Russians tried to speak German. The British radio moderator Chris Howland who worked for the North German Radio Service was loved for his funny appearances in East London's worker cockney dialect. It reminded me always on George-Benjamin Shaw's *Pygmalion* (My fair Lady). Good English was obligatory and French or Spanish were welcome and additional world languages were years later honoured by a monthly bonus. Humanist languages like Hebrew, Latin and Old Geek did of course not count. Later I came to know that Lufthansa had understood the importance of languages for the cabin staff and had established a modern language laboratory where CA's (Cabin Attendants) could train during their standby duty at the airport or in their free time could train our languages abilities. Our fitness was checked by the manager of the laboratory Mr. Selten, who was in his private life a renowned saxophonist of the "Barrel House

Jazzband". When exotical languages had to be checked like Arab, Japanese and Mandarin experts from Frankfurt University were asked to do the job.

The tested person should be able to converse about the subjects of general interest and daily life and make announcements with public address on board if required. I had already had contact with Americans, British, French and Russians in my childhood. My mother had been taught French by her governess when she was a young girl. In school I learned English and when I joined the economic high school, commercial Spanish was added. At the German Air Force I was encouraged to book an evening course in Russian. In the following Hotel Academy English, French, Spanish and Italian were taught. I perfected my English by reading a lot of English and American world literature.

At the Alliance Francaise in Paris I polished my French. Italian I had also learned from nice Italian truck drivers who gave me a lift as a hitch-hiker exploring Italy up to Naples. They also taught me to sing famous opera melodies from Enrico Caruso and Benjamino Gigli. On my way back to the North I made the acquaintance of Ernesto Oppicelli and his family clan, who invited me to stay some days in their home in Genova- Certosa. In his later life Ernesto became a respected Opera singer.

Back to Lufthansa: The head of the commission Mrs. Tautz was flabbergasted about my treasure of languages. I explained to her that my example had been my great-grandmother Ida-Nadieshda Baroness von Reibnitz, who had spoken seven languages fluently. Her reason to learn Italian had been the wish to read

"La Divina Commedia" by Dante and "Decamerone" by Bocaccio in its original language. The job as steward would give me the opportunity to practice my languages continuously. I surmounted the language and other hurdles easily probably because of my life experience. I had learned discipline and could also present a document that stated that I was a trained air force medical orderly. In addition I had already been to four continents.

When my grandfather had successfully finished the Prussian knights academy his father gave him the opportunity of an extended tour through Europe to "sow one's wild oats" before the seriousness of life began. His mothers roots were in Sweden and Russia and she spoke still with a heavy Russian accent from her frequent stay with her Krohn family in St. Petersburg. My mother enjoyed to imitate *Momo's* Russian accent.

She had a great affection for my mother whom she called *Bibi* and took her whenever it was convenient on extended trips through Western Europe. It was in 1923 when a dreadful inflation hit Germany and destroyed many livelihoods. The President of the Reichsbank Hjilmar Schacht put finally a stop to this insanity in creating a new solid currency based on real estate and public property. That clever initiative healed the economy and reduced the unemployment rate. The following years with an economic boom and joy of life were remembered as "The Roaring Golden Twenties" until the crash at the New York stock exchange 1928 started the catastrophe of the world economic crisis.

Momo had in wise precaution invested her capital already a long time ago cleverly in Sweden and Switzerland and was not afflicted by the crisis and could afford her usual standard of living when she became a widow. So my mother came to know the relatives and friends all over Western Europe. There were especially the relations from the Krohn family, who after they had been expropriated at the Russian Revolution 1917 by the communists in St. Petersburg, had dispersed over Europe to create new existences. Some of the clan were even found in Brazil, Morocco and in the Cape colony of South Africa. At the Danish court she was introduced to the Royal family and had a special affection for Prince Harald. She also met some noble friends of my grandmother who had as young Comtesse von der Schulenburg been Lady-in-waiting at the imperial court in Berlin. Those contacts extended the horizon of my mother enormously and friendships from this time lasted to her death like those from her boarding school.

Sorry about my sidestepping. I seem to have inherited this weakness from my beloved grandmother. My appearance was also accepted. I was plain shaved until the rules were loosened later on. Only my hands rough from the farm work needed some treatment. At the final interview Mrs. Tautz reverted to my hitherto professional career and told me that I was the only one; who had such good preparatory training. My age would be advantageous in my later position as superior and in the cooperation with the cockpit crew and ground staff. I received the official invitation for the training of the cabin staff just some days later. The acceptance of all of us was celebrated with champagne. There were 16 Ladies and 4 Gentlemen.

A special office existed in charge of accommodation for us with good bus or city train connections to the Airport and Lufthansa Basis. Together with another participant Rolf N. we got a room rented out by a widow in Kelsterbach at the Main river close to our training facilities. The young aspirants were much favoured by the Landlords as they had good manners, were busy with learning and caused no problems. Our time was filled out with the digestion of the versatile matters of instruction.

My room-mate came with his own car, a VW Ghia Karmann, that allowed us to explore the surrounding area on weekends. The cold winter time did not entice us to stay much outside. It was January with a lot of snow and minus Celsius temperatures. There was however one highlight, it was the visit of the OPEL Car Factory in nearby Rüsselsheim. Opel is a reputed name of a German noble family who was forced to sell the factory to General Motors Company in Detroit right after the Wall Street Crash 1928. They started successfully with building practical hand & feet operated sewing machines, then bicycles and motorbikes until they discovered the automobile market. Especially Opel lorries were a common sight on German streets. Both Opel and Ford were busy before and during World War II to produce military trucks and staff cars for the German forces. After the landing of the allied forces 1944 on D-Day at Normandy both sides were surprised that the spare parts of the captured American and German trucks were interchangeable. Even the practical "Jerry petrol cans" were taken over. Just the English military equipment was still produced in inches and feet and petrol was measured in Imperial gallons which caused a lot of problems especially at the dessert war in North Africa.

After this short side step I return to my LH course. Breakfast was our own business and not provided by the landlady. Milk, Yoghurt, Müsli, Banana and Tea/Nescafe were sufficient. Lunch was provided by LH from Monday to Friday and dinner or weekend provision was our own business. The chinaware, cutlery and glasses in the canteen were the same as in the First Senator Class on board. After a couple of years the design of the table ware was changed and the former one offered to the staff or to frequent travellers. It always found an easy market. LH had at this time still cult status. The course participants were taught the fundamentals of gastronomy fitting the special conditions on board like the international clientèle, narrowness and weather conditions. There happened to be cases of stewardesses who left LH after just some flights because they could not endure the claustrophobic condition on board. They were also told to avoid unnecessary injuries of passengers who let their limbs hang over the armrest and block the aisle especially while sleeping. When offering tea and coffee as after service one should always use a small tray with cups of sugar and cream portions and lemon slices. If the beverage spills over it remains on the high boarded tray. When during the service a sudden turbulence arises the CA immediately activates the brake and seats on an armrest and even on the lap of a pax asking the surrounding aisle side sitting passengers to hold the service trolleys tight. I never experienced that a passenger complained about such a handling of the situation. Additional tea and coffee should be offered from the trolley where the used meal trays are stowed away after the service. At breakfast coffee and tea should be offered several times. When on long range flights of over 12 hours a second meal and even an additional snack was on the program passengers had to be informed that meals could not be cooled with dry ice for such a long time. Ice cubes for cocktails were also melted after some hours. Depending on the route, special wishes of customers were taken into consideration like Oosake/rice wine for Japanese customers, chopsticks and the popular noodle soup and green tea were offered on all Far Eastern routes.

The cooled and sometimes deep frozen in aluminum foil wrapped portioned meals should never be heated too short or too long to have the right consistency when served. Routined CA's work of course much faster than a "newcomer". They should slow down a bit and adapt to the speed of the colleague. It is fair and makes a better impression. Special attention was given to the peculiarities of customs of other nationalities.

When Indians nodded their heads it meant "NO", but sidewards it meant "YES"! Perhaps that was an ancient habit left by Alexander the Great who managed to reach the Indus because it is a habit of the Greek people until today. It can happen that a stewardess asking an Indian Lady for her wishes is interrupted by her husband's words: "Sorry, but my wife does not talk to servants!" The Japanese habit of knocking at the WC door before entering is answered from inside in the same manner in the case the WC is occupied. Presents are given in Japan with both hands. That also should be observed when duty free articles are handed over while sales on board and it should always be accompanied with the words: "Dooso arigato gozaimasu!" (Thank you very much!). The often rude manners of Russians who claim everything especially wodka without saying "Please or Thank you!" should not be considered as an offense but as an interesting experience. Anyone who has experienced the overwhelmingly Russian hospitality will forget these negative experiences fast. It is very expensive for a Russian to fly with Lufthansa compared with Aeroflot, that should not be forgotten. The often offending manner of Jewish passengers on the always fully booked flights to and from Tel Aviv should not be taken personally. The Jews have never forgotten the shoah and holocaust. With charm, friendliness and humour we should overcome this hurdle. Reciting the famous Israel satirist Kishon will also help. On longer flights Muslims especially pilgrims should always be given the opportunity to practice their prayers at the exit areas where they could spread their carpets. It was my job to inform them in which direction Mecca was situated. The high consumption of Scandinavians or European contract workers from companies like Aramco or Hoch & Tief returning from Saudi Arabia always managed to drink us dry when in groups. The highly paid contract workers had been under stress for several months without being permitted a drop of comforting alcohol. In Scandinavia alcohol is extremely high taxed. In the early 70th we had to charge for the drinks but it was too complicated and time consuming to handle that without international credit cards and so this system was abolished. Just the LH charter company Condor kept it because the pax paid in German Marks. Duty free sales on board was at this time still a very important source of income because duty free shops came only slowly in existence. Flying was still something for wealthy and privileged people. Those CA's who were responsible for sales on board received lead-seals, pliers and a sturdy purse. A small folder contained lists with all regular stable currencies with their actual exchange rates. The CA in charge checked the seals of his sales trolley, broke the customs seal, checked the contents according to the attached list and closed the trolley again with his own tiny padlock and stowed the trolley in the galley.

The CA's had to know where spare articles like toilet articles, blankets, pillows, board magazines etc. where stowed. Greatest care was taken on First Aid knowledge and the ability to react fast and professionally In emergency situations like fire on board, decompression, turbulence, emergency landings and evacuations of passengers. For every aircraft type existed a dummy where regular training was done. The three types of fire extinguishers foam/gas/water were practised at a reserved safe place outside.

Before each daily flight rotation the CA's were handed out check-lists for their section on the aircraft and returned signed to the chef de cabin. So it was guaranteed that the plane was not leaving with missing equipment. The cockpit crew had its own checklist. The big stationary aluminum Doctors kit had to be checked for unbroken seals. A smaller medicine box was loaded fresh at the beginning of every daily rotation. The use of every medicine was explained. The most frequently used was Asperin. For passengers with nausea problems we had oxygen bottles with face masks available. In serious cases we were obliged to inform the LH station of our next destination or our medical station to get further professional instruction and inform them to keep replacement ready for the used oxygen bottle. The chef de cabin/Purser was obliged to make an announcement to ask if a doctor or an experienced nurse was on board who could be of assistance. For regular transports of patients a seat row at the left rear exit was blocked and a bunk with curtains was installed. A doctor or experienced nurse accompanied the patient and took care of his medical needs. In most cases they were patients who had suffered a heart attack or an accident abroad. The travel insurance covered all the involved costs. The loading of provisions and other galley equipment had to be checked punctilious together with the caterer. The chef de cabin/chief steward checked the cabin technical log-book and ordered the mechanic to take care of matters if necessary. According of the passenger list he informed the cabin staff about special cases to be taken care of like UM = unaccompanied minors, MUKI's = mothers with babies/minor childs, WCHR = wheelchair cases, Blind & Deaf pax and those who were paralysed and had to be carried on board and those who had difficulties in walking and needed support. There were HON's = rare privileged passengers who got this title from the LH management, VIP's = international members of the upper nobility, cardinals & bishops, movie and entertainment stars, Nobel prize winners, leading industrialists and politicians, police officers who accompanied criminals and deported persons to their homelands, a rather costly expenditure for the tax payers and last not least employees of LH and other airlines who travelled with industrial discount on standby basis. The CA's had to instruct passengers sitting adjoining disabled pax how to assist them in case of problems. A sad theme is still the international terrorism that started with hijackings from and to Cuba. The PLO, IRA often supported by Muhammad Ghadafi and other terrorist groups had put the world upside down. Just Jassir Arafat of all received the Nobel prize of peace to keep him quiet. Rather necessary were the security controls all over the world. That caused many pax to miss their connection flight. Like the engine drivers of the railway security staff discovered very fast in what a powerful position they were and started to strike for higher wages, paralyzing all airports causing enormous financial damage like the air traffic controllers before. The training of cabin crews by LH had such an excellent reputation that many international airlines decided to send their CA candidates to LH for instruction and training. Next on the agenda was the psychological handling of terrorists. Single actions should be avoided even when the chances for success were favourable because nobody could be sure how many "sleepers" (terrorists in disguise) were members of the passengers. Terrorists should in spite of the dangerous situation be treated respectfully and should be obeyed.

Bomb warnings were taken seriously. The intensive search was done by the whole cabin crew by means of flexible mirrors to check even the areas underneath the passenger seats. When the search of the bomb including the passengers hand luggage was successful the bomb was carefully placed at the rear exit and covered with hand luggage and layers of blankets. That promised to cause the minimum possible damage that did not impair the plane's flying capabilities.

After this unpleasant instruction was time for the physical side of flying.

Even technically ignorant CA's should be in the position to understand and explain the basic facts of flying to curious pax. A relative ot mine was manager of the spare parts department at the wharf at the base. I was well informed about the superior quality of the parts. The stainless steel screws were even x-rayed to avoid mistakes. Even the smallest stainless screws surpassed by 5 times the prices of regular ones on the metal market. Everything on board was very expensive because there were no mass products. The calculated time of use should be very long and the items should be checked in regular intervals. After a certain amount of miles aircrafts had to get a general check that could last weeks. At the slightest damage to the turbines the whole engine was changed. That was faster done than to repair it on the spot.

Seat Covers and floor carpets were fire resistant. Then we dealt with the different types of aircraft's. After this "Tsunami" of knowledge that had to be digested we were acquainted with with the actual flight network of LH and the 3-letter codes of the destinations and the functions of the IATA (International AIR Traffic Association) and the ICAO (International Civil Aviation Organisation) and next the organogram of LH (administration structure) of the management with seat in Cologne where Lufthansa had been new founded 1953. At my time LH was still over 51% in ownership of the German Government. The employees had practically the status of civil servants. The administration was accordingly puffed up until LH became a public stock exchange company.

Now all of us had passed the general test and the medical

examination that had to be regular duty all two years. We got injections against Cholera and Yellow fever. Privately I added Tetanus. Malaria prophylactic was taken directly before flights into affected areas.

All participants were accepted and bestowed with a diploma. The occasion was celebrated with "Fürst Metternich champagne". Our measurements for the uniforms had been taken some time ago by the tailoring department and we were asked to appear for a fitting. The tailors had done an excellent job, only minor changes were required like an adapted waist, trouser length and buttons for the double breasted jackets and the sleeves. Then we got white shirts with shoulder flaps and extra long sleeves that could be worn with cufflinks. For the tropics lighter uniforms and short sleeved shirts were available. The air hostesses got a beautiful silk scarf with the crane the LH logo. The headgear of the stewardesses had a kind of potform. The outfit was completed by a dark blue shoulder bag. The stewards got the same peaked hat like that of the cockpit crew. Each airline tried to have its own sometimes exotic style.

In addition we got a winter overcoat with on-buttoned lining, a wool shawl and leather gloves. Black leather shoes we could acquire at a specialized shop at the airport. Most of us used the sturdy "Samsonite" suitcases. When they were damaged they were replaced by LH. For me it was not necessary to buy new shoes because I had a collection of fine English shoes which I loved to polish regularly. My grandfather taught me that it was possible to estimate the character of a person by looking at his shoes. He told me also to appreciate the use of the old fashioned slip over rubber galoshes in rainy weather. I was asked to get him new ones from Moss & Broth. when in London because they were unavailable on the continent. The stewardesses still got a beauty treatment by Mrs. Katke who also surveyed our appearance at the check in before the start of a flight rotation. Stewards had also to have well treated fingernails and a decent haircut. Beards were until much later not permitted. At the first flight rotation we were accompanied by a check-steward who assisted the "newcomer" to integrate easily into the crew and to supervise his working proficiency. With the routine the newcomers developed the necessary self confidence and later on everything worked like clockwork. Hectic leads to mistakes. It reminds me of a wise remark of the Chinese philosopher Confutze: *There are three ways to act, thinking before you do something is the noblest way! Imitating is the easiest and learning by experience is the bitterest way!*

At the start it is the most difficult situation to remember the storage positions of the different containers and trolleys in search for a certain item. You had to check the galley with the newcomer to avoid mistakes. Once the aircraft was "Off Blocks" it was too late to correct it. Just the missing of coffee/tea pots or pax meals leads to embarrassments. Only after a meticulous check of the loading the delivery papers should be signed. Spilled hot drinks by carelessness of pax or CA's should not interrupt the service. The chef de cabin or chief steward is called to take care of the matter immediately. In certain cases when the CA is involved the

Purser will issue a cleaning voucher as compensation. Excluded are damages caused by turbulences. I remember one case where a pax was expected to make a long speech at an international conference. Spilled coffee spoiled his trousers. I asked him to take his trousers off and gave him a blanket to sit on my jump seat. I placed the trouser over the open WC door and took the coffee spots away with a kitchen sponge with hot water and a galley towel. After I dried the trouser by means of my hair dryer that I had always in my flight kit and had an adapter for board electricity. The problem was solved and the pax was happy.

An initiative like this one is only possible when there is enough time available and the service does not suffer on short range flights. The idea with the hair dryer came after I was often drenched to the bones by leaving the crew bus to deposit first our crew luggage at the storage at the rear and then to board the plane. The jacket could be taken off but the wet trouser was a problem. Thanks God I used my galoshes that kept the feet warm and dry. I always felt very sorry for those who had to hurry from the bus to the plane and sat drenched on their seats. During the flight the cockpit crew tried to help by turning the air condition heating on full power. At this time flying was still very expensive, not frequent and reserved for a privileged wealthy clientèle and employees of the industry.

In Frankfurt the passengers came by bus from the old terminal and had to wait until the ramp agent gave his sign "thumb up" to the bus driver for boarding. In the meantime the loading of luggage and cargo continued. During the fuelling procedure passengers were not permitted to stay on board. Exceptions were fuelling procedures at transit airports where no passengers were boarding and disembarking, In this case a fire brigade had to be parked beside the aircraft. That was one of the many rules by the ICAO that were accepted by 98% of the official world airlines.

Let us return to our "newcomers". After having absolved their first European 4 – 5 days rotations with a satisfactory check, they were left alone and got their next flying order into their personal company mailbox. On their next rotation they were obliged to inform the chef de cabin/purser about his/her actual status. In Frankfurt the division-chief took care of them.

The organization assigns that except on European and Middle Range flights the CA's are, according to their wishes and language abilities, appointed to certain flight divisions. The first served Europe, Near East, North & East Africa with Boeing 727, 737 and Vickers Viscount 814. The next served routes of the Boeing 707 Intercontinental Jets followed by the Douglas McDonnell 10 and the Boeing 747-200 Jumbo Jet. In Europe there existed normal rotations for up to 5 days with changing layovers in Amsterdam, Brussels, London, Stockholm, Moscow, Athens, Budapest, Genova. Milan, Barcelona, Lisbon, Paris, Geneva, Vienna, Düsseldorf, Hamburg, Bremen, Cologne, Nurnberg, Stuttgart and Munich and outside of Europe in Beirut, Damascus, Baghdad, Teheran, Cairo, Khartoum, Saana, Dar-es-Salaam, Tripolis.

For reasons of strikes, weather conditions like fog, snowfall and ice, Aircraft breakdowns schedules could change. In this case we had standby service at home or at Frankfurt/Main at the LH-basis. Most disagreeable were short range flights in winter with storm, over frozen rain, snow, frost and fog with delays and diversions. Important was always the fitting combination of clothing in the suitcase. On long range flights the clothing should be adapted to the climate of the destination.

For any case I always had some liquid soap and a brush with me to eliminate blots on the uniform. Chinese "Tiger Balm" and "Japan Oil" in my washing pouch was a good prophylaxis against a bad cold. For any case I always had a thin clothes bag containing a gray trouser, blazer and decent necktie with me to be in any case correctly dressed when going to the theater, opera or a concert. Clever stewardesses often had a fitting small black dress for such occasions with them. I always felt sorry for the colleagues including the cockpit crew who were happy to dress mostly in bluejeans, T-shirts and sneakers.

In the tropics I wore like before in South Africa a safari dress in khaki, white or reed-green. The buttoned pockets were a slight protection against pickpockets. My small boots I normally wore privately were inside fitted with small pockets and were even better. I felt sorry for the stewardesses who often dressed too frivolously and complained when they were pinched at their behind by passers by, especially in Arab countries. The mini skirt fashion promoted by Twiggy in London was just in swing and made everyone crazy. The indignation when being treated like prostitutes was pure stupidity, when one considered the strictly moral rules women were subject to in Arab countries.

Many CA's were smokers. The custom rules were that each crewmember was allowed two packets of cigarettes. So, some of the non-smokers were also asked to take two packets in order to "support the addicts". After having passed customs they were collected. As an occasional pipe smoker I was not concerned. My round tin with "Dunhill Special Mixture" lasted a long time and I never became an addict. For a long time it was allowed to smoke in reserved sections on board. In the First Senator Class even expensive cigars were offered until the ICAO enforced NON-SMOKING on all airlines. With that rule all ashtrays in the armrests and lavatories disappeared overnight!

My grandfather mothers side was a cigar smoker and a cognac treated cigar belonged to the afternoon "Mocca hour". I supplied him regularly with good cigar brands from Davidoff and Dunhill. My grandmother was always happy when I brought her some of the Ambra smelling cigarettes from the Orient.

Because of my formation in the gastronomy, knowledge of languages and my advanced age I was promoted soon to "chef de cabin" that signified that I was superior of up to 5 CA's responsible for the cooperation with the cockpit crew, ramp agent, catering and check-in ground staff and cabin staff. I had to make announcements in up to 3 languages and coordinate the medical treatment of sick passengers if required. Before the custom barriers and borders in Western EUROPE were abolished bureaucratic hurdles were (custom reports, distribution of landing cards, health declarations and spraying of the cabin in some exotic countries) had to be performed. I was responsible for preparing the Hotel Voucher with all full names, LH personal account numbers, arrival and departure dates with Flight numbers and a cabin flight report mentioning extraordinary incidents worth to be reported during the rotation.

With the introduction of the wide body Aircraft like the AIRBUS 310, the DC 10 and the Boeing 747-200 with the new "On-Dock Positions", the communication with the check-in staff was far better than before. In bad weather conditions pax could board without getting drenched by rain or snow. The Chief steward could proceed easily to the gate to see if assistance was needed. In coordination with the cockpit crew pre boarding for a certain circle of passengers (HON's, VIP's, Mothers with babies, disabled Persons etc.) was possible. I also tried to solve one problem by asking them to make an announcement to inform the passengers with high seating numbers in the rear to board first to avoid the usual chaos on board while boarding. But this procedure still took a long time until it became an international standard. The problem with oversize hand luggage was a permanent chagrin. Pax want to save extra charges for that and try to smuggle it on board. Others want to avoid the often endless waiting time at the luggage delivery point. When the aircraft is not fully booked it is no problem and easily overlooked, but fully booked there is simply no extra storage space available. There was only one solution, I had to take care of delivering the overweight/oversize luggage into the freight compartment.

I was always interested in the boarding cards. Besides the Class & Seat number the name was mentioned and often the origin and nationality could be guessed and the passenger could be greeted in the national tongue if possible and being asked for his whereabouts, that took away their feeling to be just an anonymous number in this mass transport. If I found out that a group of passengers of a certain country was on board I wished them a short pleasant trip in Japanese, Mandarin-Chinese, Arab and Greek.

It may be of advantage to fly with the same coordinated crew, but in practice it is impossible to organize. It is rather exerting to adapt always to a new crew. On the other hand it was rather interesting to meet different people and exchange live experiences. It was amusing to see the changing habits/fashions of Stewardesses and passengers. Suddenly everybody ordered Johnny Walker whisky with Schweppes bitter lemon or Bloody Mary cocktails (Wodka, Tomato Juice, Salt & Pepper). Then "Benson Hedges" cigarettes became the favourites. Overnight had a black beauty kit called mockingly BUKO (Beischlaf Utensilien Koffer =Sexual intercorse equipment case) became the fashion. After this trend ended the BUKO's were converted into picnic cases and tool kits. Pax and stewards suddenly carried diplomatic cases called in China "Ling-ling-shi = 007". I really cannot remember in which James Bond movie they were promoted by Sean Connery or Roger Moore? Rolex watches for the cockpit crew and pax became a hit like perfumes and other articles from Ralph Lauren, Givenchy, Christian Dior, Paco Rabanne or Lacoste. With many fakes they inundated like a Tsunami the world markets of the Jetset. I did not bow to any of those fashions but stayed faithfully to the old fashioned golden repetition pocket watch of my grandfather for that everybody envied me.

I always had a soft spot for fine dresses. As a bachelor I could afford to have first a tailor in London and later also in Taipei/Taiwan, Bangkok and Hongkong. You cannot imagine how comfortable it feels to wear a tailored dress with a fitting white silk shirt with fine cufflinks and initials stitched on the breast pocket.

I never owned bluejeans in my life! At home I usually wore a mechanic outfit because I was always busy repairing something or taking care of my classic car. Since the time of my service at the German Air Force I permitted myself later on a rather costly hobby collecting vintage/classic cars. The first one was a"joke" and I set it a literary monument. It was published in my Club Magazine and even abroad under the title:

MY FIRST CAR

I am a war product, born 1941, so I still can remember those battered-pre- and post war cars, that jolted over the pothole littered roads of post-war Germany, the trucks fuelled with wood gas (methane) and the coal fired steamrollers.

After our escape from the Russians we finally settled down in a small lower-saxony village in the British occupied zone. Later we moved to the nearby university city of Göttingen for educational reasons. My school there was accommodated in the former barracks of the air force at an abandoned airfield.

An old Nissenhut there housed the local glider club. Already at that period I was interested in everything concerning flying. I was permitted to assist the team that was in charge of towing. I soon got the opportunity to sit at the steering wheel of the old- "AdlerTriumph- Junior" to learn driving. A driving license was not needed there. This car's job was to tow the gliders in case the electrical rope-drum of the winch refused to turn ... and that happened quite often. The battered gray "Adler" did just have one problem, the gear lever situated at the dashboard was broken, there was just a stubble left. Changing gears worked with the help of "hammer and wrench". Instead of a fuel cap there was just a wooden plug.

At the start of the 60's I served at the new established air force base near Munich (Bavaria). There I finally got my driver license. In spite of the fact that my pay was miserable, I managed to acquire a tiny little car ... or you can call it more appropriately a "motorbike with umbrella". It was one of those many ingenious cheap constructions that were to be seen on the roads of that time. Mine was a "Kleinschnittger" built 1952 by a former aircraft engineer. I am sure part of the used aluminum material to build the car originated from the remainder stock of a former aircraft assembly factory.

The 4-wheel, open, door less, 2-seater vehicle did have a simple canvass rain-hood. The spare wheel was originally mounted at the rear, but I moved it to the side to gain space for a luggage box. The 125 ccm two-stroke motorbike engine brought the "Kleinschnittger" to a maximum speed of 80 kmh with "tailwind". There was no electrical starter. The motor was activated with the help of a wooden handle and a wire rope like a lawn mower. If you missed the timing you could hurt your fingers. There was no reverse gear. If necessary you did have to get out and push it backwards by hand. No problem with this "Super-Mini" that caused people to remark mockingly "that you needed a shoe-horn and a boot-jack to get in and out. Thanks to the simple construction its weight was just 160 kg. The oil/fuel consumption was accordingly about 1 1/2 l for 100 km. The parking procedure was very simple: You drove the car into the parking opening, then you lifted it with both hands in the rear into its correct position. The brake cables had to be checked continuously, they did have the tendency to rust tight in their slides. As ready spare brake pads were not any more available in the 60's you did have to prepare, fit and rivet them yourself.

I did have a good relationship with the local police force in the small spa-city where I was living at that time. They soon knew my address. Often I was woken up in the night or early morning by one of the squad officers who informed me that my "Kleinschnittger" had been dragged by some rowdies in front of the Emperor's monument, the water fountain or into a tulip bed of the neighbouring park. One night they even managed to lift it onto the empty loading area of a truck. The police never managed to get the culprits "in flagrante delicto". Finally, fat up with the silly tricks they played with me, I chained the car to trees and lampposts. But even then one morning in January I found a discarded Christmas tree in my vehicle. There was of course no heating in the car. As I drove it in winter too. I improvised and used a small smelly safety catalytic-petrol oven to keep the windscreen free of ice.

The small motor flap/bonnet was secured with a padlock probably to avoid fuel or the engine to be stolen. The aluminum bumper was just decoration. I replaced it with a more solid one from the Italian "Fiat-Topolino".

An Englishman who happened to park his giant Rolls Royce behind in front of the local De-Luxe Hotel remarked jokingly: "How about exchanging cars, everybody seems to be interested in your funny little thing". 1964 this kind of "means of transport" were already a rarity. Finally I sold it to a collector who made me a good offer.

The next car I acquired was a real vintage one, a BMW-Dixi from1928, a license production of the English "Austin Seven" with an 750 ccm/4 cylinder engine. It was an open 2-seater with spoke wheels. It had to be started with a crank.

Until I discovered my first Rover 2000TC in Switzerland I did own some other classics like an Austin-Healey 100/4 2600 ccm built 1952.

Maybe it is just "nostalgia", but when I think about all the cars I owned, I must state that no one has given me so much pleasure than my funny little "Kleinschnittger". A collector told me recently that those vehicles achieve astronomical prices nowadays because of their rarity.

Before I finally acquired my first ROVER P6 I drove a couple of other interesting vintage cars. The DIXI was followed by a tough English 2-seater open sports car with spoke wheels, an AUSTIN-HEALEY BN1 with a 4-cylinder 2600 ccm engine from 1952. I could only afford this hobby because I had some friends with the same interest, who could teach me the essentials to keep a car going and to keep the workshop bills low.

Later I was in the position to do most general repairs myself.

After some years being an employee of LH we got the privilege to fly standby for an industrial discount with my company and on application with other cooperation partners like PAN AMERICAN AIRLINES and TRANS WORLD AIRLINES at this time. Often I flew to London with LH or BEA/British

European Airways. I got the ticket at the employee travel center and waited patiently at the boarding gate until I was called (or rejected in the case the plane was overbooked). In this case I went to the next to London leaving flight gate. As LH flying staff with emergency training I had the privilege to fly with permission of the captain on a jump seat at the emergency exit or even in the cockpit. Most colleges knew me and it was enough to hand over my name card through the check in staff to be accepted. After the bothersome security checks, my English tool kit had to go into the luggage compartment together with the passengers luggage. Why LONDON? It was the best place to get used spare parts for my English classic cars from the car recycling scrap yards outside London and even near Heathrow Airport. Spare parts ordered from Germany took a long time to be delivered, were very expensive including freight and often unavailable because of strikes, the English disease. So I was in a privileged position to dismantle the needed parts with the permission of the manager of the recycling place which were often very cheap. My target were cars which had suffered a crash where I could be sure that the parts were working. A friend of mine David Hamilton allowed me to use his Morris Minor in search for the recycling places around London. I came already dressed in a mechanic outfit. Customs fee in Frankfurt was no question for my intentionally kept dirty spare parts like starter, generator, brake parts, petrol pumps, rear reflectors, instruments, bumpers, carburettors etc. How did I come to meet David? Not far away from Heathrow Airport in Osterley at the Piccadilly Tube Line I had booked a

Bed & Breakfast place. In the evening I spent some time in the midst of some car enthusiasts and traded stories. David was an oil driller of British Petroleum in Libya and just on holidays. He drove one of those fabulous Aston Martins. He found my way of getting spare parts for my Austin-Healey very clever and invited me to use his guest room insead of the B & B place and became acquainted with his charming wife who was the daughter of a British colonial officer and an Indian wife. She worked in the cosmetic section of the distinguished department store "Self-ridge" in the Oxford Street. David and I became good friends and he even entrusted me with the key of his home to use the guest room whenever I wanted and the key and papers for his second shopping car a Morris Minor That is only one example of how I met extraordinary people in my life. Bigger body spare parts had to be packed and went into the passengers luggage compartment or I got them from a scrapper in the Netherlands where I could pick them up by car.

An especially ludicrous acquaintance of mine goes back to my school time. Dr.Dr. George-Philipp Ranke, bestowed with academic titles, had been a member of the British secret service in WWII supplying Josip Tito's partisans with military information, explosives, weapons, ammunition and radio equipment. 1944 he had jumped by parachute and had joined the partisans in their fight against the German occupation forces. Because of injuries he was picked up at the coast by an English submarine and spent the rest of the war in a military hospital in Southern England. His father was Canadian and his mother Greek. He went to Greece to get a training course as a ship's helmsman. Much later after having worked on ships for some years he decided to study natural sciences at the renowned German university of Göttingen, Lower Saxony where my elder brother got acquainted with him. George was often invited to us together with Hosseini, a student from Afghanistan, for Sunday lunch by our world open mother. George, who was always clad in a practically military outfit, got first a doctor degree in Mathematics followed by Physics, Chemistry and Germanicism. He was a walking Encyclopedia Britannica. He lived modestly like a Buddhist monk and practised yoga. When his savings were gone he left for Greece to get a job as helmsman in Piraeus on a tanker or on one of the "rundown" soul sellers. When he finally returned to Göttingen he was again absorbed in his books sitting cross legged on the ground meditating from time to time. I was away and somewhere in the world, but helped him from time to time financially. As compensation he promised to leave me his library in the case of his death. Whoever was in charge when it finally happened, I was not considered.

This time it was a "Kneipp cure" I took as health providence after the inventor of this method the catholic priest Kneipp. I went to Bad Lauterberg Spa at the Harz mountains in Northern Germany famous for its attractive landscape and many touristic sights. In WWII in nearby underground facilities the famous V2 rockets were assembled by forced labor. A son of Bad Lauterberg was the former explorer and first governor of Tanganyika/German East Africa. While I took my regular water cures I made the acquaintance of a pleasant old Lady from Berlin, who had difficulties in walking and came regularly to the Spa and knew the area and its sites quite well but came by train. I offered her to join me on my regular excursions by car. Before her marriage with a glazier she had been a teacher. Her son had died young while studying at the Free University in Berlin. When the cure came to an end she gave me her address asking me to see her when I happened to be in Berlin. My godson Hubertus used to live in Berlin and when I happened to visit him and his clan I took the opportunity to see my Lady-friend Elli Schröter in Reinickendorf in the Northern French sector of Berlin close to the wall that separated communist East Berlin from the West. In spite of heavy bombings in WWII her impressive apartment house from the end of the 19th century was unharmed. All upper apartments had tenants and the whole right side including the former glazier's workshop was Ellie's sphere of action. Her husband had a prosperous job during and after the war time. The former shop windows had been curtained and the room had become a spacy guest room. A janitor and his wife living at the other side of the ground level with countless cats took care of the building.

There was a wide gateway to allow coaches and trucks to enter and drive to the rear where there was a pleasant flower garden now. The nearby S Bahn = City Train Station "Schönholz" was closed with bricks. It belonged to the Soviet Sector. With Ellie I undertook a lot. Our friendship lasted until her death. I met her cousin Dr. Ernest Jaeger in Toronto/Canada. He used to come once a year to see Ellie and his old friends in Berlin before he started his "Grand Tour" through Europe. As a Canadian tourist from overseas he had the privilege of a General Railway Card/ Pass valid for all European railway companies that saved him a lot of funds for expensive hotels using the sleeping cars overnights if available. Ernest was often our guest. Ellie had pledged him the right in her testament to live in her apartment when he came to Berlin. Ellie had handed down her apartment building to the Free University where her son had studied until his demise. Every year in May Ernest came to Berlin to celebrate his birthday in the presence of some relatives and old friends. The party included a generous lunch, a ship tour on the Tegel Lake and Havel and afterwards we assembled in a coffee house near the landing pier where the "cake battle" took place. At last Ernest was seated at the piano and played freehanded whatever his guest liked to hear. With them were some typical "Berlin primary rock".

Before the war Ernest had studied law, music and Russian. In the war he first worked at the "Reichs Music Chamber" creating military march melodies. The chamber was under the supervision of the propaganda and culture minister Dr. Joseph Goebbels. Later he was engaged to interrogate Russian prisoners of war. To get a visa to emigrate to Canada after the war he had to supply a document that he had learned a practical handicraft. He trained welding and emigrated with the widow of a killed in action comrade, who was a nurse. In Toronto he got a job as assistant of a Jewish lawyer. Whenever it was possible he took his backpack and traveled through Europe and the World. His last visit in Berlin was 1998 and missed his 100th birthday for 1 year. He was a remarkable personality.

The operation centre of the flying staff was at the beginning next to the controllers tower from WWII at the East of the airport. Opposite on the other side of the runway was the US-Airbase. In the first floor of the building was the branch of the DEUTSCHE BANK, where I had my account and the CA's had to depose the currencies from the duty free sales on board. Soon I made friendly contact with the employees and provided them with exotic small items from abroad. Mr. Otto was in charge of my depot of shares. Soon I had started to invest my surplus savings into shares and continued to do so all my life. Down were the "Briefing Rooms'" where the cabin crew was informed by me about the cabin relevant information before the cockpit crew came and the captain informed us about the weather condition, the estimated route and flight time. Before we were called to the crew bus we spent a short time in the "Blue Saloon" which even kept its name after having changed the color and location in the new Lufthansa Basis. The Blue Saloon was also the area where the Standby crews had to stay waiting for their call for a flight. That was also the place where rumours were circulated. It was a meeting point of young people burning for action who were released onto mankind.

At this time I decided to take a correspondence course of "Cybernetic Management Science" that lasted 3 years. I also took a Spanish course in Madrid.

In the meantime I had moved to my aunt in Bad Homburg near Frankfurt.

She had provided me with a room in the souterrain until my new apartment near the airport was ready. The date was delayed from month to month until I was finally handed out the key for the accommodation that I shared with my colleague Rolf for a short time until he moved in together with a Portuguese girl friend. The apartment was very cosy on the upper floor of the building. It had 68 square meters and consisted of a small entry, a windowless bathroom, kitchen, a spacious living room with a big window, a sleeping room with a slanted side and a glass door that led onto a balcony with a nice view on properly tended neighbours gardens. All ceilings of the rooms were planked with lovely pine wood. There was a storage room in the cellar. The famous new take-off runway was not far away and sitting on the balcony we could recognize the planes and guess where they were going. The noise was not bothering us, it belonged to our profession. By car to the LH base it took us just about 20 minutes, but the search for a parking space often took much longer in the underground or highrise garage. Opposite the runway near LH Cargo is the General Aviation centre for smaller Aircraft like Lear Jets. The Eastern section was in the late Twenties and Thirties reserved for Zeppelin Airships until the catastrophe of Lakehurst/ New York put an end to this means of air transport.

During extension & excavating works at the Southern side of the Airport one discovered poisonous gas ammunition and grenades from WWI. The whole area was closed including the direct route to the LH-base for 1 year. To drive to the LH-Basis took a long time. With the help of mine searching equipment the work could be ended successfully and the short cut street reopened. In my apartment house was a colourful mixture of tenants. Besides me there was a master-engineer of Rolls Royce & General Electric turbines and a Ramp Agent (both LH): On the middle floor was a senior Lady LH check in employee, next a LSG catering service coordinator and a computer specialist (all LH). On the ground floor was Jose Munoz a Spanish Cabin mechanic with his wife Mercedes and two kids His parents came often from Spain and lived in the souterrain apartment. There was also a Stewardess and a cabin electrician (all LH). There was plenty of parking space available because some tenants were always away.

The trader of a wine & spirit wholesale business in Frankfurt had cleverly invested in several apartment buildings of the same type near the Rhein/Main Airport and had offered them to the LH staff. He appeared rarely and seemed to be only interested in the punctual payment of the rent. It took a long time until the property was in a civilized state. I took the initiative and planted first a bush with marvellous yellow tea roses at the rear corner of the property. At the Southern side of the house I planted a couple of grapevines and finally I installed a high bed in the other corner where tomatoes thrived well. Before leaving for a flight rotation of a couple of days, I left a tin watering can for Jose to water my plants. Jose had become janitor taking care of the house and coin washing machine.

My cellar storage was situated besides the basement window where my car was parked. With a short step ladder I could leave the cellar saving me the long way around the house. In winter time with frost and early flights I put a cable to the car in order to preheat it. I never needed to free my windscreen from ice and the car started easily later on. I also took care that the battery was always fully loaded. As my storage was too small for my needs I constructed a sturdy shelf that reached to the ceiling. The illumination was insufficient so I used a neon light when it was necessary. Two short airplane trolleys that I had acquired cheaply from the LSG and repaired served super to store my tools and tiny spare parts. Underneath the basement stairs was a space that nobody used.

For me it served as storage for a spare engine of my later ROVER P6.

I am thankful that my eccentricities were endured by my LH co-inhabitants.

Each apartment had its own separate electricity counter. The costs for the central heating were fixed according to a distribution key. In the first winter season I noticed that my rooms never became really warm in spite of good sealed double windows and balcony door. There was always a light cold draught from somewhere. Finally I climbed to the attic and discovered that the insulation above the pine ceiling was completely missing. I informed the Landlord who was corpulent and had never inspected the attic above about the situation also of our two neighbours and he sent the necessary insulation material immediately. That brought me to the idea to use the spacy attic of about 200 square meters for my own advantage by closing step by step the gaps between the beams with boards from the LH cargo department where I got the special permission to use this waste material. The whole area was covered with used carpets from the aircraft's. First I used this space for drying laundry and to store bulky light spare parts for my cars. 3 windows in the roof delivered sufficient light. Up in the attic was only the container to provide hot water to the inhabitants. When my mother from Munich or my brother from New York came for a visit they could stay in my apartment while I slept on an air mattress or on a military camp-bed with a sleeping bag on the loft. While I was often away for about 22 days per month I offered friends to stay in my place when they had some business in Frankfurt or its surrounding to do. They picked up the key at a friendly neighbour opposite of our house, who was always available. I had 3 bicycles and my visitors could explore the surroundings alone or together with me.

I never had the chance to learn to play the piano. I only knew how to play the flute, mouth organ and fanfare. The opera singer Hanappel de Maes was the neighbour of my aunt in Bad Homburg and took me under his tuition training me in opera pieces from Benjamino Gigli, Enrico Caruso and Ruggero Leoncavallo. He told me that I had a wonderful voice. My favorites today are J. Iglesia, J. Pavarotti, A. Bocelli.

The advantage to flying on short and middle range flights is that we did not suffer from climate and time differences known as "Jet lag". The crew hotels were good to excellent ones. LH had contracts with international hotel groups like Hilton, Intercontinental, Sheraton, Holiday Inn or individual ones. All were located near the centres of the cities that signified a longer crew transport. A certain regular reservation of the rooms was advantageous for the hotels. The 5-star hotels were much interested to have also a young clientèle who normally could not afford to book such hotels. With our petty expenses we preferred to take our meals in restaurants in the environment. Early pickups were around 05.00h a.m. An apple and a banana plus a piece of chocolate with mineral water were sufficient. On board we were supplied with tea and coffee, so everybody was happy. My personal motto was: *Early to bed and early arise, makes a person healthy, wealthy and wise*. While the cockpit crew was busy with the flight plans, I informed the crew about matters concerning the passengers and the cabin service. Then I distributed the check lists for the emergency and medical equipment. Then we proceeded by crew bus to the aircraft to deposit our luggage at our storage compartment and boarded the plane. After we supervised the loading of galley equipment by catering. In some cases the cockpit crew was already on board when they had already flown airmail. The postal sacks were belted on all passenger seats. There were also A/C types where the seats were fixed on palettes and unloaded through the cargo door and replaced by cargo palettes. That cargo plane flew to Frankfurt and returned later in the night with new cargo to become again a passenger plane. Those A/C were the most economical ones because they were operating day and night. They had an earlier General Check that was performed according to the flown flying hours. Because some flights did not operate on Saturdays and Sundays it could happen that the crew had one or even two days off and could enjoy a cultural program.

A special attraction in Hamburg was the Sunday morning fish market where also flowers and whole banana shrubs were auctioned by eloquent Dutch merchants. Unique in the world was welcome/farewell station high on the side of the Elbe river. Every ship was greeted by loudspeakers with its National Anthem. Near the central railway station was the "Witthüs Teahouse" where one could play chess if one found a partner or study international newspapers. Some curios crews could not refrain from visiting were "Salambo" and other sex clubs where mud battles between nude women and life sex was shown. The "Reeperbahn" was world famous especially among seamen. The following story about my grandfather mothers side circulated in the family clan. As a young "Imperial Garde-Chasseur" officer he stayed in Hamburg to participate at a special training. With comrades he did not miss to see the "red light district". My grandfather was reputed for his extraordinary power. He could tear the thick telephone of Breslau in half. While strolling over the "Reeperbahn" a pickpocket tried to pinch his wallet he had carelessly placed into his rear trouser pocket. He managed to get hold of the thief's hand and broke some of his fingers, but let him run away (probably to the next hospital). I liked Hamburg because of its world open Hanseatic atmosphere. Near our crew hotel at the botanical garden "Planten und Blomen" was an unusual store for second hand books where I loved to browse looking for rare literary treasures. On demand the nice owner could find everything that was not so easy when computers were not yet ruling the world. At a lively carnival ball in my hotel I made the acquaintance of a pleasant former mannequin and fashion model. We liked each other and a friendship developed between us. I was invited to stay in the pension she owned nearby whenever I stayed in Hamburg.

Besides Hamburg, Munich was my favourite layover. We stayed in the Lufthansa owned Penta Hotel close to the Isar River and the "Deutsches Museum" and the oldest public baths "Müllers Volksbad" that was still operating. My enterprising mother was living in the green belt in the North of Munich with a good S-Bahn (city train) connection. My brother had found a nice apartment for her before he emigrated to the USA. In and around Munich were living a lot of relatives and friends. Depending on my flight rotation I visited her by train and we made an excursion by bike into the "Moos", where many healing plants were cultivated or to Schleissheim castle with its beautiful park where the aircraft department of the "Deutsches Museum" was situated. On more frequent occasions we arranged to meet at the Penta Hotel where she already expected me in the lobby upon arrival or came to my room where I had just finished my shower. According to the weather condition we started with a snack in the "Schneiders Weisse" nearby at the centre of Munich were on Sundays the delicious "White sausage" = Weisswurst was offered with sweet mustard and potato salad or we went to the Hacker brewery beer garden to enjoy the grilled sweet water fish on wooden sticks from the Lake of Chiem or we went to the Hofbräuhaus near the Maximilianeum to enjoy a rustic Bavarian dinner (not to confound with the famous tourist trap near the historical city hall). We walked along the Isar river or took the tram (that had been so satirically described by the popular comic entertainer Valentin). In the museum district was always something worth seeing. I knew something about painting because in school I had tried my luck in water colours and even in oil paintings. Then we strolled through the "English Garden" to the distinguished Coffee House "Luitpold" where we ordered coffee with "Schlagobers" (whipped cream) with cognac or an Irish cream whisky and an apple pie or another delicacy. We checked the local newspaper to find out if something interesting was happening in the theater or cinema world and acquired two tickets at the "last minute" cashier counter when we were lucky. In this case it became late and my mother slept with me in the crew hotel. When the wake up call came for me at 04.45h a.m. I left her and let her sleep by hanging a "Don't Disturb" sign outside at the door knob. A frugal breakfast was available in the fridge and a cooker for preparing hot water for tea or nescafe. On other occasions we went to the "Nymphenburg castle and park" or to the "Lake of Starnberg" or we went to see relatives and friends of my mother by S-Bahn after my mother had announced our coming the days before. For these visits I was dressed correctly and took with me an appropriate present or at least a bunch of flowers. It was amazing what kind of interesting personalities I happened to meet. Many were former friends of an intellectual university circle in Silesia, where my father happened to have been the leader. My mother, the widow, had been asked to join this formidable group. What a pity I never kept a diary.

When my mother was absent I spent my time with Patricia Chou, an old friend of mine who came originally from Manchuria and had fled to Europe with her father, a professor of music. She owned a cosy coffee-house where literacy and intellectuals used to meet.

At Stuttgart layovers I often invited my aunt von der Schulenburg for the generous brunch in my hotel where we exchanged family gossip. About our common ancestor Marshal Matthias Count v.d.S. are remarkable facts to report. After a long career on the battlefields of Europe he became with the support of Prince Eugen of Savoie the order by the Doge in Venice to reorganize the decayed Land Forces of the noble republic within 3 years. He managed to discipline the troops in a far shorter time and concentrated himself on the restoration of the fortification of Kerkira on Corfu Island in the Aegean Sea. His strategic idea was to block the way to Venice for the Turkish fleet. If they passed Corfu they were hopelessly trapped with the Marshal behind their back cutting them off from all military supplies. When the day finally came the "Pasha" concentrated himself with his naval forces to destroy the fortification of Kerkyra, but the Marshal was well prepared and rejected all attempts to invade it. At the end, having lost too many fighters, the Pascha, son of the Sultan, gave up. Before leaving the battle place he met with the Marshal alone on a small island for a confidential talk and presented the

Marshal with his diamond studded scimitar as acknowledgement for the tactical achievements of his adversary.

The scimitar stayed in the v.Schulenburg family until it was taken by the American soldiers or officers as spoils of war hanging probably at the wall of the living room of a war veteran and all are ignorant of its real value.

During my layover in Düsseldorf I never missed to contact the younger sister of my father, who had been killed in action in Russia 3 months before I was born. She was a jurist and became the first female district president of the federal German Postal Services. With 45 she stepped finally down to concentrate on raising her lively family of three lovely girls and twin boys. Her husband had been a tank commander and had lost one eye. The rest of the war he trained young artillerists. After the war he had studied law and happened to meet my aunt. When the German forces were again established during the Korean conflict my uncle was responsible for the counter-intelligence service. When the communist East German STASI with a clever spy had managed to infiltrate his organization he was blamed for this disaster. He was so furious that he stepped down and started a new career at the ARAG, a big insurance company in Düsseldorf. Sitting together and sharing a fine bottle of wine he could relate exciting stories about the war time and after. Fascinating were his accounts about big insurance frauds that were handled behind the screens and never reached the media. As a layman I had not the slightest idea of such criminal activities.

In the following example I like to demonstrate how nice it is to have contacts everywhere.

Besides London with all its enormous offers in all domains Paris where I had studied for some time had grown close to my heart. When I landed in Orly for a layover I called Jane Fiedler in her office and made an appointment at the "Fouquet Coffee House" at the Champs Elysees or at the "Cafe de la Paix" at the opera when it was convenient. Sometimes she invited me to her apartment in "La Defense" behind the Arc de Triomphe where she lived with her partner, a well-known radiologist. She was the widow of a Swiss diplomat and enjoyed still working as foreign correspondent for Siemens. How did I come to know her? Her mother was a born Martignoni and her father was the manager of the today still existing 5-star Luxury Hotel "Baur au Lac" in Zurich. To provide her with a good gastronomic training he sent his only daughter to Davos. While at this time the people in Europe butchered each other the Swiss kept neutral like always except by providing the Swiss Guard for the protection of the pope and the Vatican. The Swiss economy was based on technical precision work, international banking, chocolate and milk products and last not least tourism to insure full occupation. The last however failed as a provider of foreign currency. The famous Hotels were empty. But the clever government in Bern found a solution. With the assistance of the Swiss and International Red Cross wounded and sick prisoners of both conflict sides were exchanged 1:1 to be healed and rehabilitated in Switzerland in the upper Class Hotel where all necessary facilities for recuperation were available. The patients of both sides were kept in different hotels to avoid fraternization. The costs for this initiative were shouldered by the warring parties. After the patients had recovered from pneumonia and other infractions they were not allowed to return to the battlefield.

My grandfather had managed together with a companion for 2 weeks faking British officers until they were finally caught. As prisoners of war they were treated badly enduring thirst, hunger, frost-bites and missing medical care. My grandfather had a bad swollen injury at his leg caused by a grenade splinter followed by a heavy pneumonia. Here I attach the personal report of his time as French prisoners of war.

***

AN ACCOUNT OF MY CAPTURE AND TIME IN FRENCH CAPTIVITY

HANS FREIHERR VON REIBNITZ, LIEUTENANT, GARDE-JÄGER BATAILLON

8.9.14 On the 8th of September 1914 we were in heavy contact with the English near Boitron. At about 11:30 we received the order to break off from the battle, and that the Garde-Jäger battalion was to withdraw towards La Capelle. Captain Stephan gave the order and we all tried, in short stages, to disengage from the English who had advanced to within 200 meters of us. We managed this quite well, having lain together in a narrow gorge, without any of us getting badly wounded, although we were under heavy fire. Ringhardt followed me, and we withdrew under reasonable cover.

We had covered 200-300 meters when one of the many shells landing close to us burst 15-20 meters half left of me and I was hit so hard in the right knee that I lost consciousness for a moment. When I came to, I felt a piercing pain in the knee which got worse with every movement. I called to Ringhardt, who lay not far from me, that I could only use the leg with difficulty and that, if I was to crawl back in this state, the English would certainly catch us. So he stayed with me and we crept into a thorn hedge, hoping to fight through to our troops under cover of darkness.

Barely five minutes had passed, which seemed an eternity to us, when the hostile artillery fire, which had intensified, died down and we heard English voices. There was still isolated firing, and soon afterwards we heard the march of troop formations, followed by enormous columns of vehicles carrying English and French troops. We were barely 50 meters from the big road, so we could make out every sound. We were so afraid of being discovered that we scarcely dared to breathe.

In the end, we disguised our hiding place further with branches, and checked what food we had. Unfortunately we had precious little; of course neither of us had counted with such bad luck. Three pieces of chocolate the length and width of my forefinger and half a mug of red wine – that was it. We calculated that we could just survive for six days on this, and were much more worried that we had so little to drink. However, we hoped to overcome this with blackberries and green apples. We both also expected a counterattack by German troops. Who could have believed we would suffer such a reverse after that unstoppable advance!

Towards evening there was a violent thunderstorm with pelting rain. Ringhardt's coat and tarpaulin had to cover us both as far as possible against the rain. It was very unpleasant that the heavy ground on which we lay became soggy from the rain and that our uniforms became completely glued with the thick clay mash. The march of enemy troops past us continued through the night. For short moments we both dropped off, to the wildest dreams, until a vehicle horn or a movement of one of us in restless sleep woke us both up. Only then did we slowly recall where we were, and our desperate situation would again become clear to us. These were the worst hours. My leg, which had swelled up badly, hurt a lot but I found out by moving it that it wasn't broken.

9.9.14 At daybreak Ringhardt had gathered a few blackberries and also managed to bring back some apples. It was wet and cold, and we were freezing. The traffic on the road continued without interruption. French soldiers approached our bush a couple of times and picked berries. At such moments our hearts almost stopped for fear of discovery. In the afternoon it cleared up. About evening we heard a few shots and we hoped that our own patrols were advancing. About 10 o'clock in the evening the rain and storm started again, and this night was as disagreeable as the last. We gave up our hope of being freed by German troops and decided to try to cross the enemy lines by ourselves.

10.9.14 The rain stopped towards morning. Ringhardt went again to gather breakfast. We now made a plan for travelling at night. Above all my leg had to be made capable of moving. Although it hurt a lot, I continuously exercised my knee joint and concluded that despite the intense pain I would be able to walk. We prepared everything to start walking that night, but had to delay our plan because the movement of enemy troops continued unabated. We were terribly tormented by our awful thirst; we licked rain and dew from the leaves to wet our tongues, which seemed to stick to our palates. This night passed as terribly as the last.

11.9.14 The rain had settled in again overnight and still continued. Our clothes were soaked through, our thirst so bad that we could no longer swallow; we tried to satisfy our intense hunger by eating berries and green apples, which resulted in terrible diarrhoea. One thing was clear to us: one more night here and we were finished. All day I exercised my knee, which was very painful but absolutely necessary. We thought everything through once more and selected only the most important things to take with us. We were shaking with anticipation of the evening, with its uncertain future. We bundled together everything we wanted to leave behind.

At about 7 o'clock it had become dark enough for us to leave. It bucketed down. When I stood again for the first time on my leg, I became so faint with pain that I had to catch hold of a tree. With all my willpower I first had to overcome this state. The pain in the knee was hardly bearable for my first steps. Carefully we went forward, step by step through gardens and orchards, first to the Petit Morin to drink our fill. Making progress in this totally unknown and rather difficult terrain cost us many bruises. When we reached the stream we drank so much that we felt quite ill. The canteens were filled and then we tried to cross over to the other bank of the Petit Morin. We discovered with the help of branches that the water was more than two meters deep, so we had to look for a bridge, which we had hoped to avoid as it could possibly still be in enemy hands.

We continued upstream next to the Morin towards the east, as we hoped to meet up with German troops in this direction. We finally found a bridge over the stream and, to our great joy, that it was un-occupied. We had already considered how we could deal with any sentry quietly without injuring him. It poured down so hard that we no longer had a dry stitch on. We were encouraged by our success so far and determined to make progress, so the walking became less and less arduous. On impassable tracks on a pitch-black night, thick forest to the right and left of the track, we made relatively fast progress because we could move without taking particular care. To support my leg I had got hold of a solid branch as a walking stick.

At about 11 o'clock we came across the tracks of a small railway which we followed again towards the east. About 1 o'clock we reached the end of the forest, and in front of us we saw the lights of a village and a long column of vehicles with their lights on, just beginning to move. We repeatedly crossed roads made for troop columns, almost all of which headed north. The sky cleared up and now we could see bushes, dirt heaps and corn stacks which we had mistaken for in the harsh moonlight, as people and various monsters were lying in wait for us. We carefully avoided the villages. Of course we again found only green apples to eat. I had no more feeling in my leg, but as soon as we stopped for a short break it started to throb and cramp up, as if it had fallen asleep.

We kept going until 3.30 in the morning. In that time we had to remember to look for a hiding place for the day. Near an old English bivouac, we crept into a wood with good undergrowth. We dragged some wheat sheaves into the wood and made a camp as far as we could with our wet things. Towards sunrise it became very fresh; nevertheless we took off our whole uniforms and let them dry. Our underwear was also sopping. Covered in the damp sheaves of wheat we tried to sleep. Unfortunately our efforts were in vain because we shook with cold.

12.9.14 The morning remained clear, and the sun warmed us wonderfully and dried our things. A French airplane flew quite low over us. We envied the lucky men in it. No price would have been too high for us if we could have swapped places with them. Soon a nearby village showed signs of life, and we heard voices and the movement of many vehicles. Creeping closer to the noise, we found a wide road on which there was heavy traffic. Refreshed by the short sleep, we ate our last little piece of chocolate and decided to try in the evening to find something edible in the village. After the big exertions of the previous night I again had great pain in the knee, but I decided that, as in the previous night, the pain would gradually ease off with walking.

We were tormented by the thought of not being able to give our families any sign of life, and that they would have thought we were dead. We spent the long day sleeping and telling stories; this was rather interesting for me as Ringhardt had guided our Emperor often during the stag season in Romiten. So we tried for a moment to forget our desperate situation. At about 4.30 in the afternoon it started to come down in buckets again, and the storm howled. In the beginning the leg hurt just like the day before, and was perhaps even stiffer.

Coming through an orchard we arrived at a farm. A small room in the farmhouse was lit. Around the stove sat a ragged and poor looking family. When we asked for food the people told us they had nothing and were themselves starving, but they offered to lead us to another farm where we would certainly receive something to eat. There we were both given an egg. How delightful that tasted after those five days in which our food consisted only of unripe fruit. The farmer showed us the big road to La Ferté Gaucher. In that direction we hoped to meet up with German troops.

It poured down, but this didn't stop us from stepping out briskly on the road to La Ferté Gaucher. The further we went, the better the leg warmed up and began to work like a machine. After one and a half hours walking, we had seen the flash of firing at three different places in the sky, and we told ourselves that where there was firing there were also German troops. We picked up the pace and came to a long village. From the last house, a smithy, a wide beam of light fell onto the road. Standing in the shade of one of the neighbouring houses, we tried to understand a loud conversation in French, to learn from it anything of interest to us. Unfortunately we couldn't understand enough and we decided to make enquiries in one of the nearby farms. A beam of light came from a barn, and I thought that I could make out a lot of beds in the poor light.

We carefully approached the dwelling, which was an inn. On my knock a pretty, cleanly dressed woman appeared who asked us what we wanted. I said that we were Englishmen and would like something to fortify us. She asked us to step closer and called her husband. Unfortunately, the lovely lass had recognised us as

German soldiers and had whispered her discovery to her partner. While warming food and drinks were brought to us, the landlord locked the door. I immediately drew my pistol and threatened to shoot him if he did not open it. This worked, and we were quickly outside and disappeared into the night and fog. As we hurried past the barn in which we had peered earlier, the pretty landlady stood at the door and shook sleepy Frenchmen awake, urging them to arrest us.

We hurried to get out of this hole, wanting to get around the village and head east. We now really pushed ourselves. Clambering over thorn hedges, barbed wire and ditches, climbing and wading through the completely soaked fields, we circled around the place and continued in an easterly direction towards La Ferté. Just this side of it we bumped into the heavily guarded railway line, which carried heavy traffic. Sentry fires burned every 100 paces and made it easy to guard this stretch. So there was no way forward here. The whole difficult and exhausting journey had been for nothing.

We retraced our steps and turned into a big road which led directly north. We dragged ourselves along this for hour after hour, wet through and near desperation. Only the thought of captivity pursued us like a ghost and drove us on.

After many hours of walking we came to a seemingly isolated farm. Here we hoped to find cover for the next day. The house was locked, so we went into the cowshed and warmed ourselves there, but left again as the people had discovered us there straight away. We went into the barn and decided to remain there for the day. Both bays were filled with straw and corn and we did not expect the farmer to enter the barn. Despite the strong draft in the building we took off all our wet clothing and rubbed each other with straw to get our circulation going again. Then we spread our uniforms out to dry and crept naked into a big mound of straw. Unfortunately, the draft was so strong that we slept only fitfully because of the cold.

13.9.14 After sleeping for about two hours we woke up. It was still pouring outside. At about half past six there was movement in the yard. Now for the time being everything ran smoothly, and nobody visited us in our boudoir. Over the morning we alternated between sleeping and standing guard. I had just taken over the watch again when, at about half past twelve, the barn door opened and the face of the farmer appeared, stiff with amazement. For some time, he stared dumbfounded at us and our spread out clothes. I told him that we were Englishmen on patrol, had lost our way and had arrived the night here; we had not wanted to wake the residents, so had settled here in the barn. For a long time, he looked distrustfully at us and our spread-out clothes, but he calmed down as he saw no helmets and only green instead of gray uniforms.

In the end, the whole family gathered around us and stared at us as though we were from Mars. We must have looked amazing. On my request the farmer's wife gave me washed German soldiers' underwear which our troops had exchanged here for the farmers' clean underwear. Once more we rubbed each other hard with hay until we were red as lobsters, and slipped with the greatest pleasure into the dry underwear. We brought our uniforms into the farmer's kitchen to dry, and were given a modest lunch of boiled cabbage and a glass of milk. In contrast to our food so far this was of course princely fare.

In conversation with the farmer I tried to find out about the military situation. He told us that the Germans had been completely routed, and we're now in the region of Soissons-Rheims from which they would soon be driven. On a map I had a look at this and ascertained that from Rieux south of Montmirail we would still have some 80 kilometers to travel to reach the front. I was taken up completely with this news when the son of the farmer entered the room and informed us that French trucks were coming on their way to the front. The farmer said, "Now you're in luck; from here on you can travel by truck". In a couple of words, I explained the situation to Ringhardt, and we started to pull on our uniforms.

When we were ready we thanked the farmer for his hospitality and headed for the barn to collect our weapons, or so we said. We left the barn immediately by the rear door and hurried through an orchard to a stack of straw, hiding behind it. Unfortunately the son of the farmer had seen us and raised the alarm. Soon after the peasants in groups of five to six men, armed with guns, scythes, flails and other murder weapons, spread out around our stack, encircled us and called on us to surrender. I had another eight bullets in my pistol, Ringhardt about 15 for his completely rusted rifle, and so, considering that we were facing civilians, and we could see French military trucks driving past close by, I agreed to the peasants' demand and gave up all further resistance as completely hopeless.

We were brought by the furious gang to the house of the local elder, whom we have to thank that we came unharmed out of the claws of those people. The elder had a lot of respect for us Germans and expected us to return. So he asked me to give him a note in which I declared that he had treated us decently. I promised him this, but only after he had delivered us properly to the military authority. At about 4 o'clock in the afternoon a military vehicle arrived to take us to La Ferté Gaucher. The French sergeant asked me whether we had been in La Ferté Gaucher the night before, had been locked up there but had escaped with the help of a pistol. I affirmed this, whereupon he told me that he had been ordered to set off immediately with a team by car to hunt us, as soon as we were spotted somewhere again.

After half an hour's drive we arrived at La Ferté Gaucher, where we were interrogated by various officers. Our statements were very scanty and uninteresting, so that after half an hour we were packed into a car to be brought to Coulommiers. To the south of La Ferté we had to cross the railway line where a drunken Dragoon was on sentry duty. He stopped our car and asked the non-com transporting us for his written orders about where he was to bring us. Because the order had been given to the non-com only verbally, the sentry did not want to let us continue. He held his gun to my head and said he would pull the trigger if the car attempted to continue.

Attracted by our appearance and the violent verbal exchange, a crowd of 50 to 100 soldiers gathered around the car. These drunken chaps let loose with the most awful invectives and terms of abuse about our emperor, and told us over and over again, "Now you pigs won't be singing 'Heil Dir im Siegerkranz' and 'Deutschland, Deutschland über alles' any more". They bawled out these songs in German, spat on us and hit our car with bats. These were terrible minutes and we were sorry not to have fallen in battle, at least to have been spared this shame. In this wild melee a little incident eased my desperation. A simple French soldier came up to the car, reached his right hand to me in the car and said to me, "We're not all like that; these pigs are drunk. I was in Germany for a long time; I know what you're like."

At last we continued on our way and at about 6 o'clock we were delivered to an old sergeant of gendarmes in Coulommiers who was in charge of the gaol there. Soon afterwards we were led away to the prison and locked in our cells next to English deserters and French criminals. At my strong plea a blanket and a straw sack were put into Ringhardt's cell and he was allowed to stay with me. I felt very low, with violent shivers, my diarrhea at its worst and strong pains in my knee. The cell walls were green with damp because an old, wide moat encircled the keep-like building. Tables and chairs were fastened with chains, the bed completely disgusting with pus and human excrement. The contents of our cell were completed with a wash basin and a bucket in which we had to relieve ourselves. We were of course very depressed, as we were also physically at the end of our strength.

With my funds I procured for Ringhardt and me at exorbitant prices a pair of rough boots and two pairs of underpants, shirts and socks. After washing them we slipped into the clean underwear, ate some bread and chocolate I had bought, and tried to catch up on our sleep. We now had nothing else to do. In the morning we could go for 20 minutes into the courtyard of the gaol to get some fresh air. All day we cleaned and mended our very ragged uniforms so that we could travel through France in reasonably decent clothing.

After five or six days which passed by in much the same way, we received the order to prepare ourselves for our departure to Mulin. Up to now all medical help had been denied me, and now I rebelled – I felt unable to walk the 50 kilometers or so on foot. The railway was working again, a carriage for which I wanted to pay was available, but the French refused me everything and ordered me to go on foot. The going became very hard to me, and my leg swelled up again.

Finally, after three days of walking in which we spent the nights in village gaols and infirmaries and were shown to the people for money, we came to Mulin near Paris. Here we were led before the commanding general of a division and were dismissed after lengthy questioning. The people, who was very worked up throughout our transportation and insulted us everywhere in the most vulgar way, were completely over the top in Mulin and wanted to lynch us. We received strong military protection, and the people were driven back partly with rifle butts.

Leaving the division HQ, after a short march we came to a pleasant, modern building and learnt that this was the prison in which we would be held for the time being. My uniform and all my other clothes were taken from me and we got under the shower. This was a rare pleasure. But instead of allowing us to put on our freshly washed clothes, which I had recently purchased, we were made to put on brown convict garb and confined in solitary cells. I was rigid with fury at their cheek, but all my protests were in vain.

My cell was No. 39. It was clean in contrast to Coulommiers, the bed was freshly made, but the table and chair were again fastened with chains to the wall. I had to relieve myself in the one open bucket in the cell. Reveille was at 6 o'clock. By 7 we had to have our beds made, the cells tidied, and to be washed and dressed. We got a pot of coffee early and a quite decent piece of bread for the whole day. At midday there was a vegetable soup with a bit of meat in it every third day, thrown in by hand; in the evening we got a rather thin soup prepared from onions. If this food was poor fare, it was wonderful compared to what I had enjoyed earlier, between the 8th and 13th of September and in my time in the Coulommiers prison.

In the morning we were allowed 20 minutes in the large courtyard, but had to go around in a circle. It was forbidden to speak or smoke. Of course I refused to take part in this, and in consideration of my injured knee I was allowed to sit it out. During my first afternoon I was led to the office of the prison superintendent and my personal details were taken down in the prison records. My parents and my wife still feature today in the prison records of Mulin. There was no use in rebelling or refusing to cooperate, I was threatened that if I refused to provide the information I would be put in a dark cell without food. I asked for medical treatment for my leg, which was refused with the comment that the doctors were at the front and had more important things to do than treat Germans like us. I made cold compresses for my leg, which did it a lot of good.

At my request I received a writing paper, for which I had to pay, and could write to my wife. Although I knew that not one of these pages would ever reach Germany, I still wrote long letters every day in which I poured out my feelings, which I found very calming. To read, I received a book called 'The Raising of French Youth'. To help me sleep I did read a few pages. Next to the prison was a beautiful old church, and I took pleasure each evening in the ringing of its bell. These were the only bright moments of my time in prison, which comforted me through all the menial duties I had to perform, including emptying and cleaning of the latrine buckets. Through regular hot food and rest the state of my stomach had improved considerably.

It was rather tiresome for me that the warders sought me out all day, as they knew I spoke fluent French. I was told of the greatest French and Russian victories. They claimed that Breslau and Königsberg had been taken and that their troops were outside Posen. When I just laughed at them, especially about their Russian news, and told them how I estimated the Russians would at most only temporarily occupy any German land, even if we had been defeated in the East, they became suspicious of my confidence, said I was crazy and left me more in peace from then on. It was interesting that these people were already then counting with the intervention of Italy. As the main fruit of their victory they all expected that Germany would be declared a republic, and would disintegrate into countless small states. It was disgusting how rude they all were about our Crown Prince and our Emperor, though they presented the Emperor more as a victim of circumstances in Germany.

On the whole the days passed much the same, but my desperation grew from day to day that I was incarcerated in such disgraceful circumstances in such a small space, without being able to talk things out with someone. After we had spent about two weeks in these cells, we were woken up one morning at half past four, and we were assembled again in the big ablutions room and informed that we were to be transported to a camp. With delight we took off our brown convict garb and donned our torn, dirty but precious uniforms again. It was wretched that both my shoulder pieces and several buttons had been cut off my uniform. After breakfast we got back all our valuables which had been taken from us when we arrived. After all we had experienced until then, that surprised me the most.

At about 7:30 we marched to the railway. We were of course immediately surrounded by a howling crowd, insulting us in the most vulgar way, decent looking women not averse to spitting on us, poking us with their umbrellas and passing their hands across their throats.

At last, after a two day, difficult and strenuous journey we arrived at Cholet. In Tours I was separated from Ringhardt, who had meant so much to me over this difficult time. Even the railway officials had vented their fury on us during this journey. For the shunting at the railway stations our guards climbed off, then the carriages carrying the prisoners were pushed together so violently that we were thrown everywhere in the compartments. In Cholet I was brought to a convent being used as a camp for officer prisoners. It was wonderful to be together with fellow officers again, especially as I caught up with several close friends. I will not go here into the defective and, from a sanitary perspective, quite untenable state of this camp.

Then on the 5th of August 1916 I came to the officers' camp at Montoire near Orleans. Here everything was even worse than in Cholet. For example, for the whole winter of 1916/17 we were accommodated on a plaster floor in horse stables. The slate roof had holes, through which it rained continuously onto our heads as there was no ceiling, the lighting was very poor (two paraffin lamps for 40 officers) – this was our accommodation. The food was vile, no surprise then that my lungs got a lot worse, and I had a high temperature all the time and lost blood.

Because of this, in May 1917 there was a request that I be interned in Switzerland, and I was moved on the 5th of June 1917 to Moulins to be examined there by the Swiss doctors. On the 10th of June the examination took place and I was assessed as a serious case to be sent immediately to Davos. Until the 8th of August we remained in Moulins because the French did not want to let us go. As a reason they claimed that Germany had released too few French lung sickness cases to them. On the 8th of August we arrived late at night in Lyons. Here we were kept in a completely louse-infested school for medics where we were stuck until the 24th of August. As only half of us were to leave that day for Switzerland by troop transport, we had to cast lots, and I had the great luck to draw lot '11 departure for Switzerland'.

In locked cars we were brought to the railway and with another 450 soldiers we climbed onto the Swiss ambulance train. After a wonderful journey we crossed the French frontier that evening, and with that our time of suffering came to an end.

***

He was lucky to be selected for an exchange by the IRC and taken over by the SRC for Davos in the high mountains. Thanks to the excellent treatment in the Hotel "Bellevue" he soon restored his health. That was the time when he became rejuvenated and fell in love with the daughter of the hotel Manager Signore Martignoni. A hot affair started but was kept secret. When my grandfather returned home to his "Guard- Chasseur" unit, he was employed training young recruits for their engagement at the front in France. My grandmother was also busy as a nurse in a military hospital in Potsdam where my grandpa was stationed. Shortly before the end of the war November 11th,1918 "Spanish flu pandemic" introduced by US-American soldiers spread over all Europe and the world and caused more victims than killed soldiers during the whole war. My grandfather who had survived the whole nonsense of the war became a victim and died in January 1919 when my mother just celebrated her 4th birthday. On his deathbed he confessed his Swiss love affair and asked my grandmother for forgiveness. My grandmother did it in an unusual way. When the first political unrest after the abdication of the emperor had soothed the nation, my grandmother invited the Swiss Lady Ricarda Martignoni to the manor "Bellevue" of my grandfather in Upper Silesia (German Far East).

At the first go they got on very well and they developed a friendship that carried over for three generations. In the family clan she was well known as "Aunt Riekchen".

After our escape from the Russian occupied zone of Germany we found a primitive kind of hut without water supply and electricity in a small village near the university city of Göttingen/Lower Saxony in the British Zone. We had just rescued our life but were without means. We survived somehow the next 2 years by our mother working as a farm hand.

Through the International Red Cross "Aunt Rieckchen" arranged, that my 9 year old brother was sent to her for a couple of weeks to be cosseted back to health. All fellow pupils envied him for this trip by train to Chara Land. He returned with delicious chocolate in his backpack and valuable experiences. After aunt Riekchen came often to Germany to see us and my grandparents. After aunt Riekchens demise our attachment was transferred onto her daughter Jane, my Paris connection.

My layover Hotel "Diplomat" in Barcelona was situated close to the Placa de Catalunya where underground all RENFE railway lines met. At one side there was the upper class apartment store "Corte del Ingles" that could easily compete with London's "Harrods". In the centre of the huge place was a fine sculptured fountain where hundreds of pigeons loved to assemble and take a bath. Leading to the upper ranges of the city you find the finest shops of Barcelona especially for interior architecture. Down to the harbour leads the famous Rambla alley passing the market, the opera and the medieval city with its convents and cathedrals. The Rambla is a paradise for impersonators, musicians and pick-pockets. Shortly before the port stands the high pillar showing on its top Cristobal Colon (Columbus) pointing with his out-stretched right arm to the West. Close by is the naval museum with the gorgeous galleon real.

The port does not only give space for cargo ships and cruisers but again for ferries to the Balearic Islands and yachts. There lies also the replica of the *Santa Maria*, the flagship of Columbus. In one of the side streets of the Placa de Catalunya the artist Gaudi had created some colourful apartment houses. The Sacra Familia church was also one of his works that could be compared with the Austrian artist Hundertwasser. In a book store nearby I made the acquaintance of a pretty student from Cuba. She was the nice of the revolutionary Fidel Castro and studied in Barcelona. She took me to a coffee house where I met some compatriots and students from other Latin American states. We engaged in hot discussions about international politics. I mentioned the senseless civil war of the dictator Santos in Angola and Machel in Mozambique where they created only streams of refugees and poverty in both once prosperous countries. After the end of the civil wars no Western industrialist dared to invest in these ruined countries where economical contracts were not complied with, nationalization was the "Sword of Damocles" that was pending above them. Our "improvement of the world" discussion led to endless propositions and widened the horizon.

Unfortunately we never had a layover stop in Nice/Côte d'Azur, but had the opportunity to buy carnations at a flower farmer beside the airport.

One cabin attendant was ordered to get them. The initiative had only sense, when the flight rotation ended in Frankfurt or one had the chance to make somebody happy at the next layover. At one time the Stewardess bought one bunch too much. We presented them to the female pax at boarding. At the intercontinental routes the F/C senator guests got a rose in a little plastic container to keep them fresh for some time. Pax of our cooperation partner "Thai International" got a "Royal Orchid" in first and Business Class.

Here I have tried to compile a list where we got the opportunity to acquire desired items/articles on the European network:

Dublin/Ireland Wild Salmon, London/UK Tea & Parker pens, Copenhagen/Denmark Decorative Tin Boxes with Butter Cookies, Paris/Orly Perfume, Cosmetics, Accessories, Amsterdam/Netherlands Gouda Cheese, Stockholm/Sweden Reindeer Steaks, Brussels/Belgium Fashion Ornaments, Zurich & Geneva/Switzerland Watches, Chocolate, Coffee, Davidoff Cigars, Prague/Czech Republic, Pilsner beer six packs, Malaga/Spain. Sherry, Lisbon & Oporto/Portugal Filigree Gold and Silver jewellery, Vinho Verde and Port wine, Madrid/Spain Serrano ham from Extremadura, Istanbul/Turkey Leather articles, pine seeds and pistachio. Athens/Greece 5L basket bottles of Demestica wine, Olive oil extra Virgin, 7-star Metaxa Cognac, leather articles., Tehran/Iran, Caviar from the Caspian Sea. Khartoum/Sudan. Hibiscus flower tea. Nairobi/Kenya exotic fruit basket & local vegetables, Cashew nuts. All these articles had to be ordered through catering or ground mechanics or got from the airport shops. Upon presenting our yellow LH ID-Card we got some reduction.

Beirut/Lebanon was for me at that time of the early 70th the most fascinating destination all over the world. It had a charming blend of Arabic and French culture. It was an international business and banking Center and wore the designation "Switzerland of the Middle East". Many Nationalities and religions, even Jewish were existing peacefully side by side. Here the rich oil sheiks had their holiday homes and banks to enjoy the Mediterranean coastal atmosphere. A clever old law had laid down that the President was always a Manonit Christian and the Prime Minister a Sunnite Muslim. That had worked so far perfectly. The Lebanese national flag displaying a cedar tree was a joke. Unfortunately the once extended cedar forests had disappeared already in the antique for shipbuilding and other means and no political power had taken the initiative to start a systematic reforesting campaign like the Chinese started some years ago in Inner Mongolia called the "Green Wall".

The only cedar forests that survived are in the High Atlas mountains in Morocco/Maghreb. Some beautiful examples exist in "Botanical Gardens" all over the world. The two most splendid specimens at the park entrance of the castle of Bad Homburg v. d. H., the summer residence of our last Emperor William II. They were a present from the Duke of Cambridge to the former Landgraf of Bad Homburg 1822. Originally they came from the "Kew Botanical Gardens" near London. They are now over 200 years old.

The landscape of Lebanon is rather versatile. While snow is covering the two mountain ranges and inviting sportive people for skiing the temperatures down in Beirut allow water skiing near the "Corniche".

A former German ship captain, who was married to a Lebanese Lady took me one day to his farm high up in the mountains. He cultivated an excellent red wine. From up there you had a marvellous view over the Mediterranean Sea. The Lebanese wine is so good and rare that it is barely exported and consumed only in the country. Only a few bottles found their way into the wine cellars of the Ritz Hotel/Paris and the Adlon Hotel in Berlin. The same situation can be found at the wine growing areas at the Lake of Geneva and the Rhone river in Switzerland. In the Southern part of Lebanon are the remains of the ancient city of Tyros. The as invincible classified fortified city was finally defeated by Alexander the Great through a new siege technique. Large towers of cedar wood on wheels were protected by animal skins that were continuously kept wet he managed to bring his fighters to the parapet of the walls. In between of the two mountain ranges was the Beeka valley. Here the terrorist groups like Al

Fata and others had their training camps. Beside this there were remains of an ancient unknown culture that had moved giant stones for a wall where nobody knows how they did it.

In the Northern direction hidden in the mountain is a fabulous dripstone cave that was colourful and illuminated. On another excursion with the whole crew we passed the famous "Casino de Lebanon" in the northern direction to enter Syria. We had no passports but a copy of the Crew General Declaration and LH ID-cards to get the permission. Our destination was the giant fortification "Krak des Chevaliers" on the top of a mountain that had been erected by Arabs and the Crusaders and is the best con-served fortification in the Middle East. I am sure some historical movies have been created there.

Lebanon has always been a shelter for foreign nationalities like minorities of adventurers from Russia, Armenia, Kurdistan, Cossacks, Cherkessians, Persians, Yemenites, Syriens, Jews and last not least Palestinians. Our Crew Hotel was situated at the Corniche and belonged to a Syrian. It happened that he and his son became a friend of mine. Thanks to him I had got admis-sion to the finest business club of Beirut at the other side of the Corniche. It became a ritual that I celebrated my birthday there together with nice friends and acquaintances where I also invited the LH station manager. To hide the fact that I was a Western tourist I dressed in a white or sand coloured burnus/jalabiya with a fitting headgear and sunglasses which are comfortable to wear in great heat. Unmolested, I could mingle with the crowd on the "Place de Canon" or in the Souk/Bazaar. My first autodidactic knowledge in Arabic helped me to make some nice contacts with merchants in the bazaar.

Later on I was informed by my French friend Jerôme in Paris, that there happened to be a 6-week course in basic Arabic for French catholic missionaries in the St. Mark High school in Alexandria/Egypt during the summer holidays. As some places were vacant I applied for a participation and was accepted. Of course I had not mentioned that I was a protestant and had to learn the catholic rites. Arabic-Egyptian was taught by French Jesuits from Lebanon. The sleeping place for about 50 missionaries and students was in the auditorium and the atmosphere resembled that of a convent. Wake up for the first prayer was at 05.00 a.m. Only a simple breakfast was offered. For other meals we frequented the Egyptian eating places in the nearby surroundings that were rather cheap. We had little time for sightseeing in that overcrowded city. Besides the palace of the last deposed Egyptian king Faruk and it is now a public park there was a well maintained British military cemetery for victims of the El Alamein battle the Germans and Italians lost. The Arab-Egyptian distinguished itself from the minor Arabic dialects. A merchant from Morocco could hardly understand the Egyptians. What are the key phrases that helped to learn fast Arabic vocabularies?: "What is your honourable name?" and "What is that called in your language?"

It was easy to remember names as nearly all had a meaning. Abd-el-Calif = Father of the sultan, Ibn Saud =Son of the Saud, Ibn Wassir = Son of the counsellor. Greetings could be very colourful like Sabah al Jasmin = Morning of the Jasmine flower, Allah karim = Allah may have mercy with you. Grammar is not as important as in the Western languages. The Osmans have helped to enrich the Arabic languages. The last Osman king Faruk I. had resigned by force of a military uprise in the early 50th of the 20th century.

Now let us come back to Lebanon, where many nations and religions were coexisting peacefully. The only ones who did not contribute to the flourishing economy were the Palestine refugees living in camps at the outskirts of Beirut. The continuous support of the UN and the Western Nations did not prevent them from destabilizing their host country and border region to Israel by terrorist acts that provoked retaliation acts. Long before the unrest I could handle some jobs easily. My aged Austin – Healey had a covering that leaked and the rear window was nearly blind like the door windows. The job was perfectly done and the costs were moderate. The knob of my gear lever was worn out and I ordered a new one of brass with my initials on the top. One artisan specialist in welding stainless steel copied my standard exhaust system that fit perfectly. In those early years only Bentley and Rolls Royce limousines were equipped with those expensive systems. It would have been convenient to repair or produce bigger body parts, but I could not declare them as crew luggage even though I enjoyed some privileges. Instead I learned some manual skills to maintain and restore classic cars that saved me a lot of money. A friend who owned a beautiful "Art Nouveau" villa in the Taunus mountains showed me some of his worn door brass fittings. I took some samples with me to Beirut where an Armenian artisan prepared some mold forms which were filled with melted brass. When cooled the fittings were polished, all done immediately for a fair price. In Germany that would have been impossible. All my bachelors interior of the apartment was decorated with such brass fittings. Just the outside door knob was of an inconspicuous standard aluminium door knob. At home I usually wore an overall, because I was often busy repairing or tinkering at something. With my Lady friend I often made a bicycle tour in the adjoining forest or to a lake to take a swim. A funny thing happened when the owner of a large aquarium got the stupid idea to get rid of his growing crocodile by depositing it into the lake where we used to swim. When the first swimmers discovered the harmless animal the media took care of the matter and placed a newspaper article where the little crocodile grew to a dangerous size. The lake was closed to the public and the authorities sent a fire brigade and soldiers from the army to catch the harmless "Monster". They were successful and delivered the crocodile to the director of Frankfurt's Zoological Garden.

The choice of the right presents for birthdays etc. caused always some headaches. At the brass specialists in Beirut or Karachi I ordered fitting name or house number plates, hand operated door bells, mother-of- pearl whippets or hand painted fans were received with great pleasure. Some noble relatives and friends ordered escutcheons with their name or device underneath.

Beirut was a paradise for antiques. Some stupid Bedouin's exchanged their beautiful decorated flintlock muskets against modern guns. My interest was however in ancient Roman, Greek and other coins. I still own a couple of safari chairs made of leather and wood that can be taken apart, beautifully decorated round camel seats, oriental lamps of brass or copper tin, fine carpets to cover battered floors where high in demand. Textile shops were frequented by the local women folk. For the sales staff it was fun to get roll by roll with artistic verve to spread the different textiles in front of the Lady's. On one occasion I acquired a sturdy gold colored fabric of some meters to exchange the seat covers of my battered chairs at home.

Another exotic layover I loved to stay at was the port city of Karachi in Pakistan. It could not be compared with the French-Arabic atmosphere of Beirut but offered something unique on the LH network. Because of the always latent danger of dysentery of crewmembers, LH had decided to rent a complete upper floor of the old "Metropol" colonial hotel and established a crew casino with a kitchen where we could take all the meals and non alcoholic drinks. The fixed costs were charged automatically from our expense account in Frankfurt. Mr. Muneer, the German speaking manager of the casino, took care that everything was working smoothly and that a nicely dressed service staff took care of our needs. Even after meals we could always order a sandwich. The old experienced English speaking chief took care that the hygienic rules were strictly observed by the kitchen staff. Before the partition of India and Pakistan 1948 he had worked for a British general. Day for day he surprised our crews with one of the local delicacies. The staff and the cook were all refugees and victims of the partition of the nation. Mahatma Gandhi had been strictly against it, but was murdered. India, Pakistan and Eastern Pakistan in Bengalia that became after a military putsch the independent nation Bangladesh came into being. Mr. Muneer was always helpful and reliable. I used to always take one bottle of fresh squeezed lime juice with me to use it for the promotion of fermenting fruit and regular vine grapes that need natural acid. We could of course order beer, which we had to pay separately, but were warned not to take it outside the hotel in this strict Muslim country. On the flights from Dubai or Abu Dhabi to Karachi and vice versa Pakistani season workers flew regularly with LH. They spoke no English! Later I came to know the initiator of this business deal Mr. Chaudri. His travel office was close to the Metropole Hotel. Sometimes I carried some urgent business papers to Frankfurt for him to avoid the unreliable and slow regular mail. The Metropole had once been the only big Hotel before the Hilton and Sheraton hotels opened their gates. Instead of a swimming pool there existed an extended roof terrace with deck chairs and a changing room, shower and piles of towels to make us happy. In a frigidaire were a couple of assorted soft drinks for free use. That was the place where most spent the hottest hours of the day. The view from up there over the city with its prominent mosques and their minarets was spectacular. Close by was a church with a catholic girls high school, the officers club of the Pakistani forces and the distinguished business club. Before sunset masses of crows circulated over the city and uttered a deafening noise. The stewardesses could register in the hotel for a beauty treatment or a massage. Opposite of the Metropol on the second floor of a building was my barber with his little office which was only known by insiders. A simple haircut costs only 1,10 DM. That moderate fee was the result of the inflation the Pakistan Rupee suffered. The white haired old blade was always happy to see me for a chat. Rarely a foreigner found his way to his barber shop. Like many others he was refugée from India. He survived by the recommendations of his customers. Before the partition of India he had been for many years the personal barber and manicurist of his Lordship and General-Governor Louis Mountbatten and had accompanied him on all his inspection trips through Greater India and to the summer residence Simla in the Himalayas. He remembered Mahatma Gandhi and the Pakistani General Governor M.A. Jinnah.

Like in the Middle Age in Germany in Karachi existed corporations/guilds in the handicraft and business areas. There were streets reserved for carpets, textiles, cabinet makers, glaziers, smiths, welders, potters, stone masons, sewing machine dealers, metal- and leather dealers. There existed even a camel market. It was a paradise for curious people like me. I brought my boots of Russian leather with me and they were repaired (soles and heels) right away. A nice old refugee who owned a tiny haberdasher store I supplied with used garments I had collected from friends and relatives in Germany. The chemical dry cleaning of my uniform and washing and ironing of my white shirts was done right away or overnight depending on the flight schedule

and was rather cheap. When strolling through the streets leading towards the centre I observed at all strategic street crossings
and roundabouts soldiers with machine guns behind sand sack
positions. From time to time upheavals against the free elected
governments had taken place. When the crew members had got
enough sun, they changed into blue jeans and t-shirts and hired
3-wheeled "Tuk-Tuks" to drive to the bazaar to buy something
useful like towels, replica polo shirts from Paco Rabanne, Gucci
and Lacoste and copied Levy blue jeans. Once I found something
rare, a fur cap with the head and tail of a Kashmiri fox.

An unusual sight was the city's laundry place at a side arm of
the Indus river. It was done in ancient big stone basins where it
was cooked, milled, rinsed, dried and finally ironed with old fashioned charcoal operated irons. In Pakistan and India the people
usually buy fresh vegetables every day, so the markets are always
busy except on Friday the Muslim holidays. Few people owned
fridges. The famous central "Victoria Market" from the 19th century reminded me of the former "Halle's" in Paris. How colorful
were the fruit and spice departments with their indescribable
smells. In the meat department the intestines were thrown into
big 200 Litre former oil- and petrol barrels that spread a horrible
smell and attracted uncountable swarms of flies. At some shops
I discovered simple cotton bags made of recycling material of
the cotton industries offered as shopping bags to the customers
in 3 different sizes. That gave me an interesting business idea I
realized later on. At first it was only Laundry Bags. My design
was an elephant taking a shower with the words in German =

Wäsche, English = Laundry and French = Blanchissage. All was done in simple black and white screen printing.

The bag was closed by a sturdy string and had a handle at its bottom to facilitate the emptying of the "environment friendly" cotton bag. For smaller sizes I created some pleasant drawings like for example a "Mexican with a wide brimmed hat sleeping while leaning against a palm tree". My initiative in this venture I'll explain later. On the Victoria Market I acquired some kg of dates to ferment it at home to wine. The outcome was excellent and while ageing it became even better. I also took some Arab specialities like canned Hummus and Tahina with me.

In the fitting season we hired an old fashioned dhau/sailing ship in the harbor of Karachi for an excursion to an outlying sandy island where giant turtles laid their eggs and buried them in the sand and left the hatching to the sun. The whole action happened in the darkness of the night. The ship's crew provided us with torches to observe the action. The island had armed guards to protect the turtles. The meat of the animals and their eggs were known as delicacies. Some km far away from the port exists the most effective ship recycling company of South Asia. Directly at the beach workers were busy day and night to dismantle the old freighters and oil tankers. They had no special protection gear. I doubt they had an accident insurance. No wonder the company was working so profitably feeding the blast-furnaces of Europe and China. It took just one week to dismantle a 20.000 BRT vessel. It was interesting to watch but it was an environmental disaster because of the wasted oil. Another big ship wrecking corporation is in Kaohsiung/Southern Taiwan where they work under more civilized conditions. The artisans in Karachi are as skilled as those in Beirut. I own a villa on the countryside. The doors of the double garage are opened and closed by means of a remote sensor. Because it did not work any more I called the company in charge and asked if a repair was possible. The answer was negatif, so I should have ordered a new expensive one. I had just Karachi and Kathmandu/Nepal on my schedule and took the defect sensor with me. Arriving in Karachi I took my shopping list and sensor with me and went to the shop where I had often ordered brass items and explained my problem to the owner. He closed his shop and asked me to follow him to a relative nearby who got a radio repair shop. There we sat down and talked about God and the world. Finally he opened the sensor, took his soldering iron and connected a loose wire and gave it back to me. When I took my purse to pay him, he rejected it with the words "You are my friend, it was a pleasure for me!" After about 25 years my remote sensor is still working perfectly.

On my drive with the shuttle bus from Heathrow Airport to the city terminal I made the acquaintance of the Pakistani businessman Amin Hassan. He asked me to contact him when in Karachi. We had exchanged our name cards and it really happened that I met him at his home in Karachi. This coincidental meeting developed into a long friendship even when he emigrated to Canada later on. It included his charming wife and his lively two boys. They were members of the modern sect of the

Islam religion the Ismailis whose leader is the Aga Khan. They had excellent schools and modern hospitals where even foreign specialists were employed. The Ismailis lead an advanced and enlightened lifestyle. Their image was to be honest and successful businessmen with international connections. He took me to the exclusive business club where I met many other Ismaeli business people who played a certain role in the Pakistani economy. The most remarkable was the chief of the Karachi police. I told him about a funny happening that involved my wife and my daughter I had taken with me. While I was on a shuttle flight to Kathmandu/Nepal and back, the Ladies had taken a regular taxi to explore the city. On the trip the driver had been stopped twice by policemen and asked to pay a fine without visible reason. The chief of police explained this situation as follows. The policemen are paid poorly by the government and always looked for a little side income. The easiest targets were foreigners who paid an exaggerated price for the taxies and TucTuc's and two foreign women alone, who did not speak Urdu were a wonderful target. Foreigners paid in the rule much more than Pakistanis except for some clever ones who knew the general prices by heart. When foreigners used a taxi, the meters were all defective. By law they should all be working. There must be a little hidden switch to stop the taxameter! Everyone knew about these habits but it would take an eternity to change it "Inshallah!" I was amazed about the frankliness. I got the name card of this gentleman with his words that mentioning his name to the police officer or the taxi driver would solve the problem on the spot.

What impressed me was the visible discipline of the members of the Pakistani armed forces who had been until the separation of India and Pakistan under the command of the British Royal Army had with small forces managed to keep law and order in this giant subcontinent.

Compared with the unhampered dress code of the Indian Ladies in colorful often silken Sarees that of the Pakistani women was chaste and all in white. Because of the strong sun the head was often also covered. The footgear for all are sturdy sandals. The men were dressed in white Kurta Pajamas (the word "Pyjama" originates from there). On their head they got a small black cap similar to the Jewish one. Western style habits are only worn in the air plane when travelling to the West or at international congresses or diplomatic reunions in Pakistan.

The cultural life in Pakistani cities is very restricted: there is no theatre, opera or symphony orchestra, just some run down cinemas with impossible old movies. The abominable TV was running often around the clock in households that made it difficult to lead a serious conversation. I want to mention that there existed a couple of universities in the largest city of Pakistan. Omar Kayam, Rabindanat Tagore, Khalil Gibran and other oriental authors were well known by the upper class, who flew to Cairo, Teheran or London when they wanted to enjoy some foreign culture.

Hockey is the national sport and the worldwide victories were well remembered. Nowhere I found a Western book store.Only in the bazaar I found a merchant who traded some second hand bestsellers. In spite of the ever-smoldering tensions between Pakistan and India caused by the Kashmir conflict the trashy love productions from "Bollywood" could be seen everywhere on TV. Western movies are rarely shown because of their permissiveness. Always present are the exclamations by loudspeakers from the minarets reminding the prayers five times a day. Not only the believers were summoned to the mosque but also the countless beggarmen because every Muslim is obliged by the Quran to donate once a day for the poor. In some cases begging became a profession.

Male babies of some irresponsible poor families were intentionally mutilated to destine them later for a beggarmans career with a regular income. Some were horribly disfigured and moved on simple boards with wooden wheels. Near the "Victoria Market" I discovered something unusual. Underneath the alley trees of the crowded street freelance dentists offered their services to the people. I checked their equipment and discovered that it was the same my dentist at home used to employ.

So, there were professional dentists who could not afford a regular consulting room. With their reduced means they worked very carefully.

They attracted their customers with a board displaying a picture of a mole tooth. I have forgotten how much a treatment was, but I think it was only a trifle. Just some steps further an old white bearded Gentlemen sat under a tree with a small table where an old fashioned writing machine was placed. He was typing official letters and applications to authorities and private parties in Pakistan and abroad. He was also a translator of English letters into Urdu. For my wife I acquired a beautiful practical hand operated "Sheeba" sewing machine. It was the replica of the famous old fashioned American "Singer" type. My wife is still using it nowadays.

At the Western outskirts of Karachi was the workshop and the exhibition hall of a qualified cabinet maker, where he displayed different pieces of furniture. Once I gave him the order for a chest of drawers made of solid Rosewood from Kashmir. I was so satisfied with the outcome, that many orders followed. The transport was easy, because all pieces could be taken apart for air cargo. The furniture was executed in a mixed Arab/British Colonial Style decorated with fine brass inlays. I was still a seasoned bachelor and had no space in my apartment, but I could store the furniture in the spacy attic for my later "Dream House". The most attractive piece of furniture was the writing desk with a secret compartment and the coat of arms/escutcheons inlaid in the centre of the desktop. During a longer layover I risked taking the train to the Northern border city of Peshawar. All rumors about this city situated near the Khyber Pass and not so far from Kabul/Afghanistan were not exaggerated.

Everybody carried a gun and could have been a bandit or a Mujaheddin fighter. For a stack of US$ I could have bought drugs, weapons or faked documents. I was impressed by the artisans replicas of the old fashioned English "Lee Enfield Gun". A Kalashnikov gun was not expensive. Alone the train ride was an adventure. I was able to sleep a little bit in the First Class on my return trip.

The stationary LH board mechanic in Karachi took me one

time on an excursion to the countryside. He showed me one side branch of the Indus river artifacts from the Mughal period that were dispersed freely over the sand. Nobody seemed to have been interested at this discovery place, but a law determined that the export of such items was strictly forbidden. The same happens in Greece and Turkey where the governments are completely overtaxed with the maintenance of the antique heritage. At this occasion we paid a visit to one of the poor farmers to see how they were living with a bunch of children planting mainly wheat and cotton. The children did not go to school, they were needed to work the fields. One can imagine what the future had in store for them!

Because of the climate the Pakistani Rupees were in an incredible unhygienic state. It was advisable for Westerners who were not used to it to treat their hands with disinfectant towels we had on board. It was very convenient that we could return our unused Rupees in our LH expenses account at the reception of the Metropol Hotel before pickup. The long drive to the airport was very strenuous because the air condition never worked. The street to the airport seemed to be the most frequented one of Karachi with endless convoys of trucks. Something extraordinary were with lamps, colorful illuminated and richly decorated trucks that really could not be overlooked at nighttime. It surely would have been an attraction at the Colognes carnival procession.

LH had just received the new fleet of the after special LH specifications constructed Boeing 737, when the "Energy Crisis" hit the world. After endless disputes the members of the OPEC (Organisation of Petroleum Exporting Countries) had reached an agreement to drastically limit the output of oil. It was meant as punishment for all Western industrial nations for their support of Israel in the victorious Yom Kippur War. The world came to a standstill. Petrol prices rose astronomically, highways were closed on Sundays and became a paradise for bicycle drivers. LH reduced its flights consequently and grounded a part of its fleet near Phoenix/Arizona/USA. Most other airlines followed soon and ground- and flying staff were reduced for the time being. LH employees were enticed to leave the company against a financial settlement. I decided to take another solution and took unpaid holidays for a couple of months and registered for an intensive course in Mandarin-Chinese at the National University of Taiwan in Taipei. The Uni helped me to find a pleasant accommodation nearby. Since 1895 Taiwan/Formosa has been a colony of Japan until 1945 when it became again a part of China. The same happened to Manchuria and Korea. In the occupation period many Japanese professors were lecturing at the university. They were residing in a compound with typical Japanese wooden houses, Tatami floors, sliding doors and windows. The main building was surrounded by a high wall and an exotic garden. The owner was a refugee from Shanghai where he had been a banker. He had relatives in the USA and spent most of his time in California. While he and his wife were absent his brother Mr. Hsu was taking care of the house. He spoke no English so I was forced to converse in Chinese. The side tract to the building was my domain. The student restaurant where I took my lunch during the week was managed by a widow. I was the only foreigner among her customers and she soon took interest in my person. The reason was that her son's English reading and writing capacities were not bad, but his conversation ability was zero. He never had the opportunity to meet a foreigner to talk to. That was a general problem of the young Chinese students in Taiwan. I took her son under my wings and after a surprisingly short time he could converse fluently to the delight of his mother. At the same time my Mandarin was making good progress. Another Taiwanese was happy to make my acquaintance because he had studied German in a Jesuit college. He introduced me to the Jesuit Dr. Wang who had widely travelled and seen much of the world. He again introduced me to an agriculture scientist who was much respected by his country fellows and the president. He was responsible for the introduction of a certain pineapple and asparagus species that flourished later in Taiwan and were exported in canned form all over the world. The islanders however preferred the green asparagus that was more crispy and was rich in vitamins. At the open markets only green asparagus was offered. He arranged according to my wish for a weekend a stay with a farmer who showed me how to plant rice seedlings. It was much fun for the farmer to see a Western "Long Nose" doing such work. My German speaking acquaintance offered me his local brand motorbike to explore the area around Taipei. Unfortunately the Tamsui river and its side canals were terribly polluted by the flourishing industry. Strict laws have eliminated this problem later on. As a side job at the weekend the student had an interesting occupation as night watchman at the "National Palace Museum" outside of Taipei at the slopes of the Yan Ming Shan mountain. There are displayed all the artifacts of the Imperial dynasties the Marshal Chiang Kai Shek had rescued from Maos plundering "People's Liberation Army ". When Mao occupied Peking, all treasures from the Imperial "Forbidden City" had already been transferred to Taipei. There goes the rumor that there are so many artifacts stored in the vaults of the Palace Museum that one could easily compile every day of the year a completely new exhibition. I had the chance to see the exhibition in peace without being molested by the many visitors in the daytime. Besides the treasures were some samples that demonstrated the unique patience and skill of Chinese artisans who for example were carving a complete historical scene on a peachstone. It could only be admired by means of a magnifying glass. It must seem strange that such a connoisseur of fine arts was speculating successfully at the Chicago Board of Trade with agrarian products.

Another acquaintance I met through the connection of the Jesuit Dr. Wang was Lucia and Luke Chou. She had a leading position at the Taiwan telegraph office and Luke had together with his brother taken over the company of their father in Taichung at the centre of Taiwan. They were busy in melting recycling/waste material mostly coming from the ship dismantling corporation in Kaohsiung like copper, tin, pewter and zinc were used to produce brass and formed to manifold items like fire side frames, bells, Buddha and animal figures, tableware, decorative handles for walking sticks, banker lamps with green glass shades, picture frames and many more touristic items. They were shipped to a wholesaler in Los Angeles. Luke was responsible for the export to the USA by means of standard containers. It often happened that the containers were half unused, which meant wasted freight fees. To fill his container completely should be something that was compatible with his brass goods. At the fair in Taipei I was en-lightened. I saw light furniture of bamboo, chests of sandal wood, decorative coat hangers, rattan seats, cosmetic tables with mir-rors, baskets and small bamboo bookshelves. For a trial I ordered some items under my name. I acted as a German importer with a fitting business card with the address of Luke Chou. His wife assisted me as a translator. It worked perfectly and the wholesaler in Los Angeles was happy about that additional business.

Later on Luke left the handling of the export to somebody else and concentrated himself on his original special field, the just promising computer science. Often on Sundays he picked me up to join his family for the catholic divine service with the result that I could quote soon some of Jesus Christ's famous parables from the New Testament in Mandarin.

That just a few foreigners dare to learn Mandarin/Chinese is the strain to learn the four sounds Chinese speaking is based on. There are absolutely no rules existing that could help. Any character can have at least 4 meanings and even more depend-ing on the context. There are existing some funny phrases who demonstrate this: *Mama chi ma, ma man, Mama ma ma!* = *Mama is riding a horse, the horse is slowly and Mama insults the horse!* and here another one: *Sisi shr sz shr sz shr*! = *Sisi died when she was 44 years old*! The last example demonstrates how difficult it is to handle the hissing sounds we also know from the Russian language. Compared with French, Italian or Japanese, Mandarin cannot be considered to be a beautiful language, but in expressiveness it comes close to the German language. A foreigner is always in danger of dropping a bridge. That starts already when being introduced to somebody when answering: "Wo hen gaushing sien ni !" = "I am pleased to meet you!" After having exchanged name cards follows the usual "Djou jiang!" = "Also very pleased!" Often this expression is mixed up unintentionally with the word "Djang djou" = "Soy-Sauce". That caused, of course, a lot of cheerfulness. When I happened to make a similar "Faux pas" I had always an expression ready that was created by the last Emperor of the Qing Dynasty:

"Tien pu pa, di pu pa, jou pa jang gweize swuo chung kuo hua!" = "Don't be frightened of heaven nor the hell, just be frightened of the devil from overseas trying to speak Chinese!" Thunderous laughter avoided losing my face. All Chinese people have a decided sense of humor and express their feelings cheerfully. Even Western jokes are understood when the situation is clear.

Since 1949 the communist flag has been flying over mainland China, but few Westerners understand its meaning. The big star symbolizes the central China of the "Han" people, the other four stars are representing the autonomous regions Manchuria, Inner Mongolia, Tibet and XinJiang where the Uigures (Moslems) are living. For Mao, tze-tung refined Western culture were capitalist vices he tried to eliminate. He also tried to destroy 5.000 years of Chinese history. In the so-called cultural revolution intellectuals were killed or sent to the countryside for rehabilitation. But he failed …. What are just 50 years of communist rule compared with over 5.000 years of history. With Deng, hsiao-ping and his successors a careful change has been set in that surprises the world up to now.

The present business model mixes capitalistic and socialistic strengths where speed and unobtrusiveness are prominent. As typical examples I mention the new silk road and the successful investments in Africa. In the meantime China maintains a Navy Base at the horn of Africa to join the Western powers in their fight against pirates and Huti rebels.

My old conservative teacher and university professor of literature who not only knew the poetry of the Sung dynasty but also the Greek, Romans, Voltaire and Goethe, recommended me to read the modern Chinese author Lin, yu-tang. He lived in the USA and wrote in English and acquainted me with Chinese literature of modern times. His bestseller was "My country and my people". He had a fascinating curriculum vitae, traveled a lot and spoke several languages. I had always wished to make his acquaintance, but he died already in 1976 and was carried over to Taiwan where the government gave him an honourable burial place in the Yangmingshan National Park.

To please friends, relatives and collectors of postal stamps I sent them tasteful picture postcards or airmail letters with many exotic stamps. Compared with the prosaic German ones they were colourful and diversified. While standing in the long queue in the central post office waiting for my turn to get a couple of stamps and deliver some mail I started a conversation with the also waiting Gentleman behind me. He was the manager of a big Golf Course near Taipei. Jokingly he asked me that he would be pleased to get a nice picture postcard from somewhere in the world. We exchanged name cards and I really sent him picture postcards from all corners of the world. He had the citizenship of the USA and also managed two golf places in California. One weekend he invited me to his golf club near Taipei and gave me a basic training in playing golf. Golf was invented a long time ago in St. Andrews in England as a game for Royalties and developed itself into a healthy pastime for stressed business people, politicians and members of the upper class. The maintenance of golf places is quite expensive and is paid for by the membership fees of the regular members. They are practically the owners of those installations and a highly paid qualified manager is in charge of everything. Because of those financial exclusiveness playing golf still got the air of snobbishm. I suppose that many political decisions of importance have especially in the USA and GB decided on golf places. Except president T.D. Roosevelt, who was a wheelchair case, all following presidents were good golf players.

During a layover in Geneva I made the acquaintance of a charming Taiwanese Lady, who had attended the famous Hotel Academy in Lausanne and was working as a trainee at the reception of our crew hotel. I invited her for dinner and we exchanged our experiences in the hotel business. She asked me to meet her in Taipei whenever I happened to come to Taiwan. On account of the energy crisis and my stay at the university there I came to know her open hearted parents and her younger sister. On one occasion they invited me to an excursion up in the mountains to the "Taroko National Park" were we could admire the subtropical nature in all its glory. This mountain region is the largest butterfly habitat in the world where some species exist you find nowhere else. In Taipei is a small museum dedicated to all those colourful creatures. Down at the rocky coast of the Pacific Ocean near Hualien some clever fishermen had established their sophisticated enterprises where they bred selected kinds of fish. What could be more delicious than living fish from the saltwater aquarium and prepared by the cook in front of your eyes. Sashimi (raw fish) from the sea salmon is one of my favourite specialities, of course only with the unique Japanese "Wasabi" (horseradish paste). On weekends after sunset there was a market around the Kung Fu Tse temple where they took me the next time. There was fresh seafood of all kinds like octopus, sea snails, mussels and sea urchins offered. Completely new for me however was Cobra-soup. The cobra snake is very well-known in Taiwan and populates the rice fields and gardens. The farmers have so often been bitten by the snakes that they were immune against the poison. The cobras were brought by the farmers in cages and jute sacks to the night market. According to the consumption they were one by one pierced life on hooks and the poison is collected for medical use by pressing the thumb onto the glandular. Next the cobra is slit open lengthwise to collect the blood that is sold on the spot as medicine against male impotence. Underneath the head of the snake a circular cut is applied and the skin of the cobra is drawn lengthwise off. It is used in the fashion industry. The cobra in spite of all is still alive until the head is separated. Now the body is chopped in short pieces, boiled together with spices and served in big bowls with some lime juice. My hosts were surprised when I enjoyed it so much that I asked for a second take. One had to be very careful while eating the tender meat because the tiny ribs are like needles. The soup is similar to the "Consommé Double" of the French Cuisine. The farmers catch cobras bare handed. It is confirmed by Chinese doctors that cobra serum helps against pancreatic cancer in an early stage. For my Greek friend Michailis Metzogiannakis it was however too late, because the doctors in Athens had first provided a wrong diagnosis, dysfunction of the gallbladder. Hippocrates would have probably done better without all our modern medical equipment. The parents of my acquainted young Lady invited me to a party with many interesting people from Taipei and surrounding areas, most of them Kuo-Min-Tang refugees from the communist mainland China. Besides other guests I was introduced to an old companion of the Marshal and President Chiang, Kai-Shek. While chatting with the general I mentioned that my granduncle had been a friend of General von Seeckt. In the years 1933 – 35 he had been ordered by the German government to become chief of the economical and military group to train the Chinese officers corps at the war academy in Whampoa. Surplus stock of the smaller sizes of uniforms and helmets from WWI were part of the agreement. As a present to the Chinese government General von Seeckt had also brought a dozen of Heinkel111 bombers with trainers for the Chinese pilots. The German General was also responsible for the coordination of economic relations, that means, the exchange of industrial products against raw materials. When I mentioned General von Seeckt the old general was delighted and told me that this disciplined training by the German officers had been the best time in his life. All nicknamed the highly respected General "One Eye" because he used a monocle. Within a short time he had established Law and Order in the Chinese officer corps. In his farsighted opinion von Seeckt should have been elected Reichs-President instead of the old von Hindenburg. In this case Hitler would never have had the chance to become chancellor, but he would have disposed of him in a penitentiary for his crimes. Together with Chou En-Lay he had been trained in Whampoa. He had decent character but was lured by Mao to become a communist and its right hand. He had always felt sorry to see him as an enemy. Some time later when General von Seeckt had already left China the excellent relations were disrupted by Hitlers pact with Imperial Japan, an enemy of China. I enjoyed talking with the old charger who told me about his countless adventures, successes and defeats in the 9 years against the well equipped Japanese army and the following 3 years of civil war with the communists. I told him that I was also a refugee from the German "Far East" and related some stories from my early youth in the West of Germany.

The energy crisis lasted and I applied again for unpaid holidays of two month's. I booked a six weeks intensive course at the Taipei Language Institute. One weekend I treated myself to an excursion by express train to Kaohsiung, the southernmost industrial city of Taiwan, to explore the famous beaches around the "Olambi" (goose nose) region. I already knew the lively port city from many years ago when I was employed as steward on the *MS Schwabenstein" of the North German Lloyd, Bremen. The ship recycling corporation was still the most important employer of the city. In the meantime all those ugly improvised refugee camps had disappeared and at its place attractive small houses with gardens had been established. The Marshal and President with his wife had kept their promise to support the refugees from mainland China. Through a Spanish engineer, who was busy with a technical job in Taipei for his company in Barcelona, I came to know his vivacious Chinese girlfriend. I met him at my tailor in the Linsen Pei Loo where he had just given the order for a light summer dress. When his girlfriend came to join him I invited them for lunch. When she heard that I stayed longer in Taipei she mentioned that her girl friend Wang, Tz-Lee, needed a tutor to practice her English. She proposed that I meet her girlfriend who was just taking care of the children of friends. I had become curious and drove to the indicated address by taxi. My coming was announced and she expected me with the same curiosity and a lovely smile. There she stood, my graceful princess I had always longed for. She became the greatest love of my life. Probably she considered me as honest, sincere, decent and attractive. As a bachelor I had of course some affairs with charming young Ladies seen through. Wang, Tz-Lee gave me her address but begged me never to pick her up there and never to call her. The necessary communication was done by her girlfriend or my conspirational tailor, who was living nearby Tz-Lee's home. Her parents were very conservative. Her mother was a former ballet-dancer from Shanghai and her father was a colonel in the Kuo Min-Tang Army Corps based in Kaohsiung and chief of the counter intelligence department continuously busy with covering up infiltrated spies from communist China. I was feeling extremely sorry that I never had the chance to meet her interesting father, but his mental attitude would have never allowed an affair of his single daughter with a Western "Long Nose". The Internet was not in use yet, so my mail from abroad went to her Lady friend or the indicated sender's address was that of a fictive Chinese student in Germany. My official Chinese name was *Lei, Kwei-Shr*. In spite of the fact that her father was a member of the secret service he never had the idea to check the foreign mail of his daughter, otherwise he had the authority to block my entry into Taiwan at the airport giving notice to the immigration department.

The first occurrence we had to see through was a very sad one. On April 5th, 1975 the father of the "Free China" who had led the country in good and bad times passed away. All flags went on half mast and the country fell in shock and numbness. My

tailor prepared black armlets for us to demonstrate our affliction when no fitting mourning dress was available and we joined
the defile to wish farewell and show respect to this significant
personality. The president had influenced the destiny of China
since the death of the founder of the Republic Dr. Sun. Yat-Sen
from Canton. He was present as member of the Great Powers at
the WWII conference in Cairo, where the first plans of a Peace
Order after the end of the war in Europe were documented. At
the next conference in Tehran he was not present because he detested Stalin and did not want to meet him. With his initiative
the UNO was founded after the war, where he represented with
Taiwan the whole of China. Mao, Tz-Tung extorted however
the world powers to exclude National = Kuo, Min-Tang China
(Taiwan) from the UNO and admit the Communist People's
Republic of China to the Security Council of the organization,
were they blocked from now on together with the Soviet Union
all important decisions of the General Assembly in New York.
Chang, Kai-Shek maintained in Taipei a well informed Shadow
Cabinet, that in the case of an upheaval or revolution could be
taken over the Government in mainland China immediately in
Nanking the former modern capital of the pre-war Republic.
Very ambitious and clever but unfortunately in vain. Taiwan developed itself from that time on to a real democracy including
the minority of the original Taiwanese citizens and the economy
boomed in spite of the boycott of most of the world nations, who
cut their diplomatic relations with Taiwan to establish new ones
with the People's Republic in Peking later renamed Beijing. Even

the USA followed this international example but kept as protector of Taiwan a cooperation office in its former embassy!

After President Nixon's official state visit in Beijing the former political tensions relaxed and profitable economical connections were established between the USA and China. Thanks to the defensive alliance with the USA, independence from the People's Republic was guaranteed. There are now even strong economic connections existing between mainland China and Taiwan. There are even some regular flights existing between the two countries for business people and visitors now to see children of relatives of the refugees who had found a new existence in Taiwan.

Accompanied by my darling Tz-Lee I happened to know Taipei and its environment very well. In all seasons it was a pleasure to visit the Yang MingShan National Park. At the North-Eastern National Pacific coast near the port city of Keelung were strange sandstone formations formed by the sea. It is most natural that young lovers are looking for lonely places away from the crowds, but wherever we went we were always surprised by a hidden soldier looking for invaders from "Da Lou". They were always happy for the interruption of their monotonous job. I always had some American "Lucky Strike" cigarettes and Chewing gum with me to offer and we had a nice talk. A young "long nose" from far away Europe with a charming Chinese Lady that was something to relate later to his comrades in the barracks. To be together with Tzi-Lee was a unique pleasure and she was interested in everything and drew my attention to special matters. Despite all reciprocal mutual attention we did not neglect our studies. Tz-

Lee showed me to easily remember Chinese characters and to converse in Mandarin and I trained her in remembering English vocabularies and to converse. She was very attentive and learned fast. I had been lucky to get my Japanese residence in the Wen-zow-chie 25 with Hsu hsien-cheng = Mr. Hsu again.

He really agreed with my choice of girlfriend and permitted us against all the conservative rules to study together in my nice tended room. The shadow of the bamboo leaves reflected on the sash-sliding window. Multicoloured subtropical birds amused themselves in the papaya trees and banana shrubs. Punctually the recycling truck passed by announcing his coming with an opera melody. Next came the 3-wheeled sales bicycle rickshaw offering "Siao Lung Bautse" = a kind of delicious filled dough-pockets calling and using a bell. In the school where it was free and at home I used to drink great amounts of the healthy "Green Tea" that has an advantageous effect on the brain. Everywhere on the walls of my room I had pinned sheets of papers with difficult characters I tried to memorize by heart with closed eyes by using an imaginary brush starting always from the upper left of the character. That is the rule. The brush was introduced in the time of Confucius over 2500 years ago. Before this famous philosopher carbon and in even earlier times brass or wooden pens were used to scratch characters/picto- graphs on clay (argillaceous earth) or beeswax tablets.

In the times before Confucius the SUN was represented by a circle with a point in its centre. With the introduction of the brush, ink, papyrus, parchment and paper, the circle became a square and its point developed to a stroke through the centre = the sun which rises from or settles at the horizon into the sea. Originally all characters were simple pictograms. Today only a few hundred can easily be recognized at those when good explained, the others had been worn out and cannot be recognized as such ones and have to be memorized by heart …. a life long never ending task for Chinese citizens. Here are some more examples of simple characters. Human being = Torso of a person with two legs. An added horizontal stroke symbolizes outstretched arms and signifies Big, a person with a big stomach that can bear after-growth = Woman, a person resting underneath a tree = Retire, a women underneath a roof = Home, two nuggets in a mine = Gold, several tributaries joining = Water, sun and moon together = Bright, steam and sedan chair = Auto mobile, a bird squatting on a mountain = Island and a crane/heron with spread wings = Flying. I could continue endlessly with that subject, but will spare you from doing it. Whoever thinks Chinese characters are easy to learn now will be very disappointed. Only a few old characters can be recognized as former pictograms, the others are artificially combined strokes who had to be learned by heart. For this reason Chinese people have an excellent memory and have no problems acquiring foreign languages. I was always astonished about the fact that even in the university in Taiwan the students were never confronted with the etymology of Chinese characters. A master of this science was the German Jesuit Dr. Wiegert who compiled all old characters and explains its formation. His work is a compulsory lecture for students of sinology all over the world. The Chinese pupils have no other choice than to grind what starts already in the kindergarten. There exist about over 40.000 characters. To start studying at the "Da Shue" (university) and to understand a popular newspaper one needs about 7.000 characters. Chinese can be read from left to right and vice versa and from upside down like on the beautiful old fashioned scrolls.

I did not intend to give here a boring lecture of Chinese characters, pronunciation and grammar of Mandarin Chinese but want to make understand how difficult it is for pupils and students in the Chinese settlements like Vancouver, New York. San Francisco, Washington, Los Angeles, Sydney, Taiwan, Hong Kong and Singapore to learn writing in the classic Chinese form that is a precious cultural asset. One human life is not sufficient to master it. During the so-called "Cultural revolution" Mao's young guards persecuted the intellectuals, systematically sent them to the countryside and even executed them. The historical characters were brutally and radically simplified in order that the badly educated masses of people could digest and could be brainwashed by his "Red Bible". I had no opportunity to learn the new revised characters, but consider them as ugly. The few critics who dared to open their mouths were sent as dissidents into the prison. The communist government had until recently never the courage to concede its mistakes in order not to lose its face. My brother, film producer from Los Angeles and president of the *Monarex Hollywood Corporation* got as first foreign regisseur the permission to produce the historical documentary movie *Burma Road and Flying Tigers* where the Kuo, Min Tang President and Marshal

Chiang, Kai Shek was shown in his 9 years lasting fight with his poorly equipped army against the mighty Japanese invaders. To govern a giant nation like China was always only possible with rigorous measures. A Mandarin who was corrupt and did not obey the orders from the yellow Emperor on the Dragon Throne in the "Forbidden City" in Peking was sent a silken rope that meant that he had fallen into disgrace and had to hang himself. He obeyed!!!

In the time of our last German Empire we were not so extremely rigorous. Culprits especially "Black Sheep" of the nobility who did not act according to the old rule of *Noblesse Oblige* who gambled away their property, who entered into an embarrassing misalliance with the wrong partner or fought deadly forbidden duels were discharged from the army and sent to the German penal colony South-West Africa. That was the reason, that nowhere in Africa were so many "blue blooded" settlers and their descendants than in this colony. My uncle fathers side who still got a huge hunting farm North of Okahandja in the third generation told me about this fact and to prove it he gave me an old telephone directory.

One of the last members of the government of President Sammy Nujoma was the Minister of Agriculture Baron von Wietersheim. After the peaceful takeover at independence supervised by the UNO some settlers gave up and emigrated to South Africa, Australia, New Zealand or even Brazil. The new masters of the nation were members of the SWAPO (South West African Peoples Organisation) in reality terrorists who had persecuted and killed many of their own black people and white farmers. They took over the now free farms and ran them down. They were not taken seriously by their own tribes people like the Ovambo and the Herero, because they were uneducated and only knew how to use the Kalashnikov delivered by the always trouble-making Soviet Union.

The same problem arose when at the end of WWII the German "Far East " was by allied decree taken over by the communists who had also expropriated their own nobility of their land holdings. Having no agricultural specialists they forced those citizens to manage the large landed property of the former German nobility. My grandfather's property and castle was given after it had been plundered by the mob to a decent Polish Count Grabowsky with the order to manage the land. When I met him on my many excursions he welcomed me as grandson of the former owner with an overwhelming hospitality and invited me to stay in his farm building and go hunting together with him. At this time the baroque castle built 1721 was already run down and in a state beyond restoration.

Another senseless dispossession happened when the black government of South Rhodesia/Zimbabwe chased out and often killed the white farmers. The same happened in the former Portuguese colonies of Mozambique and Angola.

One of the peaceful African nations that is locked between South Africa and Mozambique is the last African absolute kingdom "Eswatini" (Swaziland). It is situated high in the mountains and is protected by England as a member of the British Commonwealth. The present king Mswati III. has 16 wives, one of each tribe to keep the peaceful balance.

There exists a white minority of farmers of British origin that is well integrated into this lovely country. The moderate taxes allow the nation to prosper. The population is relatively poor but every citizen is granted a free piece of land to guarantee that nobody is starving in case of a famine or natural catastrophe. Recently there had been protests in the schools that were directed against the costly extravagant lifestyle of His Majesty Mswati III. that was however dissolved by the Armed Forces.

Concerning the theme "Good Government" it reminds me of a wise remark of the Sultan Quabus of Oman. When asked by a foreign diplomat why his country never became known for political troubles like in all the other Arab countries the sultan explained: * Between me and my subjects exists the invisible connection of a fine silk thread. When my subjects are frolicsome I draw the thread a bit more tight, when they tend to flare up, I let the tension go. In this way the connection with my subjects will never be interrupted and harmony in our country will prevail*!

The energy crisis could still be felt, but the air traffic returned slowly to its normality. The by Lufthansa conditions and concepts constructed two engined Boeing 737 became instantly a worldwide hit and proved to be an excellent economical aircraft. Because of better instrumentation only two pilots were in charge of flying the jet. The fuel consumption was much lower than that of the 3-engined Boeing 727. Both left doors had cleverly constructed automatic stairs. No board engineer was needed like that one on the Boeing 727. This middle range aircraft had an independent automatic stair in the tail.

The long range wide body DC10 jet was thanks to its three General Electric and Rolls Royce engines much more economically than the old fashioned predecessor Boeing 707 "Intercontinental Jet" that was soon sold to Asian Airlines. They were in great demand because of their excellent technical state. The prizes for flight tickets became cheaper and provoked the mass tourism. People who never before could afford to fly could suddenly go with charter airlines like "Condor" to Mallorca, Antalya, Tunisia and even Kenya. Then came the first type of the Boeing 747-200 called lovingly *Jumbo Jet* in the passenger and cargo version and started its victory flight around the globe. The big international airlines had to adapt to this completely new situation of mass transport and introduced movie shows on board.Film screens were first extended from their stowages in the ceiling and were replaced soon by a digital system integrated into the arm chairs and backrests of the seats and used by means of headsets. It offered movies, music programs and entertainment for youngsters with Walt Disney's films. I have to say mockingly that our international guests did not enjoy a healthy sleep any more like in the time of the former Boeing 707 "Intercontinental Jet".

It was also caused by laptops and mobile phones. It was the UM's (unaccompanied minors) who kept us busy. They were children of diplomats, employees of the development service, representatives of non-government institutions and international corporations. They were either visiting their parents abroad on holidays or returning to their boarding schools. For those often very coddled children I arranged cockpit visits as long it was still possible or I arranged drawing competitions or demonstrated some simple magic performances I had learned during a cure. Especially the girls I provided with some tricks of the paper folding art of "Origami" when no Japanese stewardess was available. They learn that already in kindergarten. Greater boys I taught if interested in some simple ways of self defence. Sometimes I explained to them the function of an auto mobile or a jet engine and showed them some pictures of my classic cars. At wake up time I sent them equipped with a basket and a pair pliers through the aisle to support the CA's distributing and recollecting the obligatory sauna towels. It was better to keep our single young guests busy instead of leaving them alone.

An Arab kid whose parents were sleeping thought it a funny idea to unroll a new toilet-paper-roll through the length of the whole cabin. I warned him to collect the paper immediately otherwise the supply of Coca Cola or orange juice would be blocked for the rest of the flight. When he had done so I ordered the count of the passengers to keep him occupied. Another boy had paid good attention when the safety features of the life vests were demonstrated. He managed to automatically blow up the vest to take it away home as a souvenir. That was of course not possible. According to the international ICAO rules purloining of emergency equipment was highly sentenced in the USA even with prison in grave cases. In respect of other articles who tended to disappear like aftershave and body lotion from the lavatories, blankets, glasses, salt & pepper shakers, cotton napkins, china wear and cutlery in Business Class we considered as neglecting loss of tourist souvenirs and preferred to close our eyes. When it however concerned the attractive and expensive sleeping blankets of the First Class. I asked the customer for his visiting-card and promised them that the acquisition would take care of the matter. In regard of this LH-institution our pursers/purserettes where given the opportunity to accompany an aquisiteur to take a glance behind the scene of important customer care like HON's, VIP's, CEO's of big German and international corporations, dignitaries and frequent travellers all those who were entitled to a special attention. They got the privilege to be accompanied by the Chief steward before the mass of the passengers on board having spent their waiting period in the First Class waiting lounge. Officially oversize voluminous coat hangers were discretely overlooked. Also big concert instruments were admitted but an extra seat had to be reserved for those for insurance reasons. Concerning unusual bulky items I have to mention. For the "Kiel Sailing competition" a participant had got the special LH-permission to transport his yacht's mast in the cabin because the space in the cargo compartment was not sufficient. Thanks to the convenient rear stairs of the Boeing 727 the mast was loaded into the cabin and fixed at the side of the aisle without obstructing the service trolley. Passengers on this flight from Frankfurt/M. to Hamburg were notified not to stumble when taking their seats. Sometimes we discovered a well known personality who travelled modestly in economy class. I asked them to follow me into the First Class in the case a seat was available. If a meal was on the program I explained to them that they had to dispense with it. My flexibility achieved many nice commendations.

Until late in the 1980s LH offered yellow season flight plans and attractive PR postcards with all aircraft's of our fleet as well as airmail stationary.

On the intercontinental long range flights the chief steward had two voluminous flight registers ABC from the IATA available. In addition I always took a fitting lexicon for the country of destination and the actual "Fischer's World Almanac" (a diplomatic handbook) with me to stay well informed about the nations of destination and others. Today the iPhone facilitates matters and I became later member of the advertisement free serious "Wikimedia" institution in Berlin.

Thanks to my curiosity I could enjoy a new hobby. While studying the international newspapers provided for our passengers worldwide I cut out the best caricatures and articles. At the end of each intermediate flight I collected the left behind newspapers. My favourite was the " Herald Tribune International" from New York. Some articles relevant to the USA I sent to my brother in Los Angeles. Later, when it became too much, I gave my collection to my friend D. Strasser who, after having worked for the German "Spiegel Magazine", became a freelance journalist living in Singapore. He specialized in news about South/East Asia.

Referring to the caricatures again I have to mention that some of them had reached global fame. Some from Danish and French magazines, which criticized Mohammed and the islamic world. As a consequence some journalists and employees of the French magazine "Charlie Hebdo" in Paris were killed by Islamic terrorists. The most famous and never surpassed caricature at the end of the 19th century was created by the British satire magazine "Punch". It shows the German Reichs-Chancellor Prince Otto von Bismarck leaving a big ship by the gangway. Above him leans both arms on the reeling the German emperor William II. watching him go. The caricature is titled: "The faithful captain leaves his ship!"

Because of grave differences Bismarck had been dismissed by the just installed young emperor. With his diplomatic adroitness and political experience for over thirty years the WWI would probably have never happened. The Swiss satirical magazine "Nebelspalter" has also delivered some impressive caricatures. In spite of the indignation of the US American citizens, the highest ranking and decorated general and only marshal of the combined US-Forces Mac Arthur was dismissed because he did not wanted to accept the partition of Korea and intended to continue the war until his victory even by the employment of an atomic bomb again.

When travelling a lot to foreign countries the allurement to acquire souvenirs is so strong, that at the end there is no place any more to display them. Now I got a big chest where I store items suitable to give away as present like hand painted fans, sandal-wood soap, silk scarfs and cushion covers, bird imitations and imitation flowers, notice books, parker pens, pump pocket lamps, neck ties, after shave spray, leather belts and wallets. So I always had something extraordinary instead of the usual bottle of wine and bunches of flowers to give away as a present. And when there was nothing fitting there were always books written by myself available. To present something is always associated with headaches. The Koreans and Thai people have solved this problem by handing over a certain appropriate sum of money in a sealed envelope. That is especially the rule at marriage parties. The most distinguished and environmental friendly form of making presents is that of the Japanese upper class. Every family with tradition owns a couple of inherited richly decorated silk scarfs. A present is folded into such a silk scarf and closed with a slip-knot. It will be presented with both hands. The recipient will open it carefully, admire the lovely stitched scarf, fold it and return it to its donor. Recycling in the most cultured form.

On account of the employment of the new wide body aircrafts the ticket prizes sank. In Europe a new competition for Boeing arose in form of The "Airbus Consortium" based in Toulouse/ Southern France. The French were responsible for the electronic equipment and the cabin/interior of the aircraft's. The Spanish assembled the wings, the tailplane and vertical stabilisers. England delivered the Rolls Royce Jet engines and Germany delivered the body. The planes were assembled in Toulouse. For the air transport of the different parts, especially the cell, the strangest plane of the world called "Grummi" exists. With its giant cargo section it resembles the "Bumblebee" were every observer asks himself how it is possible that it flys.

The mass transport caused that the standard of the guests, especially in the economy class dropped visibly and more medical problems had to be taken care of. The aggressiveness of passengers not only caused by alcohol rose. I had always shackles with me for any case to handle unruly and aggressive pax. Mostly it was enough to show them at my belt to discipline physically disturbed, drugged or alcoholic pax. If not I could rely on able bodied guests who were happy for some action. Best was of course when LH staff, BGS (Federal Border Guard) or policemen were on board who accompanied prisoners, criminals or deported foreigners (a costly expenditure for the German tax payers).

The use of shackles was of course never mentioned in my cabin reports, because I had no official police power, but nobody knew that. The captain was in such cases always cooperative and informed the airport of destination to send a policeman or in the US a Sheriff upon arrival to the plane who took over the troublemaker after the other passengers disembarked. On rising demands and complaints of frequent travellers and business people LH introduced the Business Class with a higher comfort and service. Other airlines soon followed this decision. Even the charter company of LH "Condor" introduced an Upper Tourist Class on their long range flights.

One of my many private holidays I spent in India and Nepal. I knew the chief-steward and manager of the "Royal Nepalese Airline" in

Kathmandu, who had been trained by LH in Frankfurt. He took me to a party where I met a couple of interesting people. Besides others I became acquainted with two brothers. Their recently deceased father was a Tibetan refugee who had left his homeland together with the Dalai Lama, settled down in Nepal and married a Hindi. He had died recently and his wife contracted tuberculosis. The elder son was in the midst of a professional training as policeman and for his younger brother Dilip Lama there was no money left. He worked as "John of all trades" in a simple tourist hotel cleaning the rooms, changing the bedsheets, heating water on a gas stove, cleaning the floors and windows, delivering the towels, carrying the luggage and calling a taxi. The Hotel had no electricity but used still petrol lamps and was very cheap. Dilip worked a lot and lived mostly from the tips given by the Western guests. In the evening he joined the classes of the American school to learn English. Being confronted with the daily life of the masses of poor people I felt like the prince Siddhartha of the Himalaya kingdom who was confronted one day with the real facts of life and death who left his palace searching for the truth and finally became Buddha the enlightened one. I was fine, and enjoyed some privileges, was yet not burdened with a family and children. I convinced myself to do something reasonable and decided to get this intelligent boy on the right path.

My brother was still living in Munich as representative of the New York based Cosmopolitan Picture Corporation, which was dealing with film rights. His friend, the manager of the Holiday Inn Hotel, promised us to employ Dilip Lama in the kitchen of the Hotel. I sent him a ticket that could not be converted into cash via our LH station and the representative in Kathmandu together with a letter of invitation and instructions for his arrival at the airport in Munich. I had also arranged a travel health insurance. It was a wonder, everything went fine. For the time being Dilip was living with my brother in Munich. In the Holiday Inn Hotel he did such a satisfactory job that he was promoted soon to work in the service of the coffee shop because of his knowledge of English. I told him to learn the menu and beverage card by heart to make his job easier. In the evening he took German courses. For the immigration authorities Dilip was simply a foreign student. To renew his permission to stay he had to travel to Austria, Switzerland or France and return immediately to get a new stamp for the residence permit for one month in his passport. I ended this costly circus by bailing for him that provided him also with a temporary working permission. To relieve my brother I found another job for Dilip in a highway motel near my place he could reach easily by bicycle. My apartment was unused for most of the time because I was away on duty so Dilip could live there and keep it clean. He got a postal savings book where he could deposit his monthly income. He also got used to western food and could prepare himself whatever he wanted. Soon he had saved so much money that he could explore Germany and our neighbouring countries. Equipped with a Youth Hostel card, a map, a cardboard with a felt marker, where he could mark his destiny and an umbrella he started to travel whenever he got some days off. He did it often by "Hitch-hiking/Auto stop" that was at this time the way of students to save money while moving around. Even the police sometimes gave him a ride. A nice correctly dressed foreigner from the Himalayas was something unknown in the early 70th. His family name Lama made the people very curious. When he happened to come to Munich again my broad-minded mother took him under her wings and treated him like a son. In my village near Frankfurt Airport he also had nice contacts with my neighbours. It happened that Dilip got a job in an Innsbruck Tourist Hotel in Austria. When he started to have an affair with the pretty daughter of the owner, that one told him in a friendly fatherly way, that he should first have to get a good education and profession before starting a family. Somehow Dilip took firmly roots in St. Gallen in the German speaking part of Eastern Switzerland. I assisted him to get accepted by the Director Dr. Tuchschmidt of the local "Dolmetscher Schule" (interpreters language school). For gaining his right to stay in Switzerland I had not only to bail for him, but I had to open an account at the UBS (Union Bank of Switzerland) with so much funds that he could withdraw his monthly expenses. He used that account not often, because he earned so much money at different jobs that he did not need "to milk the cow". He cleaned cars at fuel stations, worked as gardener and sales person selling blue jeans, T-shirts or sneakers and as part time servant of the well-known Italian Restaurant "Barbarella". The owner of the place had no son, trusted him a lot and made him his right hand man. Dilip stayed there for a while before starting an apprenticeship at the renowned Hotel Hecht in the center of St. Gallen. After his gastronomical training he returned to work in the "Barbarella Restaurant" of his Swiss-Italian friend.

Dilip took very much care of his appearance and had adopted good manners and was liked by the pretty young ladies and restaurant guests.

The secretary of the director of the Kantonal Spital Pia Sabathy had caught an eye on him. After a longer intercontinental trip I found an invitation for the marriage of Dilip with Pia in my mailbox. I had missed it.

At the baptism of his two girls some years later that was undertaken by the Bishop of St. Gallen I managed to be present.

Dilip had always pestered his wife with the wish of his own business. In St. Gallen, an Indian restaurant did not yet exist. The assumption was however that Pia gave up her good paid job and took over the management of such a place. Dilips wish to stand on his own feet was so strong that all arguments against this risky venture were in vain and I could not convince him to stay in his good job at his friend's restaurant.

Dilip had no idea of bookkeeping or how to apply for a permission to open an exotic restaurant in Switzerland. His Nepalese friend "Mounty" had two good restaurants in the West of London and hoped that the same luck would happen to him. Pia did not like him and rejected all his good professional counsels. On my few visits in St. Gallen while passing through the remaining old centre of the city surrounded by high rises of banks and insurance corporations we discovered opposite the Jewish Synagogue a beautiful frame work building that was a pub that the keeper recently had closed and went into retirement, but the license to sell the local "Schützen Beer" was still valid. The property with the medieval framework buildings next to it belonged to the UBS who had surely already plans for future skyscrapers in the drawers. Under the condition to leave the building immediately when the UBS decided to demolish it Dilip could lease it for a very low rent, With the house went a giant parking space and a whole cozy apartment where everything was in good condition. That saved my friend the enormous rent of his former apartment. After having pestered his wife long enough Pia gave up and left her safe job at the Canton Spital and took care of all the annoying bureaucratic matters Dilip was ignorant of. The heart piece and most expensive part of the Indian cuisine is the *Tandoori clay oven*. The first ordered in London did not survive its transport from England. The second one arrived safely at his Swiss destination in St. Gallen and served faithfully for the remaining years. Concerning the interior decoration I took the initiative and asked the manager of the "Air India" central office in New Delhi to provide me with some public relation items to decorate the Indian restaurant. He gladly complied to my wish and provided me with a lot of impressive PR posters showing Air India interior destinations and Indian and Nepalese tourist sights to cover the walls of *Lama's Tandoori Restaurant*. The best was the famous huge figure of the Air India symbol of a magnificent dressed bowing Sikh with turban welcoming the customers and passengers. We placed that one near the entrance. To cover the blackened ceiling and beams I found in Bombay/Mumbai a colourful stitched fitting canopy with birds, peacocks, elephants and sewn in small round mirrors. From London I brought a big laminated map of Nepal and placed it at a convenient spot at the wall near the entrance. From a garden centre we got some small palm trees and philodendrons to give the entrance area a friendly atmosphere.

I had committed on Dilip's mind that the WC is the visit card of a restaurant and contributed a big bottle of 4711 Eau de Cologne with the holder. In addition I saw to it that a hygienic liquid soap provider was installed and that paper towels and toilet paper were always available and the place was at any time in a faultless FC condition. As an unusual extra I had ordered 12 handbells of brass and some spare ones at my supplier in Karachi/Pakistan with Dilip's engraved initials. If the guests had a wish, they could use the bells instead of calling the service. Sometimes the decorative bells were stolen by souvenir-hunters. If it was noticed that the bell was missing, it was put inconspicuously as an extra on the bill. Finally we put them on chains to avoid this trouble. The rustic and exotic ambiente attracted especially young people and students to his cozy place. The prices were moderate and the restaurant was situated in the midst of the banking area of the city. At lunch time his "Tandoori place" was frequented by employees from the surrounding banking and insurance establishments. A professional Nepalese cook dominated the kitchen and a pretty Mongolian student assisted servicing in the evening.

Because of the good income Pia got the idea of acquiring a house outside of the noisy city in a decent surrounding. Eggersriet up in the mountains was the choice. The most important argument was that the children should grow up in a solid and beautiful surrounding and a good school nearby. The nice home remained as long in the ownership of the Kantonalbank until it was fully paid by the Lama's. Every month they had to pay the bank a certain amount of money according to their contract. I had warned them about this lifelong encumbrance, but it was futile and disregarded by Pia. It worked however only as long as the income from the Tandoori Restaurant was satisfactory. I have to concede however that the selection of the home was perfect. There was enough room for the two daughters and there was a guest room and a garage with a private parking space and a nuclear shelter prescribed by the Swiss government for modern houses. From the extended garden terrace one had a breathtaking view onto the alpine landscape of Appenzell and its highest mountain, the "Säntis". When you took a walk from the rear of the home up to the ridge, you were surrounded by meadows and cows, a marvellous view down onto the huge lake of Constanza with its sailing boats and excursion ships, that was shared by Switzerland, Germany and Austria. My mini dachshund "Aisha" that always accompanied me on my private trips abroad loved this surrounding too. Pia, who had three cats, hated dogs. For this reason I stayed only short in transit to my Italian friends in Magenta/ Lombardi near Milano. After some prosperous years with their exotic "Tandoori" place in that lovely old wild vine overgrown fairy tale house the owner Union Bank of Switzerland decided to demolish this and the remaining other medieval houses to build profitable high rises instead. According to the contract the Lama's had to move immediately. The search for an alternative was hopeless. Instead of giving up right away and to look for jobs as good salaried employees they stubbornly continued their search and finally decided to rent a very expensive object in the ground floor of a prosaic, matter-of-factly high rise business building in the banking area. The old flair had gone and the economy and banking crisis hit the world. Former customers stayed at home to save money and refrained from going out. All restaurants suffered and the new "Lama's Tandoori place" remained empty. Only a few foreigners from the international banking and insurance business who disposed of an expense account of their employer found their way to Lama's place. They could manage to survive for some time but their savings dwindled like ice in the sun.

The situation provoked a quarrel between the married couple and also involved the daughters. The costs not only for the rent but for the staff were such a burden that they were forced to dismiss the servant, the cleaning staff, the kitchen helper and finally the cook. The menu was reduced accordingly and Dilip started to cook himself. That did not work out and finely they gave up the gastronomical adventure they had so long clinged to. Under the first favored conditions everything had worked perfectly, but later on it was a hopeless failure. Dilip returned to his Italian friend in the "Barbarella" and was received with open arms. After all, the Lama's had raised two exotic looking young girls decently and both had achieved something. Olivia became a certified dentist and Gloria a teacher with foreign experiences … under the difficult circumstances a miracle. Not to burden Pia on my rare transit visits in Eggersriet I used my own sleeping bag and helped them to trim the lawn and bushes in their garden. Dilip's friend in London, the Nepalese Mohanta Shesta (Nickname "Mounty") had been lucky and had built up a small real estate empire and owned two good running Nepalese and Indian Restaurants in Ealing Broadway Western London. Pia did not like the influence of his friend and rejected everything he proposed. I also had some differences with her, having criticized her frequently, that in my anger I finally gave up on visiting them on my tours to Italy. My disappointment was tangible. I have some good friends in Switzerland but never involved them with this problem. Everybody must look for his own problems first.

Another person I gave the chance to find a professional way was the fatherless nephew of the chief photographer of the biggest international newspaper "The Times of India", Ravi Bedi: I knew him through my friend and journalist D. Strasser in Singapore. His nephew A. Grover gave him a lot of anxiety and headaches, because he had no goal in life and squandered it with nonsense. I had already realized a business idea in Pakistan producing tropical "Prospector" shirts of my own design and environment friendly cotton bags, but was with the outcome absolutely not satisfied because of a sloppy job done. I did not want to give up and wanted to try my luck in the better reputed India. I offered Ravi to give his nephew Atul the chance to organize the whole procedure of production, payment with "letter of credit", controlling, export paperwork and sending by air cargo to Germany. I delivered the picture designs for black and white screen printing, the measure of the three different sizes of the natural cotton bags and the number of productions. After a short hesitation Atul Grover accepted and learned carefully to handle such a responsible assignment and seemingly enjoyed becoming an international exporter. To make it short, he did a perfect job and was very proud of it, having earned some honest Rupees.

His uncle was delighted with the positive outcome of my initiative. On one of my duty trips to New Delhi I took my broad minded mother with me and he took us to the countryside to show us the real life of the Indian population foreigners rarely are confronted with. Indians are a bird loving nation and Ravi presented us something extraordinary. There existed a big centre with aviaries where orphaned young birds and injured ones were fed and professionally cared for in a country where holy cows and religious beggar men were taken care of by a strange population.

On another occasion I showed her all the famous tourist traps from the Mogul time and before. By arrangement of Ravi Bedi we were invited as only foreigners to a magnificent marriage party of a leading member of the upper class in the Oberoi Hotel. The bride and bride groom had to sit for hours on throne like seats on an emporium like robots to receive from the guests passing in review compliments and piles of presents.

Now back to Atul Grover. He started to export semi precious stones to German companies in Idar-Oberstein and Pforzheim both centres of the fashion industry. In order to help him to save money I provided him with a Youth Hostel ID-card and introduced him to the benefits of the German Railway system for foreign tourists from overseas and other continents. Several times he was our guest. In addition he traded besides semi precious stones good smelling incense sticks with exotic shops that were at this time still unknown to most people before the crazy "Hare Krishna" adherents the "Beatles" and the hippies made them popular. Later he remained in India and became a sales agent for the popular "President" car with the English "Austin Atlantic 90" engine of the Daimler-Benz backed TATA motor company. Later he married and was promoted as manager of one of the maintenance and sales centres of the TATA company, a real success story.

I was still single and could afford some private initiative to support people. I had only contempt for the big international organizations for development help like the German monster GIZ (Association for International Cooperation) that wasted funds in an irresponsible proportion, that only little is left for the original assignments especially children villages were many greedy and mendacious associations are actively supported by the ignorant public and the naive blind government. The employees abroad of those associations are paid of course to German tariffs. In addition the fees for horrendous expensive international health insurances, other insurances, social security, pension funds, air transport of private property, transport, housing, car, servants, fees for children abroad in schools together with children of diplomats, foreign representatives and sometimes protestant missionaries or boarding schools in Germany are paid by the associations from the contributions of the generous German donors and taxpayers. What is left for the original recipients like the orphaned children in the so-called "children villages" all over the world. There is a fitting remark of the famous English poet William Shakespeare that describes the whole situation perfectly: *Much ado about nothing*!

A few people like the former Austrian actor Karlheinz Böhm with his best organized children village in Ethiopia and Mother Theresa, the guardian angel of desperate poor people in Calcutta were rare exceptions. My idea is that every well positioned German should be responsible for a poor family or person somewhere in the world or preferably in Africa without making them dependent. A wealthy nation should be responsible for one poor country like for example Germany for Namibia instead of distributing funds for development projects like with a watering-can after the coincidence principle all over the world.

That would be worth a trial organized perhaps by the United Nations.

Under adventurous conditions I managed to visit the plantation of my granduncle before the start of the civil war in Mozambique. For some nights I stayed in a guest house of missionaries and sisters passing the South Rhodesian border city Umtali. It was surrounded by a nicely and professionally tended vegetable garden and orchard. Curious like I was, I searched for the good soul that took care of it. I came to know the assiduous gardener Jonathan who was just cleaning the chicken pen that was even on the top protected by a wire mesh to avoid trouble from the goshawks. He showed me the tool-shack where he was living. The only book I discovered was an old bible he read after sunset by means of a candle light. Water was delivered by a rubber hose from a well. He could wash himself by means of a tin bathtub suspended from the side of the shack. He was provisioned by the kitchen staff. Jonathan seemed to have only his green overall and rubber boots. I did not discover any more cloth hanging at the pegs and felt sorry for him, because his income was a pittance. Later on I gave him shorts and a T-shirt from my luggage. He was an orphan and had no relatives. He had learned reading and writing in a missionary school. I was pondering over the question of how to improve the situation of this nice fellow and finally found a solution. I acquired a sturdy Chinese bicycle "Swallow" brand with a wire basket on its rear luggage carrier as well as the necessary tool kit with repair material, an air pump, oil-cruet, two spare tyres and inner tubes. Last not least I provided him with a thick plastic protected chain and a big padlock. I warned him never to leave his bicycle alone because larceny was a widespread evil in Rhodesian cities. After having explained and demonstrated the use of the equipment and adjusted the bicycle to his size I gave him instructions in driving. He learned fast and was very excited about the sudden surprise from heaven. I suggested him to look for an avocational occupation like newspaper and magazine home service or a courier job to earn some pocket money besides.

Then I continued my trip to the dangerous Mozambique where the beginning of the civil war had already claimed some civil victims in the population. Finding the farm in a disastrous condition I returned soon to South Rhodesia and South Africa to Europe.

The next time I flew to Africa the white government under the pressure of the UN stepped down and black President Mugabe had established a dictatorial government. The name South Rhodesia had changed to Zimbabwe and the capital Salisbury was renamed. Just the name of the important railway junction to South Africa, Mozambique and Katanga/Congo remained Bulawayo. A giant inflation had overrun the formerly stablest nation in Africa. On my last visit to the still distinguished lively old 5-star "Meikles" Hotel a can of coffee had been 3 local $, now it was 6 Million new Zimbabwe $ and the prices were still rising. The shadow currency was the US$ provided by exile citizens from abroad who supported their relatives at home. Before I left Germany I requested the German Embassy in Harare for detailed information. Thanks to their recommendation I had filled my handbag with bundles of 1 US$ bills to handle the problem. I exchanged only a little sum to handle the small daily matters. The new currency was nice to look at but not worth the paper it was printed on. It was printed in India and flown weekly in by cargo planes. After a comfortable trip with the night train from Harare to the renamed border city Mutare (formerly Umtali) as a terminal. The highly in US$ paid English railway engineers kept the "show piece" of the SIM-government moving. The luxurious mahogany wainscoted walls, folding down leather bunks, brass washing bowls still existed. The once highly profitable stretch of the line through Mozambique to the port of Beira was inoperative. Weeds and trees have taken over in the civil war partly destroyed embankments and tracks of the railway line.

The totally incompetent terrorist government in Maputo (formally Lorenco Marques) had never even tried to restore this once so important railway connection to Central- and South Africa. England still owns sovereignty rights of the stretches right and left of the railway line in Mozambique.

An old black acquaintance of mine living in Mutare had become the first mayor of the city under the Mugabe dictatorship. In spite of being a socialist he entrusted me secretly that he wished back the government of Ian Smith when Rhodesia was prosperous and law and order reigned.

In Davidson Jahwis battered Land Rover we tried to reach the 60 km far away farm of my granduncle, that was now occupied by missionaries, but had to return soon because of the danger of getting targets of the former now jobless FRELIMO-terrorists and other criminals who were roaming the area. Instead I invited him to an excursion into the Vumba highlands, a former temperate summer resort. Despite the political tensions between Great Britain and Zimbabwe, Queen Elizabeth still owned a dreamlike summer palace up in a place called "Leopard Rocks". It was kept by the dictator in a spotless condition and was used for occasional foreign political dignitaries.

At the time of South Rhodesia the country was the greatest exporter of tobacco in the world. Further export hits were Indian corn/maize and wheat. During the upheavals under Mugabe many white farmers were brutally murdered. Most of the survivors were expropriated with the exception of a few politicians like the former President Ian Smith.

The others emigrated to South Africa, Australia and Canada. Their farms were plundered or sometimes carried on with a simple subsistence economy because the former terrorists failed the necessary qualifications. So it happened that Zimbabwe failed to export anything but had to import provisions to feed its starving population. During the internal conflict even the famous game parks were not spared. Animals were systematically killed to feed the terrorist gangs with meat. The same happened with the beautiful wild-life-park "Gorongosa" in Mozambique.

From a prosperous country that was treasured by adventurers roaming Africa had sunk to a place of starvelings and criminals. Even the streams of visitors from all over the world to see the famous "Victoria Falls" once discovered by Livingston had come down to a trickle.

Just a few daring business people from North Korea and China came to this country. Since the railroad stretch through Mozambique was destroyed the copper-ore transports from Katanga/Congo are handled on the old German railroad-line via Uganda to Dar-es-Salaam/Tanzania.

Mugabe had engaged North Koreans to train his secret service and his bodyguards. His army was compared with the starving population well provisioned. Under this conditions the hidden opposition had not the slightest chance to get rid of the dictator.

Something positive was that the former eternal hostilities between the two tribes "Shona" and "Matabele" had finally been put "ad acta". There existed many academic citizens who had studied in England and Germany who were now jobless and earned some money as taxi drivers or cleaning staff. Thanks to the financial support of Zimbabwean relatives and friends living and working abroad many families could survive. The US$ became the shadow currency of Zimbabwe. The only enterprises that worked satisfactory were the old gold mines maintained by British managers and engineers who were highly paid in US$. The profit served to pay for the government administration, the armed forces and to fill the secret Swiss bank accounts of the dictator and his family clan. The well equipped army served to maintain interests in conflicts of neighbouring countries as mercenaries. In this way Mugabe secured for himself mining rights in Katanga and the Congo/Zaire. The starving Zimbabwean population remained empty-handed.

The former name of Rhodesia reminds us of the extremely successful owner of gold- and diamond mines Cecil Rhodes nicknamed by Queen Victoria "Empire Builder". With the private army of mercenaries that was equipped with the just invented maxim-machine gun he succeeded to crush the resistance of multiple tribes. The origin of three African nations like South Rhodesia = Zimbabwe, North Rhodesia = Zambia and Nyasaland = Malawi were created through his initiative. 1879 still existed as the African kingdom of the Matabele in exactly the area where Zimbabwe is now. Cecil Rhodes crushed the resistance of the old kingdom and destroyed its residence Bulawayo, now an important railroad junction near the border to the South African Union. Thanks to his boundless spirit of enterprise a breathtaking railroad network strategically generously concepted came into being that is still existing today with the exception of the destroyed one in Mozambique. His final objective was a *Trans African Railroad* connecting Cape Town with Alexandria/Egypt at the Mediterranean Sea. Once the year a luxurious train for the upper class operates from Cape Town/South African Union to Dar-es-Salaam/ Tanzania at the Indian Ocean. On one stretch it is moved by an old steam locomotive. The Northern line was once built by railway engineers while it belonged to the German empire's colony Tanganyika as a first infrastructure measure. This colony comprised today's island of Zanzibar, Tanzania, Burundi and Rwanda. The visionary connection further through Uganda, Kenya and Sudan was unfortunately never realized. It was however a pioneering achievement of the French engineer Ferdinand de Lesseps at the end of the nineteenth century to create the first small version of the Suez canal, that was widened successively later on to adapt to the growing tonnages of the ships. It is fascinating to watch the couple of outstanding personalities realizing unbelievable projects because of the invincible urge to visions come true against all resistances. Frequently they are not acting for financial gain but for glory and fame. Often their achievements are not recognized during their lifetime. Ernest Hemingway received the Nobel prize of literature only long time after his books had been published. The author R. M. Remarque, who wrote "No news from the west", whose books had been published over a century ago received for the film version an Oscar long after his death. What starvation wages did the French impressionists receive for their paintings which are now sometimes worth millions of US$ or pounds at auctions by Sothebys or Christies. How boring would our life be without those eccentric personalities all over the world. Some very unpleasant types however have achieved to turn our world upside down like Osama Bin Laden, Yasir Arafat, Muhamar-al-Ghadafi, Trump, Kim-Yong-Il and accomplices appear to me like pikes in a pond of carps which keeps them moving.

Much later I travelled again under adventurous conditions to Zimbabwe trying to visit the plantation, now a mission in Mozambique. At the border city Mutare I wanted to stay again in the missionaries' guest house. To my disappointment it was closed. A message was pinned at the door with a phone number in Harare. The once beautiful well tended garden had run wild and was overgrown with thorn hedges. The pious gardener Jonathan has disappeared. He maybe had been recruited for Mugabes army. With the help of an acquaintance of mine, the black mayor of Mutare, I was lucky to catch a Portuguese farmer at the border station.

He knew my granduncle and admired my courage travelling alone in this troubled times. He was one of the few brave farmers who had not given up and hoped for better times. With his battered Land Rover he drove back to his farm that was not far away from Maforga. His car was mainly loaded with drums

marked as plant protective agents. But that was just a camouflage, in reality the drums contained petrol. He told me that
you got about everything with US$ on Harare's and Mutare's
black markets. After we had passed the border checkpoint he
put on his ammunition belt and pulled from underneath my
seat a box with grenades and instructed me how to use them
in case of a surprise attack. We drove slowly over the pothole
studded road in the Eastern direction. Years ago this road to
Beira port had been very busy, especially with cargo vans. Now
we did not see any traffic at all. The few villages we passed, no
people, even dogs, were moving around. In the dusk we heard
the noise of a heavy truck from afar. As a precaution we left
the road and stayed in the thicket until the truck had passed.
In Gondola the farmer gave a signal with his horn and suddenly windows and doors opened and the people animated the
place. The farmer distributed different items of shortage he had
brought from Zimbabwe and then we left again for Maforga
in bright moonlight without headlights. How great was the
surprise when we arrived there. My coming was unannounced.
The farmer rejected the offer of aunt Rosemary to stay overnight.
He wanted to reach his place in the cover of the night with his
high explosive cargo. He had prepared his farm for< any case
like a fortification and could rely on his faithful black staff. My
granduncle had managed to catch one of the last TAP air crafts
to reach that by the "revolucao dos cravos / clove revolution"
agitated and in transformation contained Lissabon. My much
younger and resolute aunt Rosemarie had however decided to

fight for the property. She wanted to avoid that it fell into the hands of the FRELIMO. "Pro forma" she transferred the ownership to the "world mission". It took care of war victims, orphans, aid cases and children of poor background.

I guess that they worked under this camouflage for the American and British secret service. The courageous aunt Rosemary with her "Never Give up" attitude was still there surrounded by missionaries and one single bodyguard, a black sergeant detached from the Portuguese Army. Formerly he had done service in the Portuguese colony Macao in the Far East. Finally she left the farm via Zimbabwe and South Africa when the civil war was in full force. After the death of my granduncle she spent the rest of her life in an old age home near the Bavarian alps.

The leaders of the mission Roy and Trish Perkinson were taken hostages by the terrorists and were after an adventurous time with them exchanged by diplomats in Malawi. The plantation had become a jungle and the extended garden that had delivered surplus had run savage. There was no missionary with agricultural interests and qualifications. The main target was to cram texts from the holy bible and the new testament into the heads of their charges. With the mission truck we went to Harare where we caught a flight to Johannesburg and further to Namibia, where I wanted to visit an uncle of mine, who had a hunting farm in the North near Okahandja.

To give an idea of Namibia I like to tell a story that happened during the Second World war in the former South-West Africa.

Two German scientists were busy to explore the wild country for its plants, mineral, resources and geological facts. The local authorities asked them to explore the lonely rocky districts of the Namib desert. The"Sword of Damocles" hung over the Germans abroad when the political events were calling them home to fight in a senseless war. Most preferred to stay in S/W Africa to keep their property. At the start of the war all male Germans were jailed in internment camps where they stayed until the end of the war. The women however when it concerned cattle farms tried to keep the farms running with the assistance of their faithful black staff.

The two adventuress German scientists were not interested in staying in the internment camp. Secretly they gathered provisions, needy items, containers with water, petrol, motor oil, guns with ammunitions, a tent, candles, matches, tools, heavy duty working outfit and much more one needs in such a situation. The sturdy old Chevrolet was overhauled and equipped with four spare tires with high profiles to handle difficult sandy terrain. One day in 1939 they loaded the car in the nighttime and left for a scientific excursion like so often before. For the postmaster they left a message to store the incoming mail. From that moment on nobody knew about their whereabouts. They had taken care to leave the settlement in the opposite direction circumventing it in the original direction. Later when in the Namib desert they tried to hide the tire traces by means of a tarpaulin dragged behind. When after some days they had finally reached their estimated final destination they first searched for an accessible cave in this rocky area where the Chevrolet and the stores could be hidden. It was found soon near a smaller cave where they established their home for the future.

Nearby was a deep gorge leading in western direction. In gorges happen to be sometimes pools of water and even creeks reminders of the last raining season. The access was very dangerous and it took a couple of days to find a relatively safe one. In their situation they could not risk any accident. That strange and lifeless country was not created for plants, animals and human beings. Even the bushmen could not survive here they thought. It took all their courage to climb down to the foot of the gorge. At a shady place surrounded by cactus and oleander bushes they discovered a small pool with glass clear water. After quenching their thirst they filled their canteens, they rinsed their clothes and took a bath. As it was getting late they decided to climb up and return to their cave. They didn't have much reading material. To save candles they did not use them often after sunset. One enjoyed smoking his tobacco pipe, the other had given up smoking and passed his time cracking sunflower seeds and chewing "Biltong" dried antelope meat that was prepared like the "Pemmican" of the Red Indians in North America. On their next trip down to the pool they took two canisters with them because their original water supply was diminishing. They left them behind while exploring. After two hours climbing over many rocks they found a deep pool supplied by a source from a steep rock. They took a bath and were shocked by the ice cold water coming from the depth of the mountains.

Refreshed, they returned. It was quite a task to climb up the steep path with the heavy load. It was too late when they reached the top and stayed in a cave they had discovered before. The water problem had been solved for the time being they risked longer excursions and started to draw maps of the area and to write about their scientific research.

Further to the west they found a steep way down the gorge and discovered a large pool with footprints of antelopes which had managed to survive in this hostile surrounding. Suddenly a big thunderstorm that lasted for three days with interruptions transformed the gorge to a tremendous river that carried even boulders with it. Step by step the waters oozed away and multicolored flowers and butterflies appeared just for some days until dust and bright sunshine reigned again. One day we suddenly heard the noise of a single engine search plane and went for a hiding. After some circles it disappeared and never came back. Their search for minerals and geological particularities went on. Then they dared to explore the opposite area of the main gorge. Here the Namib showed her wildest face with one sleeping volcano. Here the geologist found quartz and large resources of iron ore that have however never been excavated. Namibia is rich in natural resources like gold, silver and diamonds. At the time of our two scientists, diamonds were found in the coastal region. A German railway track checker whose hobby was geology had first discovered them. Today "De Beers" is in charge of diamond search in South Africa and Namibia. It came the time when the provisions of food were exhausted and they had to look for game. At the western gauge, where the lake even in the dryest times never disappeared the two adventurers managed to shoot an antelope from time to time. The leftover meat was right away cut into stripes and dried in the sun. One day they were surprised by a bushman who leaned on his javelin at the entrance of their cave. He showed them a cave in the upper part of the main gorge where they had never been before. There they found some semi-precious stones and where seemed to be always fresh water.

While the world was tormented by a crazy war they got used to their simple lifestyle and went on to make remarkable discoveries. They kept looking civilized, cutting their hair with a scissor regularly. A problem came however when one of them became seriously sick with high fever that could not be treated with the means available. They planned already to reactivate their Chevrolet to look for a doctor, when the bushman appeared out of nowhere and pulled some dried roots ans leaves out of his leather pouch and prepared this natural medicine for the sick man. After a couple of days the fever disappeared.

The rumour of their existence had however kept alive in the habited Southern parts of South-West Africa and their stay in the wilderness came to a sudden end when an aerial search discovered them. A ground search of the authorities was after years successful and both were detained in the internment camp. They were highly respected like heroes and could later leave the camp whenever they wanted. The war in Europe came to an end and they were installed in their former scientific position. Their valuable researches during their stay in the wilderness were received with great respect and helped to develop the country in the late 40s..

Now I like to report about my first visit to Namibia. I wanted to see my uncle fathers side who owns a hunting farm in the midst of the northern bushland near Okahandja. At the moment I climbed down the air stairs at Windhoek airport it started to rain after two years of drought. This coincidence was celebrated in my uncle Claus' favourite pub in the city.

It continued to rain "cats and dogs" for the next three days. Over night the parched country came suddenly to life. We drove on an asphalt road to Okahandja. From there the road became a quagmire. Thanks to our four-wheel drive we did not get stuck in the mud. Several times I had to leave the pick-up to open and close again the wire mesh gates of neighbouring properties where the road passed through. After passing a couple of creeks with rapid flow we left it to reach the farm "Ovita", that is the abbreviation of "Ogombejanavita" the name of a nearby mountain and means "the backside of the tribe's chieftain".

My uncle was in the third generation in the country. His grandfather had started with a cattle farm in imperial times. My uncle had changed this concept for a hunting farm on an en fenced property of 10.000 hectares.

Thanks to his experience with excavators he created over 30 dams to store the rare and precious rainwater. That allowed him to keep all kinds of wildlife.

Originally he was not a game keeper but a street constructing specialist and changed his job when he inherited it and created a paradise for wild animals. He managed to keep even crocodiles. Hippos and young elephants. To his stock belonged all kinds of antelopes, wild horses, kudus, zebras, cheetahs, buffaloes, giraffes, rhinos, but no lions to spare his animals. As small animals he got warthogs, porcupines, tortoises, guinea fowls, pangolins and vultures. Something very special are birds which harvest maggots from open sores of hippos, buffaloes. rhinos and the palate of crocodiles. The always present vultures serve as health police of the bushlands. Typical for this dry landscape were the prominent brown termite hills. Those workaholic occupants cultivate underground a species of mushroom for nourishment. When it happened to rain this mushroom happened to appear outside of the termite hills and were a delicious surprise and were also eaten by the wild animals. From the normally dried mud at the side of the dams bullfrogs appeared suddenly which called audible for a mating partner. There was also a fish that survived two years in the mud waiting for rain to fill the dam. Snails with magnificent shells appeared everywhere.

Beautiful coloured bugs and caterpillars had just little time to propagate Its species. Impressive dragon flies and locusts enjoyed their short life span. Just for a few days grass was growing and the landscape was covered with wildflowers. Trees and bushes produced fresh leaves.

Since the next civilized place with post office, fuel station, supermarket, bakery, dentist and doctor was the 60 km distant Okahandja, the farm tried to be as independent as possible. Every day bread was prepared fresh. In the storage were piled up elementary provisions like flour, salt, sugar, baking powder, edible fat, salad oil, noodles, rice etc. and dry goods like matches, washing agents, toilet paper, spiritus and petroleum.

A separate storage besides the workshop contained petrol, diesel oil, motor oil, lubrication grease. General repairs were done on the spot by my uncle and an experienced assistance. As a precaution the "rolling stock" was checked and maintained on a regular basis like those on the plantation in Mozambique. When greater problems arose with the excavator, dredger and chain driven vehicles a special service with a workshop car and spare parts was ordered by phone from Windhoek.

Electricity was produced by an ingenious simple solar panel system. The big panel could be adjusted manually vertically and horizontally to the sun. If more electricity was needed a generator was started.

On an elevation at the side of the farm were two big round open Zinc tanks that contained water for general use. Drinking water was pumped by a windmill from the depth of 70 meters and was ice cold.

Besides the water tanks was a with mesh wire fenced huge garden where a gardener was in charge. Even the top was protected with mesh wire to keep the birds away, that loved especially the grapes. Besides the farm was a dam that was always kept full of water. A crocodile was waiting in ambush there for a victim like a chicken that dared to come too close to the water or swimming there. The dog of Claus was also caught by the crocodile.

At the side of the farm was a fenced park where the only big eucalyptus trees on the whole property gave shadow. The park was protected by Max, a half tamed cheetah that had been an orphan, that Claus had found and raised with a milk bottle. On the top of the roof throned "Fritz" the peacock who at sunrise woke up everybody with his blood-curdling cry. Another big dam was near the farm and was also kept full of water all the time. On its far end on the crest of the dam the wild animals gathered at sunset to drink, while we watched them from a pavilion, where we used to take our sundowner before dinner. Claus had fulfilled himself an old wish and purchased three young elephants.They were baptized after the "Holy saints" from the bible Baltazar, Caspar and Melchior. They were left roaming free, but always returned to the farm in the evening. They fooled about and caused a lot of headaches. Finally the government in Windhoek had decided to do something for the infrastructure and supply some northern farms with electricity from the power station in Windhoek. Wooden masts were erected to carry the power cables.

For a while everybody enjoyed this long missed modern facility until "Baltazar" the eldest of the three got into his head to measure his strength with one of the masts. He won but was killed immediately by the electrical shock. The trained black farm-hands took the elephant apart and got their share. The rest of the poor animal was deposed in the cold storage. For weeks coming elephant meat was served at dinner, a rare delicacy. Slices of the trunk are the best of all.

The property of Ovita is so extended that it is impossible to walk around it in one day. There was ample space for buffalo and antelope herds. The hunters who had booked wild animals to shoot came from Germany, England, France and the USA. They were only interested at the head of the animals as trophies. Near Windhoek was the workshop of a taxidermist who specialized in preparing those animals accordingly.

For me it was always exciting to stay hidden in a tree near a water-hole and watch the different animals which came to drink. Fascinating are the social birds which constructed together a kind of big woven ball made of twigs where they were living and hatching their eggs. Unfortunately some snakes used to plunder the eggs.

Contrary to Angola, Mozambique and Zimbabwe it came in

Namibia to a peaceful release into independence. The UNO supervised the first elections. There was a rumour that the conservative "Turnhallen Alliance" had been discriminated compared with the SWAPO, the former freedom fighters. The first government under the leadership of Sam Nujuma was rather successful because some white specialists participated in the government. The expropriation of farms was largely avoided. The ambushes on outlying farms had become a rarity. Many of the former freedom fighters and terrorists had no jobs because they had no professional education. The government tried to integrate them into the new police force but failed.

Well armed they terrorized their own people or poached on the hunting farms for rhinoceros horns and elephant ivory tusks which achieved high prices on the black market. If the farmer caught one poacher red handed, they executed them on the spot and buried them hurriedly because they could not expect any support from the government.

Most of this former terrorists had as supporters of the Communist MLPA (Movimento Popular de Libertacao de Angola) committed many human rights violations like torture and murder of opponents in concentration camps in Southern Angola. Many returned to Angola where the civil war raged on, impelled by the Soviet and Cuban forces. There or in other African nations they continued to earn their livelihood as mercenaries. Turbulent places existed enough in Africa.

The chief of the NDF (Namibian Defence Force) was the notorious "Butcher of Lubango" who had committed countless war crimes in Angola. The president Sam Nujoma promoted Solomon Huwala to General Lieutenant. That is how it works in Africa. The international law court never occupied itself with these war criminals. 1994 the South African enclave Walvis Bay was handed over to Namibia and civilized conditions reigned over the country. The nation has ample resources at one's disposal like graphite, silver, lithium, tin, zink, uranium, diamonds, dioptas and semi precious stones. The density of its population is the lowest after Outer Mongolia. Its size is one and a half compared with that of Germany with a population of 2,5 millions. It is remarkable that most of the business is in the hands of half-breeds the Rehoboth Basters who often bear Dutch and German names. It is amazing that German is still spoken by the elder Namas,

Hereros and Rehoboth Basters. The latter were a respected group of half-breeds and originate from marriages between Boors and Namas in South Africa, who settled in the fertile region South of Windhoek. Conspicuous and lovely is the outfit of the Herero tribe at special occasions. The women wear habits that resemble those of the German women in Southwest Africa at the end of the 19th century completed with a colourful turban.

The elder men appeared in an ample decorated uniform, copies of those worn by the German colonial troops.

Some of the German development help projects was a plant to change waste water into usable water. The old railway line to Okahandja and to the western coastal city of Swakopmund was generally restored by the German Railway Company DBAG and the rolling stock reviewed. A luxurious train was created and is now a tourist attraction.

Once again curiosity has driven me to travel once more to Mozambique.

At the border checkpoint we caught a completely overloaded collective taxi to Villa Pery. I refused to store our kitbag on the roof of the Toyota and kept it on my lap otherwise it would have probably disappeared. According to an announcement of the UNO the landmines in Mozambique had finally all been removed. When that was true it was a miracle, because in Europe in northern France are existing still areas from the WWI. that were areas with barbed wire fences because of mines an gas ammunition.

On our next stage to Gondola and Maforga we have not seen any Europeans or Asians. Yet there was a hustle and bustle in the villages. I was probably rated as a missionary with his wife. From Gondola a truck left us at the branching off to Maforga. The surprise about our unannounced visit was great. None of the old team like the cook Schulz or the hunter Ravo had remained. The old settlement of the farm-hands had gone too. The extended garden had been overgrown with weeds and trees. New missionaries with practical formations as craftsmen had started to train the pupils in skills like repairing cars and tractors, making tiles, masonry, cabinet making and welding. The girls were taught by an old retired teacher in sewing, knitting, and cooking after having learned writing, reading and mathematics together with the boys. But what should happen to all those young people once they leave the mission? My granduncle had once provided many jobs for the indigenous people, but the nonsense civil war had destroyed all conditions for a prospering community. The missionaries had managed to hire an experienced and adventurous German nurse, who had no problems with the primitive conditions. Thanks to her initiative a perfect working little hospital was established where all kinds of uncomplicated diseases were treated. In this one we were allowed to register and weigh the babies of aids infected minor mothers. Depending on the case those babies were treated with a special diet from South Africa. How versatile was such a job that due to the non-existence of a regular doctor allowed small operations to be performed. I had highest esteem and respect for the friend of aunt Rosemary Dr. von Fürstenberg who had remained in Mutare in spite of the disconsolate chaotic conditions taking care of HIV positive affected citizens in a special camp. Some time or other Mozambique will return to its once prosperous society when finally good educated not by corruption influenced politicians are taking over the government and accept the council of professional foreign specialists. At the moment Mozambique is shunted by foreign investors. The reason is, that the "Sword of Damocles" of nationalization is always pending over them. The still secretly by Moscow led by the nose government in Maputo had since the end of the civil war 1992 plenty of time to bring forward that by countless raw materials blessed country. The result is a shame and embarrassment. Poverty and crime rule the country.

Another relative of mine managed after the death of her husband to manage her coffee plantation in Angola. When the communist government dispossessed her she left Angola empty handed and could not even take her savings with her.

On a private trip I met a relative Dr. Margaret Krohn a paediatrician in Nordhook/ Capetown near the the Cape of Good Hope and invited her to a trip around the Cape province. She was the widow of Hugo Krohn who left an exiting report about his life.

He was born on the Krohn property in Funchal/Madeira but spent his school time in Hampstead/London where the Krohn clan kept a large villa. After the WWI, while it was difficult to find a decent job at this time, the family decided to emigrate to Northern Transvaal/ South Africa to build up a farm. After this difficult task Hugo started a job as draughts man underground and later as a surveyor at the Rand Leasing Mine near Johannesburg. But soon he was called for a military exercise in Kenya together with Australians and New Zealanders. Then they were engaged in the difficult task to drive away the Italians from Abyssinia and restore the regime of the Emperor Haile Selassie. After they joined the English forces in the desert of North Africa against the German-Italian troupes. There he became a prisoner of war by the Italians and spent some time in a camp in Southern Italy. They were transferred to a camp near Triest were he managed to escape and join the partisans operating in Jugoslavia. In the danger of being always caught and shot.

He managed to reach the Adriatic coast and reached the just liberated Italian port of Brindisi. From there he flew to Cairo. By submarine he managed to reach England and stayed in a repatriation camp in Brighton until he was sent back to South Africa after the end of the war. This is just a sample of adventures of prisoners of war on both sides who survived in this senseless war.

Concerning the cabin staff, the Lufthansa management finally began to comprehend how important foreign languages were. Starting from the third foreign language the company paid a bonus of 70 DM per language and month. The ability and fluency was checked by the manager of the language laboratory. For languages he did not speak, a lecturer of the university was appointed to do it. Since I spent my holidays often on school benches I could count on a nice extra bonus.

We flew in so called divisions, that means that I could as far it was possible, request a desired division for example to Far East,

Middle East and to the USA. My advantage was that I spoke Spanish and Portuguese and was called to take over a flight to South America or Mexico when it was necessary. At the start I flew short and middle range routes. Considering the climate and time differences it was not so exerting. I enjoyed the short but interesting lay-overs for example at the Astir Palace Hotel at the Aegean coast near Athens. At the two days stops at the weekend was enough time to stroll through the entangled Plaka (old town) and climb to the Acropolis with its ruins from the classical antiquity. Often I was accompanied by a relative whose father was the representative of AEG in Greece. A member of the LH ground team in Athens was a musician and took me to his band's appearances. Sometimes I paid a visit to the harbour of Piraeus to proceed with the ferry to the island of Salamis. A culinary highlight was the restaurant "Vassilenas" in Piraeus near the Papastratos cigarette factory. They offered only one menu consisting of about 20 small samples of the Greek national cuisine. Included in the prize was an unlimited supply of local red and white Demestica wine. Individual extra wine of other brands and quality had to be extra paid for. Many guests could not enjoy the whole program and gave up. My trick was to interrupt the dinner and take a walk in the fresh air around the block. In this way I managed to try all the offered delicacies. A pleasant custom is to offer little tidbits when you order just a drink like it is the custom in Greece, Spain and Latin America. Even privately I discovered Greece because I loved the easy going atmosphere especially on the countless islands. Just equipped with a backpack the islands could be reached with a ferry ship that also carried trucks. One could easily find cheap an accommodations at private families that offered their rooms with loud calls "domatia" when the passengers were discharged. Often existed motorbike workshops where one could rent a Japanese scooter to explore the islands beaches, impressive churches, remains from the classical antiquity, convents, hot volcanic sources, abandoned villages and some rare icecold sources, a surprise at temperatures up to 35 degrees centigrades at noon. In the North of Greece near Thessaloniki exists an independent monk republic that can only be entered with a special permission. This strange state was until the present time tolerated by all Greek governments. On all islands one can find the influence of the former Venetian and Osman occupation. In Crete island that had lasted the longest time. In the classic time the Minoan kingdoms had existed. Caused by the mega explosion of the volcano of Thyra/San Turin and its giant tsunami and poisonous clouds this culture was wiped out. At the Eastern end of Crete exists a desert like climate that allows date palms to grow there. A peculiarity are the "Dodekanes", a group of 12 islands along the Southwestern coast of Turkey. After a conflict of the Osman empire with the kingdom of Sardinia this islands were ceded to the victorious Italians. The biggest of those islands is Rhodes, with his powerful impressive fortifications that belonged to the dominion of the crusaders after they had lost the holy land. Rhodes was handed peacefully over to the Osman empire later on. After roaming around homeless on the Mediterranean Sea they finally settled down in Malta Island. After it changed several times its ownership until it became a republic. Still today the St. Johns and Maltese orders are social institutions. The protestant branch is called St. John and the catholic one Maltese. Both are engaged in medical services and the transport of sick patients.

After this historical digression let me return to Greece. On one holiday equipped with a detailed map I took the ferry "Knossos" to Herakleon, the capital of Crete island. At 07.00 p.m. it left the harbour of Piraeus to arrive next morning at 06.30 a.m. At a pleasant temperature of 28° C.

I slept on a bastmat on the deck. The old cranky former cruise ship owned by the orthodox church in Hania whose rust scars were hidden under thick paint was rocking slowly towards its destination. The marvellous firmament and the continuously swinging moon conveyed an unbelievably feeling of comfort. A nice engineer which whom I shared experiences on sea, took me to the machine room and the captains bridge. Half an hour before landing the last still sleeping were woken up by the ship's bugle. I took my time and did not haste to leave the "Knossos" but observed the disembarkation of the trucks from the rear upper deck. Afterwards I took my backpack and walked to the bus center for East Crete and bought a ticket for Agios Nikolaos. I treated myself to a strong Greek coffee whose preparation the Greeks had learned from the Turks like the puff pastry croissants filled with spinach. After the arrival in Agios Nikolaos I rented one of those practical Japanese scooters and drove in the Eastern direction. Like planned by destiny I had a puncture near a village.

I pushed the scooter to the cafeneon and asked if there existed a workshop where my puncture could be patched? That was not the case, but there was the butcher Michailis Metzogianakis, who was just engaged in preparing "souvlaki" spits in his shop. He could help me but was busy at that moment and asked me to accompany him to a marriage party in another village where he had to deliver the souvlaki. There I helped him unload and carry the boxes to the place where the marriage party took place. There we were witnesses of the animated festival. We were invited for some drinks. At that time the music pieces of Mikis Theodorakis were popular and the people were dancing sirtaki. After many "isighia sas" (your health)" we returned a little bit tipsy to Sfaka, as the village was called. Michaelis proposed that the puncture be taken care of the next day and invited me for dinner up in the village where I met his charming and clever wife Kajopi who I nicknamed "Poppy" later on. The son Manolis joined us for dinner. The daughter Maria studied archaeology in Thessaloniki. Michaelis had before his marriage been a sailor working on cargo ships to the Far East. So we had a lot to talk about. The question of where to sleep was solved easily. Half way down to the sea existed a storage for agricultural tools "Kastri". There was a double stock bed, a metal wardrobe, a table and two chairs. A mosquito net protected the sleeper from its attacks. Always present was the chirping of the cicadas. Since the way up to the village was too laborious for "Yaya" (grandmother) who took care of her sheep and goats, she often stayed overnight in Kastri. Now the grandparents were living down to the sea at the side of the dry river

"Lutres", where "papus (grandfather)" had created a little paradise with a garden. Water was taken from a cistern.

Michaelis was visibly the "John of all trades" of the village and its surrounding. He had to take care of his extensive olive plantations, vineyards and gardens. He had given up breeding goats and sheep. Instead he had started keeping pigs, chicken, turkeys and rabbits.

The stables, silos, freezing house and storage he had built together with relatives and friends. He kept 200 pigs. The slaughter was done by Michaelis and Poppy. She took care of her garden, the orchard and a goat that delivered enough milk for daily use.

One overnight stay became five. I got along very well with Michaelis. In these few days I learned to drive a caterpillar, clear the pigsty of dung, kill a chicken professionally and to prepare souvlaki. Michaelis was the first in the region who had acquired a caterpillar to set up terraces for new olive trees and to grade ways that had been damaged by heavy rainfalls in the wintertime. Michaelis was fully occupied and discerned himself from his compatriots by his initiative and imagination.

Finally I continued my tour to the East and stayed one more night on my way back to Heraklion. So started a lifelong friendship where I was fully integrated into the local life when I happened to be in Sfaka again. Together with "papus" Georgios I helped to repair damaged walls of the terraces or to drive "Yayas" sheep. Sometimes I was permitted to ride on a donkey. Often I went for a swim at the end of a dry river where I could snorkel and dive for sea-urchins and mussels, a rare delicacy. During the hot siesta time I took a nap on my bast mat in the shadow of tamarisk trees. These trees can grow near the sea and can secrete salt.

Some of the species are able to secrete a resinous liquid when cut into its bark. It is called manna and is mentioned as nourishment in the bible.

There is another resistant tree "korupsi" carob tree that produces long dark brown pods when ripe. They are a favourite food for donkeys and are called Greek candy because they are sweet when chewed. The pods contain seeds that have the same weight and size when ripe. One seed has 0,2 g and 5 are 1 g are 1 carat. That was the original measurement for gold since the antique. Along the paths and trails are growing bushes which got flexible tender long twigs which are perfectly suited to weave baskets. In Sfaka there remained only one old man who mastered this art. At the pebble beach there were fabulous stones but their beauty appeared only under water. In spite of this fact some of those started my world wide stone collection. The most beautiful were semi-precious stones from Namibia.

At places where sheep and goats were grazing scarab bugs appear and form little balls from the manure to roll them with unremitting diligence to underground storages. Similar assiduous are the ants which carry sections of green leaves to its underground habitations for feeding its after-growth. The Greek species is bigger than the German variety. A bite is more painful than that of a German one. Like the sting of wasps and bees they are treated with onion or lemon juice. Especially in early spring time the otherwise parched landscape is covered by an ocean of white marguerites that look like snow. Suddenly countless multicolored butterflies appear and sit on the flowers to enjoy the nectar. It is also the time for the small black and yellow marked snails to appear. They are collected in fine nets and fed with macaroni noodles that cleanse the intestines. Next they are plunged into simmering water, taken out and dried then tossed into a hot pan with olive oil, garlic, onions and spices.

With a little hook the meat is pulled out of its shell, a real delicacy. The favourite place of the "salingari" are the "ajinara" artichoke plants. Once I have taken with me living salingari to Germany and set them free in my property, where they could diligently propagate with our German type of snails. Troublesome were under the magnifying glass so fascinating scorpions. For whatever reason they choose my boots to stay at night. For that reason I always had to shake them in the morning before pulling them on. A sting of those creatures could spoil the entire holiday. The way to the next hospital and physician was far.

Just for this reason the experienced grandparents had a box with dried leaves, pressed juice of plants mixed with olive oil and dressings available. Cuts and abrasions could be effectively treated with fresh thyme honey. No scars remained. No sunburns occurred when one used a mixture of half olive oil and half lemon juice. That could however only be taken away by means of home made curd soap. I enjoyed taking a hot shower in the slaughter room of "hirostatio" where I could also do my laundry. Michaelis had shown me the hiding place for the key. I was always invited to come again and had the opportunity to get acquainted with the land and people. In spring time I came often at the end of lent (fasting period) to help to capture the run wild sheep and goats which were for sale. Some were of course reserved for feast banquets at "Christos anestis" Eastern time. To catch these refractory animals and bind together its hind legs was really a difficult task that could be compared with the job of the cowboys in the American West and the gauchos in Argentina and Uruguay. I enjoyed helping prepare "kalizunia", an Eastern speciality. For the women it was fun, because the male population never engaged themselves with such matters. "Christos anestis" Christ's resurrection was lavishly celebrated by the orthodox "papás" priest in the richly adorned church. It did not only smell of incense but also of moth insect powder from the rarely used black festival habits.

Autumn was the time for the harvest of grapes. They grew far up at the mountain slopes on terraces. To harvest them was a real challenge. On difficult mountain trails I was allowed to drive the truck full "cuves" plastic boxes down to the village. I just imagine that all this work had been done once with donkeys on those since the antique existing "monopaties" foot paths. The shepherds, who could not leave the animals alone, had to stay often eight months' up in the mountain, because the animals had to be milked every evening and came to the corral voluntarily. The milk was processed to "Tiri and Feta" cheese on the spot and was picked up from time to time and supplied to the shops. If necessary the shepherds were provided with the elementary means like olive oil, flour, sugar, coffee, dried fruit, corned beef, "praximadi" a kind of dried bread that can only be used when stripped into water and milk, wine, candles, matches, washing powder, tobacco and batteries for the radio etc.

To break the monotony of the work in the vineyards the women used to sing a lot. I was told to have a harmonious voice so I did my best to support them. The women wore the traditional black working outfit even in the strong sunshine, but all had a straw hat. Just Poppy made an exemption clad in a working habit I had given her as a present showing red poppies printed on. The women envied her for it. An early kind of grape was the "sultani". They were spread on tarpaulins on the flat top of the houses or on "alonis" the former round thrashing places to dry. The raisins are an export article in great demand.

The harvested grapes were sold to the cooperated society or used to make wine. The procedure was like this: A plastic tarpaulin was spread over the loading space of the truck. A manual grape press was positioned there. The grape juice was collected in buckets and filled into very old 200 litre amphoras that were stored in the basement of the house. The contact of the fresh grape juice with the remaining old wine in the amphoras started an immediate fermentation that lasted a couple of weeks. The husks of grapes were filled into clean former petrol drums and water was added to start fermentation. After some weeks the liquid was used to distillate "Raki", a brandy. The wine contained a high degree of sugar so it never turned to vinegar. That was made with the help of a sponge like bacteria. In other years the grapes were pressed in a concrete basin by stamping on the grapes with the feet. Before the pressing instruments were invented it had been the method for thousands of years.

The EU had tried to introduce the spirit monopoly in Greece but had failed shamefully. The farmers and their ancestors had always prepared their own raki so the government gave up to enforce this new way of an additional tax revenue like in the rest of the EU. In another case the Greek authorities could not carry through what they had in mind. The islands population had discovered that the former storages near the coast could be altered into cheap tourist dwellings as far as water was available. The EU and Greek government were trying to stop the dense settlement outside the villages and the waste of precious water. The compromise was that the old dwellings could stay, but new ones were forbidden. A continuous danger were sudden conflagrations. The cedar forests of the antique had already been destroyed by fires and human exhaustion. Nowadays olive plantations are victims of fire disasters which are often caused by recklessness. Just throwing away cigarette ends can cause a catastrophe. Many existences can be destroyed by that. To plant new olive trees is a troublesome process and it takes decades until they bear fruits. The fire problem concerns all countries around the Mediterranean Sea and terrorists have used it as a political weapon against governments. The combat by means of fire fighting planes proved to be a dispute between David and Goliath.

Whenever I walked through the steep lanes of the village, the doors opened and I was urged to try a glass of wine, a cafelatchi, a fresh pastry, or a fancy cake, that meant that I was engaged in a small talk. Especially interesting it was when I finally decided to marry. I was obliged to introduce my wife everywhere. She was taught to knit, needlework, to bake and housewives Greek. Soon we felt like members of the community. We even got addresses or relatives on other islands and in Athens. There was for example Dimitri, a ships engineer and his enterprising Scottish wife Sylvia from Piraeus who owned an olive plantation near the village. When they came for a visit they lived in her storage similar to our "kastri" but very comfortably outfitted. Besides the usual hot water container on the flat roof he was the first one who equipped his place with an English wind generator for producing electricity, enough for the light, fridge, TV, radio and pump to supply water from the cistern. Water is a precious good in Southern Greece and on the islands. The farmers had meditated for a long time on this problem until they had found a solution how to save it. Coming from the big round water storages are leading downwards thick black plastic tubes which are passing several olive plantations. From those fine hoses lead to every tree and supply them drop wise with water. To avoid too much loss by evaporation, the system works only at night.

East of Heraklion where the mass tourism with many big hotels is present all the water available is used by the hotels. Very little is left over for the farmers and many have simply given up. Only few hotel companies who feel responsible got expensive waste water recycling installations. Most of the houses in Greece got water containers on their flat roofs. The circulated water is heated by the sun. This system was first invented in Israel and is now used by most Mediterranean countries.

Poppy was my age and was eager to learn. Under different circumstances she would have become a politician or a professor. She loved swimming, something unusual for Greek women. She had insisted on her daughter to study archaeology and become a teacher. Marias good knowledge in English gave her the chance to become a teacher at the high school in Sitia, the next city at the northern coast.

As an intellectual it was rather difficult to find an appropriate partner. Finally her choice was a German tourist, unfortunately a bit strange person. Michaelis, who had died of pancreas cancer, would never have accepted him as son-in-law.

In late autumn begins the troublesome olive harvest. Fine mesh nets are spread underneath the olive trees. With clubs the branches are shaken and beaten. Wealthy farmers got a tree shaking machine. The fallen olives are collected and delivered to the co-operative society. According to the result of the pressure money was assigned to the account of the farmer and a rest was given in the form of olive oil. Due to the sparingly rainfalls in Crete the olives are small but produce a concentrated oil. Michaelis had tried to grow some olive trees from Thessalia in the North where the olives are much bigger, but in Crete they also produced just small ones. A friend of Michaelis had planted some avocado trees. The fruits were small but delicious. Another farmer down near the sea at the dry river "Lutres" had a large hothouse "thermospitia" where he grew tomatoes, zucchinis, cucumbers, melons and aubergines. Outside he had some "aginara" artichokes. Its heart pieces were a delicacy with lemon juice. Growing wild and in gardens were fig trees and kakteen.

High up in the Monokara mountain was a hidden fertile valley where we discovered a plantation of almond and nut trees. In its middle existed still two open wells from Venetian times. They were constructed in a way that one could climb down to the water level by means of circular stone stairs. Nearby a shepherd was living in the summer season.

Down at the sea is the little fisher village Mochlos. In front of it is the small island Agios Nicolaos with the same name like the city opposite of the bay "Colpos Mirabello". Originally it had been part of the mainland, but had been separated during an earthquake. On its side facing the village, American archaeologists had discovered a Minoan settlement. Their findings like jewellery and tools can be admired in the museum in Heraklion, where nearby the only existing Minoan palace "Knossos" with its beautiful wall paintings can be seen. I loved to swim around the rocky island that was not so easy because of its breakers on the seaside. On my duty flights to Cairo we crossed the island at an altitude of 10.000 meters. Not far away from Mochlos behind a ridge is a giant limestone quarry. By regular blastings material was won that was carried by tipping trucks to a big steel tube that served to feed cargo ships with limestone that was brought to the big cement works in Piraeus for further processing. The owner of the quarry "Gipsos" lived in a decent villa in Mochlos and had an extended collection of petrifactions. Further distant from the quarry was a long inaccessible pebble beach where great quantities of sweet water gushed forth. It was an enigma where this water originated from. It could not come from the central mountain range because of its quantity. There were rumours that it came from the Nile in Egypt where big quantities of water disappeared in the porous ground of the Aswan dam. Up along the mountain range the street went straight down like drawn with the ruler to the drowsy little village Kavoussi. After the exit of it a small side street at the left leads to a wrapping factory. To run such a business one needs a lot of water.

Curious like I was, I followed the black pipeline leading to the mountains. Up in a steep gorge I discovered a natural deep basin with water that was provided from the gorge. After the trip in the heat I took a bath. Already in time of the Venetians and Osmans the water had been used to operate some mills and irrigate the fields. Remains of aqueducts and mills could still be seen, but the former fields have disappeared. There are just thorn bushes now.

Further down a path led to a lovely small village that was abandoned by the people except for an old couple that still lived there with a donkey, a goat and a couple of chickens. They were extremely delighted about our visit. While accepting a "cafelachi" we chatted about God and the world. The former inhabitants were living now in the cities or overseas like their son. From time to time he sends them some money to support them with the substantial for their livelihood. The papás came from time to time with his donkey from Kavusi to provide them with some necessary means and mail. In the small little chapel burned the eternal light. In Greece exists one saying: "When you have a problem finding a fire, some Saint will provide it." Another said: "There are more chapels than living quarters." The couple led us around the place. The homes were still habitable. There still existed a fully equipped cabinet-makers workshop where the old man sometimes was busy repairing something. I was impressed by an old fashioned olive press. Its vertical round stone was moved around by a donkey to press the olives. It was still in workable condition. The couple had no sorrows and were happy to live far away from the anxieties and the hustle and bustle of the modern time. Water was also sufficient, all houses still had a working cistern.

The Greek male population loves the cafeneon. Retired old men seem to spend more time there than at home. These establishments are with few exceptions tiled and white washed affairs. A bar and some simple chairs nowadays in plastic and tables complete the furniture. Over the bar a miserable TV set took care of a noisy background. In summer a ventilator moved slowly at the ceiling. In Sfaka existed four of those places. The strategically most favourable was situated beside the former oil mill above the bus station where the kiosk for lots and newspapers was situated. This cafeneon was the field of activity of Pelegia, a friend of Poppy and Michaelis, while her husband took care of a herd of sheep and the garden. To please her I got a couple of exotic posters of different airlines and fixed them at the barren walls. I am sure they still exist if the place has not been closed at the meantime.

When we sat together with the fishermen and other in the evening to enjoy the wine participating at discussions how to improve the world it happened to become a Babylonian confusion of languages. The youngsters of Crete often worked as seamen, cooks machinists and helmsmen on international vessels and learned different languages. In summertime the Danish author Mike joined us. He used to come every summer, stayed a couple of months near Mochlos and lived at a farmers place. When he thanks to the consumption of too much wine outdid everybody with his loquacity I called him not finding a fitting expression **Blablakis** what was accepted with a frenzied applause. Blabla stands for talking too much and "kis" the ending of many Greek names was introduced by the Turks for showing contempt for the subjugated Greeks. At lightened speed this new expression spread over Crete and is probably still used.

Much has changed in Greece too. People have become victims of the internet. Just the very old ones use to ride on their "environment friendly" donkeys. Since Perestroika the use of padlocks at their property was unthinkable in former times. Especially the Albanians that left their economically decayed country had a criminal disposition that stirred up the distrust against foreigners.

The Greek politicians and citizens seemed to be two different matters. Funds for urgent EU projects oozed away in the jungle of bureaucracy.

Other successful EU projects were declared unique achievements of the ruling party. One of those projects was to make use of the sweet water resource at the pebble beach near Mochlos. A specialized company solved this problem. Now a pipeline delivers this sweet water to a storage dam near the Southern coast at Irapetra to provide the countless thermospitia/hothouses with the water that provides tomatoes, zucchini, cucumbers, eggplants ans melons for the European markets.

The large scale ship owners like Niarchos, Onassis and industrialists managed it to evade the tax. There profits are hidden in Swiss and other banks abroad. The Greek government got documents that proved that, but up today no steps were taken to stop that nonsense. How can you blame the simple people when they also do it openly. In most tavernas and cafeneion you never get a bill. If asked the consumption is written on your table paper cover or a napkin. In big hotels and shops the tax appears on the bill. As consumer and tourist one is happy no to be bothered with such matters. The Greeks as a maritime nation and with their oriental character are traders by heart. There is a description of this mentality: "10 Westeners are cheated by one Jew, 10 Jews are cheated by one Greek and 10 Greeks are cheated by one Armenian!" When one is shopping on a fruit an vegetable market and having chosen 10 perfect tomatoes, when unpacking they are surprised to see that 3 are putrid. His wifes criticism is harsh. Next it is the wife that takes over to go shopping on the market with the same result. But when you are an old customer you get some extra ones and all are perfect. In the lands of the Greek exist many Mini-Tavernas with two tables. There exist no menu cards. You simply proceed to the kitchen an d take a look into the pots and pans and take your choice.

The custom to offer a glas of water with your coffee or meal is very old. When people were used to walk long ways they were offered a glas of water at their destination a cleaning and a massage of their sore feet whith olive oil.

Compared with the great expense and refinement ot the French cuisine the Greek one is rustic and most of it an most of it can be found in the Turkish, Lebanese, and Egyptian cuisine. The most common are:

Souvlaki = mixed meat on skewers

Dolmadakia = filled grapevine leaves rolled

Moussaka = hashed meat, potatoes, goat and sheep cheese au gratin

Tsaziki = yoghurt, garlic, cucumber, olive oil

Scordalia = galic sauce, dressing

Gavros = deep fried small fish (sardelles and anchovis)

Gigantes = big beans with tomato sauce

Giros = fried meat scaped from the turning skever

Mecedes = appetizers served togerher with ouzu or raki

The demand of mutton meat can't be covered by the domestic supply, the gap is filled by New Zealand. The fish supply from the Mediterranien Sea has been neary exhausted and comes now from Essoira/Marocco.

In Germany "Bockwurst" sausage of the goat is very popular, but since a long time they are made of pork meat. The original one came from Greece, but is rare to be found and only home made.

Drinks: The Retsina wine is something unusual that exists only in Greece. In the antique wines from Greece and Phenicia were shipped to Cornwall and exchanged for tin and copper. To avoid it getting spoiled during the voyage it was mixed with resin. Even the stopper of the amphoras was of resin. The consumers of wine became so used to this exotic taste, that helps to digest rich food, that it is still available now.

Metaxa is one more and less concentrated brandy that has been mixed with diverse herbs. The seven star Metaxa is the strongest one.

The first exotic fruit that is ready in early summer is the musmula that looks like yellow apricots and tastes like mirabelle plums. Rare, but with bigger yellow fruit is the khaki tree that originates from Japan and Korea.

When harvesting the cactus fruit in summer one must wear thick leather gloves. In the deserts the cactus plants have rescued many lives of people gone astray because they store water in their stems from the humidity in the night. Similarly I have discovered on the Canaries island of Tenerife. The mountains are covered with forests of a species of pine trees with long needles that only grow there. They got the attribute to absorb with their needles humidity from the seafogs in the night. The surplus water is released by the roots into the ground. It is so much that the consumption of the island is covered. Botanical specialists have tried to plant this kind of tree elsewhere, but in vain, it grows only in Tenerife.

Everywhere in the world exist animals and plants that survive only at certain places. On the Greek island of Lesbos for example and only there grows the mastic tree that produces a resin that is used in the oriental pastries, sweets, chewing gum, soap and tooth pastes. The island was under the special protection of the Ottoman sultans.

Let me now return to my Lufthansa lay overs after having narrated so much about Greece. One I liked very much was Istambul, the former Constantinople and capital of the Byzantine empire. The old city is still surrounded by a giant defence wall, but was conquered after a betrayal by the Turks. Before it was several times plundered by the crusaders.

Along the Bosporus are situated the palaces of the rulers and the nobility. From the Topkapi palace above the city you get a marvelous view of Asia Minor and the Princess islands. In the time of the Osman empire members of the upper class built their villas there. They are often still in the ownership of those families. Cars are not allowed, hamsons are still the means of transport. The European part of Istanbul is connected with the Asian part by the longest bridge in Europe. After a short time it became congested and the government decided to construct a similar tunnel like that one between France and England.

At the Northern end of the Bosporus is a little settlement of fishermen. There are a couple of restaurants that compete with each other for visitors coming by ship or owners of yachts. They are specialized on fish from the Black Sea. In Turkey they got excellent wines. In spite of the muslim population, a lot of wine is consumed.

It is considered as a blessing of Allah and a good medicine. A champagne like sparkling wine can easily be compared with that famous one from the Crimean peninsula. The oriental bazaars of Istanbul are still the lively centre of business where you get about everything. There are no fixed prizes you have to haggle for the final prize and one never knows if he had been overcharged. Anyway it is fun. Tourists have done much damage to the restaurant business, because of the "all inclusive system". A must is the visit of the Hagia Sophia, the once greatest christian church in the orient. It was the sample for all islamic sacral buildings later on. The minarets were an accessory from where the Muezzins could call the believers to pray five times a day. In our culture there are the church bells to do this job.

Something special that should not be missed are the "Hammams" steam bathes that had survived all those centuries. Hygiene was already important in the Greek and Roman antiques. The dwellings in the city had no individual water supply. For that reason common bathes and hammams were the solution. For a little "obolus" everybody could afford to use those establishments. Massage, shaving, manicure, pedicure, haircut could be ordered. The hammams were also a meeting point where politics and business affairs could be discussed. The barber was a person who heard everything, but did not dare to meddle himself into the discussion and disputes especially when he kept the razor in his hands. He was an esteemed diplomat.

In the world of the Muslim women are generally discriminated. In questions of inheritance they always get the infertile lands. That was also the case with the salty plains along the Southern coast around Antalya.

When it became a prosperous tourist region the women became hotel and real estate owners. Politically they have more power than those anywhere else in the country.

The German language is often understood and spoken because many Turks have earned her livelihood in the German industry, coal mines and other sections of the economy. The clever ones had learned a lot and later on build up their own business in their home country and brought the economy forward. Few people know that Turkey has achieved something admirable. From the water rich Taurus mountains in the South they had constructed an undersea pipeline that brings water to a dam in Northern Cyprus for irrigation. It is a present of the Turkish Government to Northern Cyprus that is only recognised by Turkey. Its currency is the Turkish Lira. Southern Cyprus is an independent Greek speaking nation that is a member of the European Community. Most people don't know that Turkey is the largest country in Europe. The greatest problem of Turkey is the vicinity of Russia that had always tried to get the Bosporus in its hands. Another problem are the minorities who are demanding their rights. Especially with the Kurds simmers an endless conflict that has caused innumerable victims. The Kurdish territory covers Turkey, Iran, Iraq and Syria. They dream of an independent country and never give up. Turkey is a member of the NATO to protect the Southeast flank of the defence organization, but Greece is also a member. Continuous quarrels between those historical adversaries about islands and resources provide for a never ending anxiety. Turkey is so rich in raw materials that I consider it as a pure show of power. What some tensions can lead to is what we see in the Ukraine – Russia conflict. When the territory in some parts of Anatolia is good for nothing. It can still serve to produce electricity with solar collectors. The mountain area is beautiful and is an attraction for tourists. In some lonely places exist still bandits who used to assault Western truckers on their way to Iran. But that is not worthwhile since the embargo restrictions against the Mullah regime are still valid and the transit traffic nearly came to a stand-still.

The overnight layovers in Russia were restricted to Moscow. I have of course taken a look at the pompous underground system that is partly outfitted with marble from Germany. How many slave workers from the gulags must have been exploited to create it? The Red Place was really something when empty without military parades. It looked like a runway for smaller aircraft's. One adventurous German private pilot had managed to land there without being detected on his way. The impoliteness of the civil service officers and hotel staff was like a disease and stuck in my memory. That changed very fast when Michel Gorbatchoff sounded the perestroika and the Berlin wall fell.

The rest of the East German Interflug Airline staff was taken over by Lufthansa and the cockpit members helped us thanks to their geographical and Russian knowledge to find our new destinations without problems. At my time it was Novosibirsk/Siberia, Ashgabat/Turkmenistan and Alma Ata/Kazakhstan.

Originally Novosibirsk was a railway junction and a main stop of the Trans Siberian Railway and a settlement for workers in charge of the construction of the railway bridge over the Ob river. The city grew when factories were transferred there out of the reach of the German Air Force. They manufactured tanks, air crafts and weapons. The railway maintained there depots and overhauling workshops. One did not expect culture in this ugly accumulation of brick and concrete buildings, but one was mistaken. In this now the third biggest city of Russia existed an opera, a ballet, theaters, museums, sport arenas, film- and TV productions. As a lover of art I was surprised to find a painting of the famous Ukrainian painter Ilja Jefimowich Repin in a small museum of fine art that can't be found in the art catalogs. Famous are his " Letter to the Sultan" where wild cossacks and a Russian officer surround a writer.

Another shows captives towing a cargo boat on the bank of the Volga.

Both pictures have adorned Russian postal stamps. Another one shows 15 most important generals assembled at a circular table discussing military matters with Tzar Nicolas II. At that time war was a matter for men only with the exception of Catherine II. of Russia, Elizabeth I. of England and Jeanne d'Arc of France.

The railway station was worth seeing. Even at night time cargo was loaded and unloaded. On some side tracks old steam locomotives and former luxury waggons were parked. In front of the station refuse was burned in open petrol barrels surrounded by travelers who tried to warm themselves. In wintertime the people were dressed in long, formless, cotton lined heavy coats, feltboots and fur caps. They all could have served Repin as character studies.

Outside the city, deep in the forest a former KGB-agent had during Perestroika acquired a big dadscha with side buildings.

There he had stored several discarded tanks, trucks, jeeps and a helicopter. Paying guests could amuse themselves by learning to drive a tank and making an excursion on the Ob in a landing boat. The provisions consisted of roasted venison and other game or fish from the river. In autumn we went out in the forest searching for mushrooms under Sergejevs supervision. LH flew only two times per week to Novosibirsk. So it was worthwhile to visit Sergejev. After a telephone call he picked us up in the hotel. We paid in US$. Some km distant from the dadcha we discovered a little village during our excursions. We were permitted to visit the elementary school. We ascertained that many items were scarce commodities. The children were enthused about the foreign visitors.I promised them to come again. On my next visit I carried everything they were missing with me in a big box like notebooks, lined paper, writing pens, sharpeners, paint boxes, brushes, drawing paper and ball point pens. The best was an old atlas. The happiness about all those commodities was great. On our visit to the datscha we met some former KGB colleagues of Sergejev who received a satisfactory indemnity or pension. Some had found a job in the economy, had started a business or enjoyed the new freedom. All spoke English and could tell remarkable stories about their former job.

Another destination was Alma Ata, the former capital of Kazakhstan. The giant steppes of this country reached from China to the Caspian Sea. It became well known for its Russian space launching basis and its unsurpassable wealth of raw materials and other resources. Alma Ata is situated at the spur of the Tien-Shan and Pamir mountain range, which is partly undiscovered and possesses the longest glaziers in Asia. We heard that the military helicopter crews had not been paid their wages for a couple of months. We were able to convince one team with a bundle of US$ to take us for a tour over the impressive mountain ranges. This unusual happening was never forgotten by the participants. Besides the former government buildings in the typical soviet architecture and the big parade places the city had not much to offer. Famous are however the steam baths and the masseurs. The new capital Astana is situated far away in the plain steppe and was designed on the drawing-board. Kazakhstan is the greatest inland nation in the world and its Northern border with Russia is 7600 km/ 4750 miles long. The majority of our passengers flying to Alma Ata were international experts for oil and gas, mining prospectors, and engineers, infrastructure specialists and representatives of big companies like Siemens, Bosch, Daimler-Benz, Thyssen-Krupp, MAN and foreign companies. Most had appointments with the ministry of economy in the hope to get mandates for factories and mines to get the urgently needed raw materials. Kazakhstan had been blessed with deposits of iron ore, pit-coal, phosphor, mangan, nickel, copper, gold, bismuth, vanadium, fluorine, bauxite, silver, uranium, cobalt, lead, zinc, molybdenum and recently oil, gas, rare minerals and opals. No wonder that Russia had problems dismissing this country into independence. To its disadvantage it must be said that all this raw materials cannot be processed because there is no industry to do it. The secret second currency is the US$. The government tries to maintain good relations with all sides. The Russian space rocket launching facilities are still operating in Kazakhstan.

On the flight back to Germany it was conspicuous that many passengers were old men with long beards holding a bible. There had been met an agreement with the Kazakhstan government that those people of a religious group of Mennonites with German roots were permitted to leave the country. The younger ones were a loss for the economy because they were estimated for their reliability and efficiency. Once Catherine the Great had invited the ancestors of those people to leave the overpopulated regions of Southwest Germany to come to the fertile Volga and Don regions of the empire with the promise of land donations and remission of taxes. The scarcely habituated regions flourished until the second world war. Stalin did not trust this minority because he feared that it would support the German army on its advance. For this reason he deported those people with German roots to Siberia, Kazakhstan, Uzbekistan and Tajikistan.

At the beginning they lived under most primitive conditions but managed to build up a new existence. The local people distrusted these newcomers and discriminated them. That changed soon when they saw their drive for survival. The young generation had managed to build up a new existence after they emigrated to Germany.

Another flight destination was Ashgabat, the capital city of Turkmenistan. I found out that here and in the neighboring countries all modern hotels belong to Turkish hotel companies. The language is a Turkish dialect.

Originally the Turks came from these regions and invaded the former Byzantine empire where Greek was spoken. At the Caspian Sea Turkmenistan has considerable oil and gas resources but had concentrated its endeavors in the Soviet time on the production of cotton. The water for irrigation was taken from the Aral lake.

As consequence the lake has completely disappeared and its former fishing boats are rotting on its dry bottom, an environmental catastrophe of the first degree. In Ashgabat you find a couple of public buildings which are completed in white marble. The airport building has got the form of a flying bird, the symbol of Turkmenistan. One of the ideas of a pompous dictator. What a contrast with the railroad station whose tracks were overgrown with weeds. Chinese engineers have been called to restore the rotten railroad net.

The Turkmen ancestors have been the Skyths, a folk on horses like the Mongols and Tartars. Their influence reached to the Black Sea. The former fortifications can be seen near the city.

Even though I had forgotten my elementary Russian I spent one evening in a theater where a play of Maxim Gorki was shown. I understood only a little but enjoyed it nevertheless. At the end I came in contact with the actors. Only a few could speak English. They knew some Western playwrights like Berthold Brecht and Tennessee Williams, but those were banned by the dictator. Far outside of the city existed a prodigy. At the mountain from centuries of use polished stone stairs lead down to a volcanic hot spring with several basins of a different temperature. Towels and a masseur were available. The water was awarded some healing properties. Ashgabat was only a short time a destiny of LH. The Turkmen Airline was withdrawn the landing rights in all Western European countries because it did not meet the liabilities of the IATA and ICAO. As retaliation Western airlines could not land any more in Ashgabat.

Since perestroika an ever growing number of destinations in Russia were flown to. At that time I was only flying on intercontinental routes and cannot report about those places. But I still will mention some short and middle range destinations.

Milan for example, was a favored city unfortunately with just a short stay.

The aircraft arrived late in the evening. It was always a combi version of the Boeing 727 for freight and passengers. While the cabin crew was picked up for the hotel the on palettes fixed seats were offloaded through the side cargo door and palettes with cargo containers were loaded. The cockpit crew flew to Frankfurt and another cockpit crew flew with cargo to Milan where the cargo was unloaded and passenger seat were again fixed in the aircraft. Another cabin crew took over the morning flight.

This type of aircraft could operate day and night. Pure passenger planes could also be used more effectively in the night by fixing mail sacks on the seats with the seatbelts. Milan is the second biggest and richest city in Italy. In this region Lombardia are existing the largest industrial companies of the country. The racing course Monza and some automobil companies are in the vicinity of Milan. An attraction is the "duomo" with its marvelous architecture, its "piazza" with countless pigeons and the galleria. The dome has no tower, but from its roof one has a wonderful view to the massive of the alps, the palace Skorzese, the arc and the railway station. Directly behind the galleria is the inconspicuous but famous opera Scala. A foreign visitor has not the slightest chance to get a ticket. It has to be reserved months before. Not far away from the duomo I discovered an unusual restaurant that offered a couple of typical Italian appetizers instead of main courses. After having enjoyed them a basket with nuts with a wooden plate and hammer were placed on the table to amuse the customers with cracking nuts. Nearby existed one of the rare food-shops where most articles were sold loose like olives and anchovies from the wooden barrel, cheese from the wheel, flour and rice from the sack, dried dates and figs from wooden boxes, olive oil from tin containers and dried peas, lentils and beans from paper sacks. Compared with our sterile supermarkets it smelled so wonderful like an oriental market. Outside the city are long "navigli" canals which lead up to the Lago Maggiore/ Ticino. They had been planned by Leonardo da Vinci for the duke of Sforzese to bring building material like marble for the palaces to Milano. Now the former towing- paths serve as comfortable bicycle ways. In summertime many boats enliven the navigli. The nobility has built some impressive summer palaces at the canals. On the way to the Lago Maggiore one passes the alternative airport Malpensa where all the intercontinental and some continental air traffic is handled. He is also used when the city airport Linate is closed because of fog.

Much in demand was the layover in Amsterdam. The American Hotel was directly at the "Grachten"-canals in the centre. Until a century ago they had served as transport of goods from the harbour with cargo boats to the storage places of the merchants. Today they are fixed tight at the side of the grachten and serve as living quarters for young people. With the chicken and potted tomatoes a strange sight. In this city the only reasonable means of transport is the bicycle. One can rent them but must always lock them tight because the theft of bicycles is the most frequent crime in Amsterdam. The second sin is drug consumption. The government has given up pursuing it as a crime except the use of heroin. So Amsterdam has become a magnet for the youth of neighboring countries which still have strict laws against it. These young people represent an important economical factor. What should not be missed is the visit to the Rijks-Museum of Art. The painting of the "girl with the pearl pendant" must be seen. A wonderful book has been written about it. The revolutionary Dutch and Flamian art was that for the first time real life with a correct perspective was presented. I can only divine how many unknown paintings of famous artists are still hanging hidden in private Dutch and Belgian houses. Before paintings were just a matter for the catholic church who ordered it of Maria with Christ, Jesus at the cross and holy persons. Often those were bloodless, stiff and repulsive persons. Later the nobility ordered pictures of themselves for the ancestors gallery. In Italy Michel Angelo and Leonardo da Vinci also started a revolution with their realistic and colorful technique of painting.

Many people are not aware of the fact that Amsterdam is the greatest trading and processing place for diamonds in the world. The monopoly has De Beers of South Africa. Scarce diamonds have always exerted a great attraction on mankind, but the main business are the unattractive, lusterless industrial diamonds used for cutting and grinding especially alloyed metals. Without the use of diamonds on drill heads the search for oil would be impossible.

For centuries the Netherlands have been fighting against the sea and had won precious greenland. A great part of that country is underneath the sea level and must be kept dry by means of pumps operated once by windmills and now by diesel engines. Whenever there were problems with draining swamps Dutch specialists were called. The noted ones are the region of St. Petersburg where convicts were employed to drain the swamps. Before this initiative of Catherine the Great many young children died of tuberculosis. In Prussia the swamps along the Oder river were dried up and won for agriculture.

Not far away from Amsterdam and easy to be reached by train is the former luxury resort Zanfort aan Zee. Now it is a place for mass tourism and provides a racing course for motor bikes. Who wants to experience really giant dams will find them near Den Hague. There one can really estimate what the assiduous Dutch have achieved to protect their country from the floods and to transform the won land into fertile agricultural soil.

Contrary to the Netherlands and its lively Amsterdam, Stockholm/Sweden Is a lonely place. The airport is far away from the city and we stayed at the SAS hotel at the airport. In spite of this fact we took a taxi to go to the city. The old part of it "Gamla Stan", for German ears a funny name because it sounds like "Gammler stehen" = where the beatniks killed their time. I was surprised about the absolute silence that reigned there except for the central railway station. In summer time it did not get dark in the evening, which was valid for Helsinki and Oslo too. In Scandinavia alcohol is highly taxed. When landing all our alcoholic drinks were gone. As specialty herring filets were prominent. As snack everywhere smörebrot with butter, salad and shrimps, salmon or reindeer were offered. Worth to be seen is the royal park in Drottningholm with its plants and flowers.

Stockholm is surrounded by endless forests and islands. Some of them can only be reached with private boats.

An extremely different and fascinating country was Jemen that was twice per week flown to. Its capital city Sana'a was in the conservative North. Aden was the capital of the communist South supported by the Soviets who had a navy base there and were responsible for the civil war. As witnesses everywhere burned out tanks, military vehicles and crashed helicopters could still be seen. The country is controlled by tribes which have been in conflict with each other since eternity. In addition they belong to different religious groups like the Wahabis, Shiites and the Sunnites that is always a reason to quarrel with each other. The villages of the tribes are always strategically advantageous on the top of mountains from where one has a good view over the surrounding countryside. The male members of the tribes distinguish each other by different beautiful stitched attire with a curved dagger in the belt that has a handle often decorated with semiprecious stones. Every Jemenite of standing is carrying such an often inherited dagger to show his manliness. It belongs to the Jemenite culture like the kilt to the Scotchman. Sana'a is the only place in the world where local architects have already created centuries ago high rise buildings that happen to be even beautiful. The prices for real estate plots were already a problem in ancient times and that building were a simple solution. As I already mentioned there are different religious groups that dislike each other. The Shiites are supported by the mullahs in Iran and the Sunnis and Wahabis by Saudi Arabia. That is the reason that peace never prevails.

Over 2000 years ago Yemen was famous for its unique irrigation system and its dam of Marib that worked because of good maintenance for centuries. It was destroyed by an earthquake and one never tried to reconstruct it. Coffee originated in Yemen and was exported through the harbor of Al Mukha/Mocha. It spread all over the world and Brazil is now the greatest producer and Yemen seems to have given up on cultivating it. Incense and myrrh came also from Yemen.

Men spend their afternoon siesta in the coffee-house while chewing quad leaves that mediate a spiritual easiness like hashish. That plant exists only in Yemen and is shown on one of the Riyal banknotes. There occurred some kidnappings with ransom claims. Because of the unsafe situation in Yemen Lufthansa gave up flying to Sana'a.

Similar happened in Lebanon. Caused by the conflict between Israel and Palestine originated the big refugee camps near Beirut. In addition the mullahs in Iran supported the Hezbollah terrorists and mixed into the affairs of the Lebanese government. I was on duty in the last Boeing 727 that landed in Beirut. LH cancelled all further flights. The crew was trapped In the hotel. During the curfews we spent our time playing chess and literature. When I dared to move to the flat top of the hotel that was at the Corniche I could watch snipers exchanging their shooting with their opponents. The nearby Hilton hotel had been the target of a bomb attack had completely burned out. The provisions of our Hotel became scanty. We finally got only pancakes without eggs. After about a week in cooperation with our station chief we decided to leave Lebanon on the seaway. Despite the civil war and chaos the bureaucracy was still working. To leave the country we needed our passports. When entering In Lebanon the passports remained at immigration and the crew got a general declaration. After long discussions I volunteered to proceed to the airport to get our passports in exchange for the general decleration. With a good paid daring taxi driver we circumvented the refugee camps and reached the airport. At immigration our passports got an entry stamp and after having paid bakshish I returned to the Hotel. I was celebrated like a hero. The station manager said that we could leave the next morning with a small coastal freighter to Cyprus. We left the hotel with a bus to the harbor. At immigration we got our exit stamps in our passports. The cargo vessel had no cabins. The suitcases had to be fixed with ropes. On the hatches. We could sit on jute-sacks leaned against the wheelhouse or walk around holding us at the criss-cross fixed ropes. The ship started with its chugging diesel engine. Officially the cargo consisted of sheep, goat and camel skins, the smell was accordingly. They were for processing leather goods in a factory in Cyprus. I was sure that underneath were hidden some smuggling goods. It was good sunny weather and from the bow was drifting a strong breeze. One stewardess dedicated her big LH silk scarf with the yellow crane and we hoisted it at the mast. We met a few other ships. Most were far away in the South on their way to the Suez Canal, Alexandria or vice versa. The diesel engine stopped twice. The sound of hammering came from the machine quarter. Technically interested, I climbed down to see what was going on. The machinist was just preparing a new seal from copper tin for the diesel oil pipe. That was inserted into the flange and its screws tightened. That happened at another place a second time, but was handled in the same manner. That was routine and nothing to get excited about.

Like so often when travelling on a ship we were accompanied by seagulls in the hope to snatch some kitchen refuse. I was feeling sorry for the birds because we had just some bottles of water with us. Finally the Eastern tip of Cyprus appeared. The helmsman radioed the first small harbor mentioning our presence on board. He did not get a landing permission and was referred to Limassol in the West. I think they were not prepared to handle the matter. At Limassol there were no problems.

Our passports were stamped and a small bus was organized that brought us to the Hilton Hotel in Nicosia. Our station manager in Beirut had handled the accommodation and arranged that tickets were ready to London with Cyprus Airways the next morning. For sightseeing of the divided city in the Greek-Cypriot part was no time, but that I made up leeway years later on a private visit. The Greek speaking Southern part of the island had profited from the civil war in Lebanon. Most of the international and local banks had transferred their business to Cyprus as well as many merchant houses. The MEA = (Middle East Airlines) had also transferred their business activities to Cyprus. Like we could see at the airport the next morning the ramp was full of MEA B707 cargo planes.

England had 1960 released Cyprus into independence but still maintained two military bases that were also used by the US Forces. In London-Heathrow we took the LH connection flight to Frankfurt where our safe arrival was celebrated by our CEO and the management.

A similar adventure survived another LH crew that were captured in Cairo because of the outbreak of the conflict between Egypt and Israel. The crew had managed to catch a train to Alexandria. There they were lucky to get on a freighter to Genua.

The danger of getting into conflict is real, when one does not observe the curfew. That happened to me in Tripolis/Libya. Despite the fact that we had landed rather late there I wanted to enjoy the pleasant evening taking a walk in the city and admire the Italian architecture of the buildings. Libya has once been an Italian colony. The colonel Ghaddafi had revolted some years ago and sent the Senussi king into exile. There were still tensions and a curfew was imposed at 08.00 p.m. what I did not know. Suddenly a police patrol stopped besides me and asked me to stand at the wall to search me. Then they handcuffed me, drove me to the central police station to put me in a cell. Finally an officer who spoke Italian and English interrogated me. Now I could convince him that I was a harmless person who did not know about the curfew. I was driven back to the Hotel whose name I had remembered. Another occurrence happened in Iran during the celebration of the 2000 years of the dynasty. We were not lodged like usual in the Royal Tehran Hilton but in a motel far outside the city. I decided to enjoy the good weather and take a walking tour in the surrounding area. Equipped with my backpack, a bottle of water, some snacks and a book I left the motel.

After a while I sat in the shadow of a kornifere to rest and continue reading "War and Peace" by Tolstoy. Suddenly I was surrounded by a group of heavily armed soldiers in camouflage dress. They searched me for weapons and took me to their camp where an officer tried to question me. I spoke no Farsi besides some common expressions. Finally they drove me to their headquarter where a civilian and an officer interrogated me in broken English. They took me to the motel to verify my statement. It was a surprise for some crew members sitting on the terrace when I arrived at the hotel with the military escort. I invited my attendants for a drink and they explained me, that I had inadvertently entered an area off limits. In the mountain was the notorious underground high security prison, where the opponents of the Sha Rezal Palevi were captivated. Unintentionally I had penetrated this forbidden area.

A layover I was always looking forward to was Cairo/Egypt. It was the hub for many flights continuing to Khartoum/Sudan, Asmara/Eritrea, Sana'a/North Yemen. Dar-es-Salaam/Tanzania. Cairo is one of the world's most tainted cities with pollution. The sun can only with difficulties penetrate the smog. Except in wintertime the temperatures are intolerable. In spite of this disadvantages is Cairo a fascinating place where unimaginable masses of people move in overcrowded buses. tramway and a "tin avalanche", donkey carriages, freight camels and bicycles moved forward accompanied by a hoot concert. Despite this chaos at the "Al Tahrir Square" the Hilton Hotel is situated there. It is a place of relaxation at its pool and garden side facing the Nile river with its feluccas/cargo boats which animate it. At one side of the square is the building of the Arab League and opposite the world famous antique museum where artifacts of the Pharaonic dynasties were displayed.

It was mostly English, French and German archaeologists that have managed the excavations in the valley of the kings in upper Egypt. The Egyptians distinguished themselves by grave robbery. Family clans knew about some extraordinary sites where the graves with their treasures were hidden and sold them step by step on the international black market of art. That is the reason that the best items can be seen in English, French and German museums where they are displayed in a fitting scope for educated and interested spectators.

Due to the continued political tensions and danger of war between Egypt and Israel president Anwar-el-Sadaat had ordered a public black out.

Everywhere at the main streets authorized persons were ready with a barrel of blue paint to apply it to the reflectors of cars that had not yet conformed to the rule. It was a free of charge service by the ministry of transport. The government prepared itself for a war, but life went on like always. The tension was only felt when seeing the passing tanks in desert camouflage and the trucks moving in the direction of the Suez Canal and the Sinai desert. The predecessor of Sadaat, Abd-el-Nasser had confiscated the Suez Canal from England risking a war. The English had lost their gushing financial source and were of course furious. It shows how risky investments are in unreliable countries. Similar happened with the Panama Canal and the Cahora-Bassa dam in Mozambique. I had a good contact with a receptionist at the Hilton Hotel Omar Assem. He invited me once to his home and I came to know his father, who was a member of the Suez Canal Commission, gave me some interesting facts about the history and the administration of the canal.

Most of the crew members spent their afternoon at the hotel pool. I preferred to explore the city to see the impressive mosques, the bazaar and exotic shops. The transport with battered buses and overloaded trams were strenuous but dirt-cheap. For a snack there existed everywhere shacks that offered "aish balatin" flatbread filled with chicken meat and fried vegetable or red beans. At other stalls you got fresh pressed juice from mangoes, oranges, pomegranate or melon.

I enjoyed sitting in a coffee-house nearby and watching the people. The coffee was very strong and served in small cups or you ordered "tshai bi halib or limun" tea with milk or lemon.

In the Champollion street named after the archaeologist who accompanied Napoleon and deciphered the "Rosetta stone" is the press club where I could study the latest news of the International Reuters Agency I made the acquaintance of an Egyptian journalist Samir Tadros who used to work for the leading newspaper "Al Acham". As dissident the government had inflicted punishment on him by forbidding him to work, but the newspaper kept him on the payroll. His wife was from East Germany and she had met him there. Marrying him had given her the chance to leave East Germany. He invited me to his home on the Nile Island Zamalek where the smog was not as unpleasant as in the city.

They took me to some nice places that were not frequented by foreigners.

Thanks to the diversified agriculture the Egyptian cuisine is multifarious and was influenced by the Greek, Turkish and Italian kitchen.

My favorite coffee-house was in the Champollion street near the "Midan al Tahrir". It belonged to a Nubian from South Egypt. He was an efficient real estate broker and handled all his business in his coffee house. Contrary to the often uncouth Egyptians they distinguished themselves by innate good manners. Opposite at the wall of an abandoned palace was the stall of a "Fakkani" fruit merchant. Despite a prohibition for such a street business the fakkani Faussi Yussuf had managed to stay through bribing the authorities. He knew all the people living in this area.

He was a christian, corpulent and friendly to everyone. I often spent some time there playing chess with him. Our conversation was a funny mixture of Egyptian, Italian and English. He was clad in a white "galabeja" (burnus) and a cap. Soon I had contact with most of his regular customers who were of course curious about this foreigner. He told me that he had to be with his cart at the central wholesale market at 04.30 a.m. to supply his stall with fresh merchandise. He was mostly sitting and could spend the day easily taking a nap from time to time to be woken up by his customers. It was a coincidence that the journalist Samir Tadros was also his customer. Much later when I was already married I took my wife with me to Cairo. When we met Faussi he asked me to come to his home and meet his family. So we came to know the workers' district of Cairo where he lived in a block of flats. The rooms were illuminated with petrol lamps. Water came from a pipeline outside. Cooking was done with gas. I had asked Faussi not to make a big show and we were happy to share the simple meal with the family. All neighbours were jostling at the door to see Faussis foreign guests. After the meal we were all sitting on cushions on the ground and I spread some useful items on the ground I had brought with me. The son got a fine dress that should help him to find a good job. On the bazaar we had bought a beautifully embroidered "galabija" for my wife and she had kept it on for the visit. One attentive woman had seen that it was a little bit too long and brought her sewing machine to correct it. Then it was time for the son to try on my blazer and trousers. It fit perfectly. For his wife and daughters I brought some nice scarfs.

Missing good education and overpopulation are the two greatest problems of Egypt. How could people with little income afford to send their children to a good school? Germany is one of the few countries where apprentices receive a little pay and where students with no means can apply to the government for financial support. When a good job is offered hundreds apply for it. Not the most qualified gets it but that one with the best connections or the highest bribing sum. The ruling upper class does not mind when the masses of people propagate like locusts. That was considered cheap labour. Sporadic unrests were quelled by the armed forces which often provided a dictator who guaranteed law and order.

Something incredible I have seen when sitting at Faussi's stall. Because of the heat for hygienic reasons the organic waste was collected every day. A Rolls Royce Phantom III. appeared for this job. The rear passenger compartment had been taken away to make place for a loading platform. Who might have owned it formerly? I guess it had belonged to the vehicle fleet of king Faruk I. who had been deposed by colonel Abd-el-Nasser 1952.

There was one means to escape the indescribable traffic of Cairo to rent a felucca and make an excursion on the Nile river. We could also take a taxi to Gizeh, the site of the Cheops Pyramids where MG/Mohammed Gomez operated a large stable with horses and camels. LH crews were regular customers and we enjoyed special conditions. The foreign tourists loved to be photographed with a camel. The dexterously camel drivers had also foreign names for the animals according to the country where tourists came from. For Italians it was called Benito, for English ones Winston and for Austrian and German ones Amadeus but obeyed only in combination with their own Egyptian names. We took horses who went quickly into the desert. The reason was that they were some km away expected by a crib with water and delicious carrots. They were not ready to proceed further. On the return trip they rode quite fast because the beasts smelled their stables. Another tour was along the green strip to the much older step pyramids of Sakkara. After such riding trips we went to the nearby "Mena House", an old luxury Hotel to enjoy a drink and the lovely atmosphere.

The agriculture of Egypt is based on a for thousands of years ingenious puzzled out irrigation system. Regular floods in spring time carried fertile soil from the African highlands. Since the construction of the Aswan dam this natural inundations are missing and the famous Mako cotton does not grow any more. When building that giant dam the Russian engineers have not considered the pressure of the water masses. A great amount disappeared in the permeable underground without appearing anywhere else again. The reduced water amount that finally reaches the delta of the Nile is not sufficient anymore for the existence of a certain kind of fish one only finds in this once ideal mixture of sweet with salt water. The fishermen had been forced togive up their lucrative job. The Aswan dam also establishes a danger for the Egyptian nation in the case of a natural disaster or of a military conflict. A destroyed dam and the resulting Tsunami could damage all villages and cities along the river. Egypt is like India a marvellous country and could be a terrestrial paradise if the population would be only a fraction of the present number. The government had some years ago decided to abolish the subsidy for "aish baladin" flatbread that burdened already for years the budget. It had nearly ignited a revolution and the Government gave up this plan. Instead it raised the tax on petrol and diesel fuel without problems. The tax did not hit the mass of the poor people who got just a bicycle, a donkey or a camel. Other countries have equal problems with poor jobless people. The upper ten in Egypt, India, Indonesia and Pakistan for example can enjoy a comfortable life. For every occupation in the household they got cheap labor. For jobs we do ourselves they have their staff of babysitters, cleaning women, cook and assistants, room maids, watchman, washing and ironing girls, servants, gardener, driver and secretary. When a person is sick a nurse takes care of it. The Lady is just busy supervising the staff and giving orders. For animals like dogs and horses there must be an extra person to take care of. In the orient since the antique slaves were taking care of everything. It is still a question of social standing to employ many people otherwise one is losing his face. In England it is a question of prestige to employ a butler. Companies that got representatives in oriental countries must tell them to adapt to the local customs and employ some people even if it is not necessary.

Whagdi Fahmi an Egyptian friend and neighbour of mine who lived also in the little village near Frankfurt airport introduced me to his family clan in Cairo where I saw the liberality in dealing with many domestic servants, I praised him for his simple household in Germany, where he handled everything himself. He was working for Lufthansa as section chief of the departure gates at the airport. He was nicknamed "troubleshooter" because he could handle passengers easily especially when dealing with fastidious Arab customers that could hardly be handled by the most female employees.

On one of the flights to Cairo I had the pleasure to meet a very interesting personality. In our conversation the Lady was amazed about my experiences and invited me to her home in the upper class suburb of Cairo. She was a German from Krefeld, where her father owned a well known spinning-mill. Her husband had been an apprentice in the factory where she met him. Her husband also owned a spinning mill and had in addition extended land holdings where he cultivated cotton. He was a member of the parliament and supporter of the president Anwar-as-Sadaat who was killed by terrorists later on. Madame Zein-el-Din loved reading and I supplied her with many books. By lucky chance I happened to be in Cairo when an opera was presented. I was invited to it and her driver picked me up at the Hilton hotel. So I experienced the famous singer and Callas of the Orient Mme. Um-Kalzum a good friend of the First Lady Gihan-as-Sadaat. For European ears the Egyptian symphonic scale is rather strange but fits the oriental atmosphere.

On another occasion I was invited to a garden party outside of Cairo.

Besides the cotton-lands that belonged to the family existed an orchard for growing oranges, mangoes and lemons. All was cultivated by "fellachin" farmhands. There was a rustic summer house with a separate stone oven that looked like those we used to bake bread in a long time ago. Three days before it had been heated and a disemboweled mutton was filled with spices, garlic, onions, oranges and completely covered with clay placed on a spit and turned from time to time in the heated oven for the three days. At the party the mutton was placed on a stone table and the cook opened the hard clay crust with a hammer to display the roasted meat. Everyone took a flatbread and the cook filled it with slices of meat that were replenished with grilled tomatoes and eggplant with tahina or hummus sauce. Never again I have enjoyed such an exquisite mutton dish. Originally the Arabian kitchen was very monotonous but the influence of the Egyptian and Osman kitchen had made it more versatile.

Here I want to mention two tragic happenings. We were accommodated in the new Heliopolis Hotel near the airport, but after some months it burned down. A steward who was in the second floor jumped out of his window and broke both legs. Other crew members who went to visit the famous bazaar "Khan el Khalili" were suddenly missing a pretty colleague. Searches even by the Egyptian criminal investigation police were unsuccessful. She remained lost forever. What else happened? After the take off of a Boeing 747 in Nairobi/Kenia it crashed because of an engine failure. Some passengers and crew members were killed.

In Rio de Janeiro some crew members took a walk along the Copacabana. One stewardess happened to lose her golden necklace by a criminal who came alongside with the car and tore it off. A steward who wanted to intervene was simply shot. A flight captain who got in conflict with terrorists who had hijacked a LH-jet was killed in Mogadishu/Somalia. Another tragic accident happened in Kenia. A copilot rented a small plane to visit a wild animal reservation near the Kilimandscharo. When the motor striked the plane crashed and all occupants were killed.

Those are just some of the happenings I remember.

The most conservative and best governed nation in the Middle East is the Sultanate Oman. Until the 19th century it had been a powerful nation. The trade with slaves, ivory, precious wood and gold had made it rich. The European colonial powers had ended this supremacy in East Africa. Presently the Sultan Quabus had achieved peace in his country. Many tribes had caused trouble before. Terrorists had no chance to spread their influence. The Sultan had introduced all positive modern ideas but kept all conservative sides of the local culture. His administration took care that the youth got an excellent education. The modern form of mass-tourism was rejected. Just a couple of individual groups were allowed to enter the country. The crews stayed in a splendid hotel outside of Mascat at the Indian Ocean. Nowhere in the world I have seen so many washed ashore shells. I could not resist and collected two bags full. The customs officer in Frankfurt made big eyes when he checked my suitcase. The little capital of Muscat distinguished Itself from all the other chaotic cities of the Arab world. Only in summertime temperatures reached 30° C.

At the time of the charismatic president Mobutu who loved to appear in public with a leopard skin and headgear to present himself as father of the nation we flew to Kinshasa/Zaire. Many of the former Belgian installations, factories and warehouses had been rotten and the railway did not operate anymore. It was a sad sight to see this country rich in resources and raw materials in such a state. At this time the copper region Katanga tried to get independent from Zaire and employed mercenaries to defend itself from the Mobutu forces. The military equipment of the different fractions was coming mostly from the Soviets or the USA. For a time the blue helmets of the UN tried to bring peace to this country, but the Swedish General Secretary of the UN Dag Hammarskjöld who was on a peace mission was killed when his plane was shot down.

Foreigners who dared to walk outside the hotel alone could expect to be threatened, robbed and stabbed. To have a better impression of the city I put on my jogging dress and could move around unmolested. All solid shops, fuel stations, restaurants and banks were like everywhere in Western Africa in Lebanese hands. They made a profit where others failed. There was for example a chain of steak restaurants that belonged to a Lebanese. The excellent meat was flown in with one of his two old Boeing 707-200 aircraft's. I happened to know him closer when our crew went to his restaurant to enjoy the service and good food. On demand he also carried forbidden goods, mercenaries and weapons. His present problem was the supply of spare parts for his two Boeing aircrafts. I chatted with the entrepreneur and took a liking to him. Beirut had been my favored place. Despite the chaotic condition in Zaire he was satisfied with his business. What he was missing was a trustworthy Lebanese partner. The money he earned he knew to exchange and had it in a reliable bank in Cyprus. Shortly after this talk I had a flight to Dallas. On the way from the Airport to our Hotel in the city we passed a fenced area with discarded ready to be scrapped aircraft's. In spite of the weekend I could reach this company by phone and got all the information. I was asked to provide all necessary details and the serial numbers. Next I called my divorced sister-in-law who was living in Phoenix/Arizona where I knew about an area where aircrafts from all over the world were parked temporary. LH pilots had trained there and told me about it. She found out that there was also a scrapping company nearby and gave me later all contact details. There existed also an area where military aircraft's of the Korea and Vietnam wars were "mothballed". I sent all information by mail to the Lebanese in Zaire. Next time I came to Kinshasa I met him and heard to my greatest pleasure that he had received my instructions and had been able to get all the used spare parts he needed. He asked me how much he owed me for my initiative. I told him that a buffalo steak medium rare would be all right. We sat together and talked about aircrafts. Another problem was that his planes did not fulfil the rules set down by the ICAO concerning pollution so both planes could not land anywhere in Europe. I told him that the solution was the old DC3 Dakotas. They were the donkeys of World War II. carrying soldiers and cargo. Just the speed was a fraction of the jet planes. In estimating the war lasting 2 years longer the US government had ordered a large stock of spare parts. So those planes were still abundant flying in South America, Southern Asia, New Zealand and Africa. I told him about my unforgettable flight from Caracas/Venezuela to Manaus at the Amazonas. There existed even an opera house from the time when caoutchouc was gathered in the jungle and the city became very rich.

Another Lebanese had established the "Golden Casino" on the top floor of our Hotel in Accra/Ghana. I am a strict opponent of all gambling, but did not want to be a spoil-sport since the chips were rather cheap.

I had a lucky chance and won considerably. When I could not exchange it to US$ I invited all present people like Crew members and easy girls for dinner in a Chinese restaurant. A pleasant band played in the background. The music created by the Ghanese is the best in Africa and resembles a little bit the steel-bands in Jamaica. The Ghananese bands are on tour all over Africa. The natives are dexterous in carving wood like animals and people. One could also order busts by photographs which could take weeks of course to complete.

As a lover of nature, Singapore the city state had a special attraction. Its botanical garden is just marvellous. No wonder, the Equator is close by and the humidity is near 100 percent. Despite the countless high rises and skyscrapers the city maintained its typical Malayan, Indian, Chinese and European quarters which are worth visiting. A relic from colonial time is the majestically "Raffles Hotel". In the evenings one meets a colourful international public at the bar that wants to admire where a courageous guest had once shot a tiger underneath the billiard table. Unfortunately no taxidermist prepared it for posterity or had the marksman claimed the tiger for himself? Outside at the bougainvillea framed main entrance are parked a couple of bicycle-rickshaws which are waiting for customers to be taken for a tour through the quiet side lanes. Despite the astronomical prices for lots and real estate the city planners had preserved such areas. They also left

a real jungle in the centre of the city to remind the citizens how Singapore had looked like 150 years ago. In the South existed a rocky bastion with a battery of canons to protect Singapore from the Japanese which were supposed to come from the sea, but they came from the North through the Malayan Peninsular by foot and with bicycles. At the bastion is a hall where wax figures remind the public of the capitulation of the Japanese in August 1945. Another ludicrous highlight is the park showing the Chinese hell and what happens to people who had sinned and were punished accordingly by being sawn to pieces, boiled in oil, blinded etc. The park was dedicated to the city by the owners of the famous "Tiger Balm Company".

My friend Rick Strasser resided in the penthouse on the 23rd floor of a high rise. As a freelance journalist he delivered good and bad news from Southeast Asia for the Swiss "Neue Züricher Zeitung" and others. The country he liked most was Papua-New Guinea whose national language is based on "Tok Pisin = Pidgin English".Here are some samples: Longfellow = White man, Yu no ken kam insait = Don't disturb, Yu ken stetim rum nau = Clean up room now, Buskanaka = savage, kalabus = convict, Me = goat, Posi = cat, Manki masta = Personal servant, Tok kuskus = fairy tale, Hambak = folishness, luk lok = see.

On my request, he recommended a good Chinese tailor. While that one was busy with another customer I discovered a ready safari dress that was very attractive. The tailor told me that it was for a regular customer, the Sultan of the Malaysian province Johor next to Singapore. I asked the tailor to make a similar dress for me. Most people don't know that Malaysia is a kingdom. One of the nine Sultans is voted to be the king for five years. If he did a good job he is voted to be king for another five years. That reminds me of the principle "primus inter pares" = "The First of equal ones".

Via Singapore or Kuala Lumpur we flew to Melbourne and Sidney. Touristic highlights in Sydney were the modern opera house and the nearby bridge at the bay connecting the city with the suburbs. A former prison near the start of the bridge was now a centre of the nightlife area.

At that time Australia suffered from the ozone hole in the orbit and all people wore hats for protection against the ultra violet rays. On a private visit to Australia I met my uncle in Canberra. He had Australian citizenship and worked for the government. We explored the Blue Mountains and he enjoyed angling in the brooks.

Except for the Northern island Hokkaido the population in Japan is incredibly dense. The greater area of Tokyo is with 37,2 Million people the greatest overcrowded regions of our world. The masses of people are living in the coastal areas. The rest of the mountainous areas consist of impenetrable forests. There are of course some national parks with good roads that offer volcanic hot springs "onsen".

Some years ago a JAL Boeing 747 crashed in the mountains near Tokyo. As helicopters could not land it took nearly a week for the rescue team to reach the place of the catastrophe. The volcanic tremors are always present. The stretches and tunnels of the Japanese railway "chikatetsu" and underground system "kokutetsu" are so extensively protected that accidents caused by earthquakes are nearly out of the question. Tsunamis are destiny that must be endured. Something strange are the "Pachinko" gambling halls where workers gamble away their wages. These halls are a curse and the government never tried to eliminate them because they belong to the Japanese mafia "Yakuza". They were a valuable informer service that helped the police to investigate cases. Their members can be recognized at the right hand where the small finger is missing.

My Japanese girlfriend did not need to work but decided after she had finished high school to work as a secretary for a foreign embassy. When that became too boring she decided to take a job as a stewardess for Lufthansa. In my experience it was better to avoid any affairs with stewardesses as superior. It was also difficult to meet each other because of the different flight plans. Friendships without sex affairs were better and one did not get a name as philanderer and superficial personality. I was not interested in an affair with a young person who had no interests and experience in life. Stewardesses had a short "maturity" and married soon. Marriages with colleagues from the cockpit and cabin crews often did not work. The longer absences were not good for the children who were in need of a father who was always available. When it was possible members of the flying staff took their partner with them on a tour, when a grandmother was taking care of the children.

Concerning affection I had a charming friend, who was secretary in a publishers company in Frankfurt. She was always available when I happened to be at home. She was unpretentious and needed only some attention. She provided me with interesting books from her publishing house. Now my Japanese girlfriend appeared on the stage. Tomoko was received with enthusiasm by my mother and clan. I had never told them about my German lover, because she was married. Her husband seemed not to appreciate what a gem he had as a partner. Normally I could tell my mother everything, but in this case I wanted to avoid to burden her. My brother was a womanizer and had many affairs. On the flights together with Tomoko I never let anybody know that she was my girlfriend. We kept professional distance and gave her Japanese colleagues no hint to chat about us. I thought it reasonable to separate from my German lover. It was effectuated without dramatic scenes and shedded tears. To be together with Tomoko we spent holidays at a wine growers place near Saint Tropez at the Côte d'Azur in Southern France. I showed her the beautiful places in Germany, especially in Bavaria, but also the sights of Berlin and Eastern Germany. Later I took an intensive course in Japanese at the Sendagaya Gakko in Tokyo. I remember a funny remark: "A happy man has an English manor, a Chinese cook, a Japanese lover and an American salary. An unhappy man has a Japanese home, an English cook, an American wife and Chinese salary." This remark is only understood by somebody, who has widely travelled and experienced the different societies and situations on our globe.

For quite a while I flew only on long range and overseas routes. I was forewarned and knew about the criminal situation worldwide. To protect myself from being a victim of pickpockets and gangsters I had my paper money in little pockets inside my small boots or in my elefant-leather belt with an inside zipper. Some small amount of money I carried in my purse. In New York city it is usual to be asked for some coins for a subway token. Often they don't ask you politely but warn you with their switch knife to hand over your money. In Colombia when you are assaulted by criminals on a street in the countryside it can happen that they cut off your finger when the goldring does not get off. In most of the countries in South America it is advisable not to stop when the traffic lights are on red at nighttime. The chance of being robbed is great.

Apart from such unpleasant happenings which are a result of poverty, there exists a joy of life and atmosphere that I miss in Europe. It is unbelievable but true that in Colombia are existing schools where pick-pockets are trained. When the pupils have passed the examination they are sent to international happenings like congresses, olympic games, exhibitions etc. to lighten participants and visitors from their financial burden. A part of their harvest had to be delivered to their instructor at home.

At the East side of Hispaniola is the Republica Dominicana. Its name reminds its citizens that Christopher Columbus landed here in the New World on a Sunday and established here the first Spanish settlement named Santo Domingo. A Lady friend I knew from Germany invited me to get aquainted with her country and people.

Her father was a respected architect who had designed some of the public edifices and the new airport. He had a fantastic library with world literature. His specialised books on architecture were to my surprise all in German. He could read and understand all, but was unable to converse in German. He simply had no chance to meet Germans.

My host was the leader of the political Partida Quisqueyana that represented the interests of the mostly exterminated aboriginal indios and environment protectors. This subtropical country possesses a rich flora and fauna and the Cordillera Central with its Pico Duarte of 3101 Meters that is the highest one in the whole Caribbeans. On one day the brother of my host took his 4-wheel drive military truck and took the whole family for an excursion to a lonely part at the East of the island, where corals had created a strange place. Snorkelling at the edge to the open sea was a real pleasure because of the under water paradise.

The Dominican Republic has only few natural resources, remains only agriculture and tourism at the splendid beaches.

Genoveva Bernard became much later consul of her country in Athens.

Venezuela is a country blessed with raw materials and natural resources. Unfortunately the different governments made the mistake of setting their efforts on the hauling and export of oil and gas from the Bay of Maracaibo. The agrarian sector was completely neglected. When the Americans started to boycott the socialistic governed Venezuela it came to difficulties in supply and to demonstrations against the dictatorial government.

LH crews were lodged near the airport at La Guaira in the Hilton Hotel. When we happened to have two days off we chartered the old fashioned yacht of Otto Meier, a German from Berlin that anchored nearby in the boat harbour. The yacht was something special and constructed all in resistant wood. The owner had been stranded here and was depending on charter fees for the continuous maintenance costs. When good weather was announced we left good provisioned for "Los Rocco's" an uninhabited group of islands in the Atlantic. In the evening a stiff wind helped to fill the sails and save fuel. Otto had taken some gulps from a bottle of rum and gave me the steering wheel and indicated the general direction some degrees left of the North star and disappeared in his cabin to take a nap. It started to rain and in spite of the staggering of the yacht I managed to keep the general direction. When it was dawning I discovered the islands at the right hand side.

Otto appeared with a cup of coffee for me and steered the yacht to a flat island that was covered with nests of seabirds that ignored us completely. A rare sight were the cormorants diving for fish. Next we moved the ship to the bay of a rocky island we took a swim and Otto dived with a net for lobsters. They had a grey camouflage colour and changed to orange when boiled. The trip back to La Guaira took several hours while we were accompanied by a couple of lovely dolphins.

At the 3-day layover we could book a jungle excursion to Canaima. With an old DC3 Dacota we flew to this isolated settlement where we took a boat to explore the tributary of the Orinoco river. At certain stretches the motor was stopped and silently we drifted down the river in order not to chase away the wild animals. When we were discovered by monkeys a noise from hell broke out. The native tour guide directed our attention to an anaconda that rested on a branch hanging over the river. It is the biggest snake in South America and can reach a length of 6 meters. It is a good swimmer and attacks only when feeling in danger. Alligators are only found in Latin-America tropics and are distinguished from the African species by the pointed snout.

I was especially interested in plants and small creatures and always had a magnifying glass with me to admire them. In Venezuela there are still existing prospectors who earn their livelihood by searching for gold and precious stones.

In 1989 I decided to improve my Portuguese knowledge by booking a 6 weeks course at the CIAL in Lisbon. The school arranged for me and accommodation with a widow. The other room was also occupied by an elderly Gentleman from England. It was a coincidence that he was in the same class as me. Edward Eates told me that he had always wished to learn Portuguese but he never had the time to do It. Now he was retired and widower and could afford to join this course. To explore the country he had come by car and he invited me to accompany him on his excursions to the countryside. I related him about my experiences in Mozambique,

Rhodesia, Namibia and Far East, and he told me about his professional experiences in Africa where he had trained the police forces of former English colonies in Nigeria, Ghana, Sierra Leone and Gambia. Some years before he was retired he had been sent by the English government to Hong Kong to handle the difficult situation there as chief commissioner of the Chinese police force. It was the time of the cultural revolution when infiltrated spies tried to instigate the population against the British administration. With his police force he had managed to quell and quench the unrest and to send the agitators back to China where Mao had turned everything upside down when trying with his young guards eliminating the intellectual class. For his diplomatic ways of handling the problem without causing dead or injured persons he became the local star. We shared literary and historical interests and enjoyed improving our Portuguese while following the TV evening news the Lady's parlour. On November 4th, 1989 we sat in front of the old fashioned TV set like usually when suddenly to our surprise pictures of the Berlin wall and the famous Gate of Brandenburg appeared with the information that the wall had fallen. Youngsters with hammer and chisel were already busy taking the stone of offence apart. Incredible but true!

I was not ashamed of my tears and embraced Ted, who had become my friend. To celebrate this miracle the Senhora opened a bottle of port wine.

When the course ended and our ways separated Ted gave me his calling card and asked me to see him whenever I happened to be in England. He was living in Exeter/Devonshire. I knew only the Southern coast of Cornwall with his harbour city Plymouth where the Royal Navy had a base. I came for a visit and we took an excursion following the footsteps of the Celts, Romans and Normans. He showed me also the infamous prison Princetown in the Dartmoor surrounded by swamps that made it difficult for prisoners to escape. Many prominent inmates happened to have been jailed there. One of them had invented the toothbrush. The prison has served as a background for many crime movies. Further in the North near Bristol exists a historical railway line that is privately owned and maintained by retired railway employees. One of the steam locomotives bears the impressive name "Duke of Gloucester". The stations, uniformed staff, rolling stock is so authentic, that it has also served for many movies and TV-series.

Exeter has already been an important place for the export of wool. Sea going ships could reach Exeter by means of a canal. The chamber of commerce and industry gives evidence of the lively trade. I loved to visit Ted as often as possible. He was like a father for me I had always missed. Finally I convinced him to visit me in Germany. He appreciated my initiative to drive his right hand steered car. For driving along the Lahn, Rhine and Mosel river I took my classic Rover P6 3500. We also went to Heidelberg, the technical museum in Sinsheim to see the "Römer" with its medieval buildings and the Art Museum. He was also interested in the bronze sculptures of bull and bear in front of the stock exchange in Frankfurt. With a special permission we could visit and watch the bustle and activities on the trading floor from the visitors tribune. In close by Bad Homburg we were invited for dinner at my aunt's villa. He knew that the English crown prince and later king Edward VII. had often stayed in the castle with his cousin the German crown prince William who had chosen Bad Homburg as his summer residence. Thanks to the initiative of Edward, the first golf course in Germany was created in the city's park.

Ted had never been before in Germany and was curious to see Berlin East Germany and the former German province Silesia that is now Poland. We went of course to all places that had some relation to my family like for example the abandoned ruin of the castle of my grandfather. The castle had not been destroyed in the war. It had just been plundered and neglected. There had failed the right people to estimate its architectural and historical value. My friend Christopher Vale from New Zealand was such a person who had the courage, knowledge and resources to restore the castle Krobielowice near Wroclaw/Breslau. It took him about 15 years. Originally it had been owned by Prince Blucher who had together with the English general Lord Wellington defeated Napoleon at Waterloo. The Prussian king had bestowed this castle on his marshal as gratitude for his performances he had achieved for the Prussian kingdom. It serves now as a hotel. Sometimes social meetings take place there. On our way back to Germany we took the Southern route through the Czech Republic and stayed one night in the famous spa Karlovy Vary. Some ancestors of mine originated from there. They had been adherents of Jan Hus a Bohemian who was a religious combatant like later Martin Luther. He had a conflict with the emperor and the catholic church. Because he did not revoke his teachings he was burned on the stake like Giordano Bruno Most of his followers left Bohemia and were welcomed by the Duke Elector of Brandenburg whose country later became the kingdom of Prussia. From Karlsbad we crossed the border, passed Würzburg and reached my home near Weilburg/Lahn. After resting some days I drove Ted to Hamburg where he took the ferry to Harwich/East England. Later Ted got a heart pacemaker and did not dare any more to undertake longer journeys. I met him several times in Exeter and London at last in the hospital. A few days later I received his obituary notice that my cousin Elizabeth had cut out of the "Times" newspaper.

A longer journey I took was a tour through Morocco with a little group.

Starting in Casablanca where the mosque is supposed to be the biggest in the world we went to Meknés where the most impressive Roman excavations can be seen. Handicraft artisans still know how to compose mosaics for floors, water basins and wall decorations. Wealthy and fastidious foreigners booked artisans to decorate their villas all over the world. In Fès we viewed the palace of the king and in Rabat the capital city we saw the fortifications at the sea, another palace and the bazaar.

Then we left the fertile plains with its orange plantations and drove up to the cold and rainy Atlas mountain range with its extended cedar forests.

At Quarzazate we stayed overnight at a beautiful lake and continued our trip through an endless date palm valley. Near Tazenakht we stayed in the endless desert with its sand dunes and made an excursion on camels. Next we crossed the Atlas mountain again and a gray and stony plain.

There we admired the still existing sceneries and backgrounds of the monumental movies like Ben Hur, Cleopatra and Moses. On the way we met a couple of German motor bikers and people with vintage cars who made a round trip like us. Near an old fortification we entered a long gorge with a river, a surprise in this dry region. We reached the Atlantic at Agadir, which had been destroyed by an earthquake some years ago and my wife and I went for a swim. We continued our trip with destination Essaouira, which is the fishing port of Morocco. Our accommodation was again a "Riad" a typical Arab accommodation with flat roof and an inner courtyard. The city is encircled by a high fortified wall and has a maze of lanes where you can easily get lost. In the antiquity it was famous for producing a purple textile colour from a certain sea snail. Marrakech has got like Essouira a maze of lanes like a labyrinth and got a unique bazaar. On the central place snake-charmers, artists and fairy tale story tellers were entertaining the crowd. Marrakech has an unique atmosphere like that in the stories of a thousand and one night.

In Rio de Janeiro we experienced something disagreeable. Instead of spending our time at the swimming pool of the hotel, we decided to stay at the beach. We took just the camera, towels, a pipe set with tobacco, a bottle with water, reading matter and the room key in a backpack with us.

As precaution I put the camera in a plastic bag and hid it in the sand. While we were swimming I observed a person feigning some gymnastic near our place suddenly bowing down, taking our backpack and running away. I left the water and followed the thief, but everywhere I was blocked. Finally the thief threw away the backpack and I gave up the chase. When I checked the back pack only the leather pouch with the pipes and the room key were missing. We decided to return to the hotel and inform the reception about the loss of the room key. When we were approaching the speedway I saw another thief who pulled a briefcase from underneath a towel and proceeded also to the speedway and crossing it. By chance a civil team of the police was passing by. I stopped it and indicated the thief at the other side of the street. They drove over the center stripe of the speedway and caught him. They told him to stand with spread legs at the fence and searched him. They retrieved the briefcase he had tried to throw away and saw that it just contained a driver license, credit card and keys, one with a Mercedes symbol. Together with the criminal we were driven to the next police headquarter where the chief of police dressed in civil white interviewed us. After the situation was cleared he phoned the hotel and asked them to change the lock of our room immediately. Concerning the other case they would soon find out the owner of the briefcase. He explained us that occurrences like ours were a common matter caused by inhabitants of the "favelas" shanty towns up in the mountains. They were breeding places for criminals. The civil policemen brought us back to the hotel where the lock of our room had been already changed. The dwelling places of wealthy people in Brazil were guarded like fortifications and the providers of observation cameras and razor wire became rich. The drivers of wealthy persons are heavily armed and the job as bodyguard had a boom.

I became curious and explored a "favela". There was electricity available but only for those who could afford it. Water was gratuit but had to be carried with buckets from a central supply. Cooking was done with gas cylinders. The roofs of the houses were of corrugated sheet iron or wood lattice covered with tar boards. They were weighted with stones to protect them from storms. The sidewalls of the shacks were done with palettes, plywood, plastic sheets or hammered sheets from petrol barrels. Who could afford it built walls of stone from houses that had been demolished to make place for high rises. For hygenical reasons the government supplied communal toilettes which were exchanged in shorter periods. Heating was not necessary because of the subtropical climate. It was surprising, but all had TV sets or radios. If not one looked at neighbours, what was happening in the world. Kids were forced to go to school, but controlling this was rather difficult. In the favelas where small shops where elementary items could be acquired. There was a shop that repaired bicycles and small motorbikes. In another shop they were busy with hand operated sewing machines to repair something.

Since the prices of housing in Sao Paulo and Rio de Janeiro had risen astronomically, even owners of little shops down town were living in favelas where the building lots were free of charge. The inhabitants of the favelas paid attention that no chaotic conditions developed and nobody was starving.

In Rio and Sao Paulo and everywhere in the world where LH-crews had a layover we had our favourite restaurants where we went for dinner.

In Rio it was a restaurant directly at the Copacabana where "Churrasco" was the favourite choice. It is the best part from the loin of the bull grilled over charcoal, something valued by the "gauchos" who took care of the herds on the pampas of Argentina, Uruguay, Paraguay and Southern Brazil. The meat of those animals is much better than ours from mass breedings in mega stables.

My godfather and my mothers brother C.C. von K. was a veterinarian and agronomical specialist and worked for the GIZ (Society of International Cooperation) a governmental institution for foreign missions. His present job was a 6 years stay in the Brazilian province Rio Grande do Sul. The reason was the combat against the cattle-plague that caused that the cows to give no birth to calves at all or brought forth only dead ones. The Brazilian Ministry of Agriculture was at a loss and asked the German Government in Bonn for help. The export of conserved corned beef was besides of coffee and tobacco an important economical factor and had cared for the rise of the harbour and the provincial capital city Porto Alegre of Rio Grande do Sul. My uncle knew about the cattle-plague under the medical term "Brucelosis". In

Europe it had, especially in England, caused a lot of losses of animals. The disease had been effectively combatted.

I took the opportunity and asked if my visit was opportune. He was happy to see me. With VARIG I flew to Sao Paulo and further to Porto Allegre, where my uncle was expecting me with his pickup. When he had loaded some GIZ cargo from Germany, he bought some items for his station and neighbours. After he took me for a sightseeing tour around Porto Allegre with its "fin de siecle", Portuguese colonial style architecture and beautiful parks. Then we left the city in Western direction on a dusty macadam road. It took some hours until we reached his station that was surrounded by a Mennonite community with houses on wheels, that could easily be transferred together with the cattle to another location. The Mennonites were a protestant group that had been persecuted and emigrated to Russia and Brazil. They were extremely conservative and were busy breeding cattle in the pampa. In Germany the Brucellosis cattle plague had already successfully been treated with Doxyelinic and Streptomycin. The deep cooled semen of bulls had to be be inserted into the sexual organs of the cows by means of arm lengths rubber gloves. The supply was regularly sent by air from Germany. I was permitted to assist my uncle at his occupation. It took some time until the disease was eliminated. I had supplied my uncle and my aunt with a suitcase full of literature. The life in the Pampa was unpretentious and the next settlement was far away. Together with aunt Jutta, son Carl-August and daughter Elizabeth we made an excursion to a lonely bay at the Atlantic coast. Some time before my uncle had, while snorkelling, discovered the remains of a commercial sailing ship with its cargo of dispersed china ware. The ship had passed the dangerous Cape Horn or the Magellan's strait unharmed until it was wrecked in a storm close to the destination Porto Allegre. We dived for some fitting fragments of plates, bowls and vases and also found some decorative shells.

I left my hospitable relatives. My next destination were the remains of the Jesuit state Encarnacion and La Santisima Trinidad at the Parana River. Once there had existed a Jesuit country that had been dissolved by order of the pope. The owners of the large landed property had problems to get agricultural labourers to work for them.

My means of transport was an old Ford-Bus. Its floor had been rusted through and was covered with plywood. It also served farmers to bring diverse animals to the market like goats, sucklings, sheeps, chicken and pigeons in cages. In Paraguay I admired the "Saltos del Monday" with the "Devil's Throat" and the famous "Iguazu" cataract on the Argentine side. In the old colonial capital Asuncion is the imposing and probably most beautiful public building in South America the "Palacio de Lopez", the seat of the President General Alfredo Strössner with German roots. Through a military insurrection he came to power and ruled Paraguay for 35 years. He was a vehement anti-communist and persecuted them and the leftist opposition. For this reason he was highly esteemed by the Western powers. About 40.000 German citizens settled in Paraguay after the Second World War and many of those were former Nazi's.

Once again I took one of those rusty buses for Montevideo/ Uruguay. The centre of the city with its magnificent buildings and places are worth seeing. The long promenade starting at the harbour and along the Rio de la Plata to the Faro de Punta Carretas is always animated by the citizens. Because of the extremely high import taxes on cars you saw many vintage cars kept going. At weekends many Gauchos come from the lonely pampa to enjoy the diversion of city life. They usually hold a silver bowl while drinking Mate-herb tea. Its light bitter taste makes it a perfect thirst quencher. On the other side of the Rio de la Plata more upwards is Buenos Aires, the capital of Argentina. Regular ferries connect both city's. During the passage I had to think of the German armoured ship "Admiral Graf Spee" that was at the start of the Second World War trapped by enemy cruisers while staying in the harbor of Montevideo for repairs after a sea battle. Against the order from Berlin to engage into a hopeless battle, the captain decided to rescue his crew of 1150 men and to sink the ship near Montevideo in the Rio de la Plata. The crew was granted sanctuary in Argentina.

Friends of my mother owned a big landed property for cattle breeding south of the capital near Benito Juarez in the pampa. I had announced my arrival and informed them that I would take the comfortable night-bus of the "Condor" company. Relaxed, I arrived in time in Benito Juarez where my host v.S. picked me up. He told me that visitors from abroad were rare. After a long dusty trip we arrived at the hacienda where I was heartily welcomed by the mistress and some lively dogs. The only news they got were from a delayed newspaper and the radio. From time to time he flew for business reasons with his Cessna-plane to Buenos Aires and stayed in the farmers club. Most of the haciendas had a landing strip with a windsock. The distances were so big that some could afford the luxury of a plane. When my host heard that I could ride he gave me a good natured black horse with the hint to watch out for burrows of pampa foxes, guinea-pigs and visachas, which are a kind of rabbit.

It could also happen that armadillos and guanakos might cross my way.I told my hosts that a relative of mine had lived in the more Southern province of Patagonia. Her husband had made a fortune importing barbed wire the rancher's needed fencing their property. When she returned to Germany after his death she lived in a manor in Silesia. Whenever she was in a bad mood she shouted: " I wish I were back in Patagonia."

My host was happy to live far away from Buenos Aires, because the political situation was hopeless. A high inflation had hit the workers and the employees depending on their salaries. Unrests and a military putsch were imminent. My host flew me to Buenos Aires where I caught the LH DC10 flight to Frankfurt via Sao Paulo and Dakar.

In Bangkok we stayed for a couple of years outside of the city in the Hyatt Central Plaza Hotel. Next to it is a big department store. In its upper level were countless stalls where one could taste the delicacies of the Thai cuisine. A distinguished meal in a nice surrounding one could experience in the famous Oriental Hotel in the open beside the Chao Phraya river. One could observe the lively river traffic, whose water taxis stopped beside the Oriental Hotel. The old tract dated from the 19th century and had a lot of charm and served at marriage parties of the upper ten. A friend of mine, the chief stewardess of Thai International Chingduang Raksanaves was often my guest there for brunch. Thanks to her I was introduced to the German manager of the hotel and could take a view behind the screen, especially the kitchen.

I had a trick to avoid the endless traffic congestion on the way to the city. Not far away from the Hyatt passed the railway line to the central railway station. With the 3-wheeler Tuk Tuk the station could be reached in ten minutes. From the central railway station one can go to the Thai border and change at the border to the Oriental Express to Singapore. Bangkok is a multinational city. Its largest minority are the Chinese, former members of the Kuomintang army, who became handicraft and business people. Other refugees came from Cambodia, Laos and Vietnam. Europeans and Americans were a small percentage of the population but were important as investors, counsellors and business people.

At the Gulf of Siam are beautiful beaches. The former fishing village Pattaya was discovered during the Vietnam war by the US forces rest and recreation organization. It became a playground for drugs and prostitution. Even the admonishing of king Bumipol could not avoid it. The temptation of the US$ was overwhelming. Despite of the tropical heat one could confidently try the snacks and specialities of the street vendors. Popular are the "satay" wooden sticks pierced with shrimps, chicken meat and vegetables fried over charcoal grills and offered with peanut-coconut sauce. Pineapples are cut in a decorative form and offered with a wooden stick. Everything was very appetizing.

Next to the Oriental Hotel in an inconspicuous windowless hall I discovered a shop that was evidently just known by insiders. I became a good customer of it. The owner had decided to rescue old handicraft and folk art from being lost. The articles were made of rattan and bamboo like boxes, chests, chairs, bowls, frames, baskets, hats. In addition there were silk articles and some of raw cotton. At the ceiling were hanging old fashioned ventilators fighting against the heat. Every time I came to Bangkok I acquired there some items that are adorning now my exotic home and are admired by my guests. In this unusual city I enjoyed taking walks through the quiet side lanes to discover old wooden houses with marvelous gardens. My friend Chingduang had such a home but it was surrounded by high-rises. The lot was worth millions, but she did not sell it.

Tourists were always shown the "floating market"where women in wide boats sell fruit and vegetables to customers living in a maze of "klongs" canals near the river.

By coincidence I discovered near my hotel in the Sukumvit district the pub "Alt Heidelberg" that offered all the German specialities like "Sauerkraut with Würstchen or Schweinshaxen with fried potatoes" etc. This place belonged to a Jew Horst Franz who had survived ...the Holocaust as a young boy. The pub was the anchor place of all the German, Swiss, Austrian and Dutch community and tourists in Bangkok. Here was also a meeting point of some strange people who stayed permanently in Thailand to enjoy the pleasant weather an low costs of living. A member of the former high ranking German Waffen SS and relative of the Cardinal von Gahlen became representative of the German medical care company Hartmanns Verbandsstoffe in Southeast Asia. One evening he stormed into the pub inviting everybody present for a free Singha beer. The US-Americans had just bombed Cambodia and the supply trail of the "clay jugs" used intensively by the Vietcong. He has just signed a contract for the delivery of sufficient material. An other steady guest in the late 80s was an industrialist from Hamburg who was specialised in the salvage of sunken ships. He was always accompanied by a charming young Thai girl who took care of him while his stay in Thailand. But his real reason to come to South Asia was a professional one. He had been informed of a German submarine that had been sent to support the Japan war efforts with a cargo of quicksilver that was needed for the bomb triggers. Despite that top secret action, the submarine had been detected by the Royal Airforce and sunk in the Strait of Sumatra in 1942. Just recently this fact was uncovered and the old man was trying to get the permission from the

Malaysian government to salvage the whole submarine or at least the barrels with the precious quicksilver. The danger of polluting the whole Strait was after 4 decades imminent.

Horst Franz the owner of of the pub found an other outlet of his energy besides chasing pretty girls. I took him once to a lonely fascinating beach West of Phuket where only some fishermen had their boats. Just at this time he had acquired a complete kitchen equipment from the US-Army.

He liked this wonderful beach and planned together with his Chinese partner, the bottled water supplier of Bangkok, to build a hotel there where the US-kitchen came into use. Over one year later I was the first one to stay overnight in this place. I should not have shown him. More hotels followed and and soon most of the former beauty and silence had gone. Years later the Tsunami hit this beach, killed many people and destroyed most of the hotels and living quarters of the population. Later I found his pub in strange ownership and heard that he had divorced from his wife, a former major of the Israel Army and had left because of tax evasion and became the manager of Coca Cola in Novo Sibirsk.

Another place of interest is Hong Kong with its high-rises and skyscrapers where people are living like ants. Just landing on the old airport Kaitak was a brilliant performance of pilots who got a special training license to do so. The runway had been extended into the bay. In spite of this fact it still happened that air crafts overshot the runway and ended in the bay. From the marking checker point hill on the landing was affected close to the high-rises that the pilots of all concerned airlines asserted that they could pick up the laundry from the balconies what was of course nonsense. Due to the extreme density of population and the mountains a lot of land had been reclaimed from the sea. That had happened too when the new airport at Landau island was built.

The time difference to Germany was so great that the crews could not adapt easily to the local time and went to sleep right away after having checked in at the Sheraton Hotel around noon. They woke up when Hongkong went to sleep. Through the mother of a Chinese acquaintance in London, who was living near the hotel in the Nathan Road, I came to know the acupuncture specialist Professor Chen, a refugee from Shanghai. He wanted to give me an example of his abilities and convinced me to an acupuncture session. "The general separation" proved to have a wondrous effect on me and I could survive the day without feeling tired. From now on I got an acupuncture treatment whenever I happened to come to Hong Kong. When I had something to do on Hong Kong island I used the Star Ferry from Kowloon pier that arrived like clockwork every 15 minutes. The ferries were very old but reliable. In the shadow of all the skyscrapers of banks and famous companies was the once prominent Admiralty, the former seat of the English governor. Nearby was the bus stop for those who wanted to drive up to the peak, the highest point of Hong Kong island, where the prominent people have their residences.

Others used to take the cable car to reach the observation point from where they had fantastic view to Kowloon, the mainland and the outlying Islands. Up there resided also a business friend of my brother, a share- holder of the HSBC, real estate broker and film distributor. My brother was a film distributor and producer in Los Angeles and had since the early 70th good relations with Ho Chapman that exceeded his business ones.

It might have been his idea that my brother started a series of over twenty "Mysterious China" documentaries. At two of those "Burma Road and Flying Tigers" and "In the footsteps of Genghis Khan" I accompanied the film team in the function of counsellor. Whenever I landed in Hong Kong I contacted Ho Chapman. His office was close to the Sheraton Hotel in the parallel street of the Nathan road in the same building of the "Bottom up Club" where the advertising showed a couple of attractive female behinds. Bottom up means an upturned glass = "Gan Bei" the Chinese expression for cheers. When Ho Chapman had time to spare we went to one of his favourite fish restaurants where the fish were alive in salt water aquariums like squid, crabs, cuttle-fish and octopus. The Chinese, Koreans and Japanese of the coastal regions are world champions in preparing seafood. Everything served will be eaten with chopsticks. After a short training every Westerner will learn to handle it. To support digestion the compulsory "Kaoliang", a rice brandy is served. Sometimes when it was convenient I was invited to a party near the peak where I got on well thanks to my appropriate dress and my knowledge of Chinese. In the case of a mistake during a conversation I had always ready a phrase that derived from the last but one Chinese emperor of the Qing dynasty: *Tien pu pa, di pu pa, jou pa yang gweize swo Chung Kuo hua!* Don't dread heaven, don't fear hell, just fear when a devil from overseas tries to speak Chinese. There are many reasons to make jokes about the "Long Noses", because the foreigners happened to "drop a brick". Chinese who did not have any experiences with foreigners rejected to shake hands for hygienical reasons. When Mao tse tung took over, all conservative customs were abolished and marked as counter revolutionary. In imperial times and later people greeted each other by forming their hands to fists, pressing them to their chest and bowing slightly. Grand children demonstrated their esteem for their grand-parents by crouching on the ground and touching the ground with their forehead. After this ceremony they were asked to stand up and to come to their grandparents to be embraced like the children of Westerners. The former used spitting bowls came from the mental attitude that spittel should not be swallowed but exterminated.

Handkerchiefs were not known in China, Japan and Korea. The people could not understand that used ones were placed in the pockets. The use of paper napkins and toilet paper was a revolution. Belching after having eaten was considered a compliment to the cook, the host and housewife. The same is valid for sipping noisily a delicious soup. A good cook was lent out to houses of friends for special events.

Ho Chapman was a decided connoisseur not only of the Chinese kitchen, but also of the French one. He planned to move to the Provence in Southern France after his retirement. Before Hong Kong was returned to China 1997 he settled in Vancouver where a big Chinese community exists. A curiosity and relict of the past besides the "Star Ferry" are the double decker tramways on Hong Kong island. From the upper deck one got a fantastic view onto the throng of people on the pedestrian ways and the crowded streets. Nowhere in the world not even in Los Angeles, London or Singapore I have seen so many Bentley ande Rolls Royce limousines than in Hong Kong – Wanchai. The most exclusive Luxury Hotel the "Peninsular" in Kowloon had the tradition to have a fleet of twelve Rolls Royce limousines to pick up important guests at the airport. When I wanted to enjoy a pleasant afternoon I booked a place in the lounge for the 5 o'clock tea. Sometimes I took a stewardess with me provided that she was decently dressed. We listened to the life orchestra playing pieces of music from Beethoven and Strauss. Of course there were offered the English cucumber or ham sandwiches and pastries. When Hongkong was taken over by the People's Republic the fleet of Rolls Royce limousines was dissolved as being considered as a capitalist provocation. One of those nostalgic Rolls Royce Corniche cars were acquired by my friend in New Zealand and general overhauled.

When I wanted to escape from the biggest International shopping paradise I went to the outlying Islands terminal near Admiralty and took the ferry to Sok Kwu Wan on Lamma island. The tiny village consisted of a large fish breeding enterprise, some restaurants and a Confutze Temple. From there a well maintained path led over the top of the island to another village Jung Shue Wan. One branch of the path went down to the sea where just one boat was pulled onto the small beach. Before coming here for the first time I had studied the map of the island and knew that opposite of my position was a bay, but to proceed there I had to clear a path through a reed and bamboo grove. I reached a marvellous bay with a long beach. The left side was blocked by steep rocks, but the other side was accessable. Between the round washed rocks I discovered a brooklet with clear water that came from the side of the mountain. Through the open side of the bay I could see the ships passing to and from Hong Kong. It was a miracle to find such a lonely place near one of the densest populated cities in the world. I was feeling like Robinson. Storms had deposed some interesting items on the rocks. Underwater I found a lot of sea-urchins and mussels. Next time I came I took a sturdy knife with me to harvest the mussels and tried them with lemon juice. I also met a yacht that had anchored in the bay and the people went swimming in the quiet water. When they discovered me they invited me for a drink on board.

Another interesting excursion was by train to the Chinese border. At this time the terminal was still near the star ferry. The train also stopped at the beautifully maintained "Royal Hong Kong Golf Club". I enjoyed watching the players from the coffee terrace. In the centre of Kowloon besides the Nathan Road is a hill that accommodates the Botanical Garden. It has some aviaries where all Asian birds can be admired. At the very top of the hill a platform with circular rails could be seen. At the war an anti aircraft gun had been positioned there. In the 1980s a fire had broken out on the cruise ship "Elizabeth I." in the strait between Hong Kong and Kowloon. It had half sunken and was for some time a strange sight. It served as the background for a James Bond 007 movie. If the fire would not have happened Hong Kong would have a unique swimming university. The Chinese multi millionaire C.Y. Tung acquired the ship to realize his idea. The upper part of the former cruise ship was recycled and the lower part was integrated into the foundation of the new container terminal 9 of the Victoria Harbor. The presumed insurance fraud was never proved.

Gambling in the crown colony was strictly prohibited. Those Chinese with a passion for gambling took a hovercraft or ship to Macau, the Portuguese colony where gambling was an old privilege and source of income. What few people know is that it is the richest city in the world. Hong Kong has another attraction that is Aberdeen on the other side of the island. There are the restaurant junks that are only open on evenings and illuminated with red lanterns. Without reservation one has no chance to get a seat. Another highlight is the Chinese version of the Western brunch called Dim Sum. Around 10.00 a.m. it starts for groups of minimum 6 persons. In the middle of the round tables are turnable plates which are offered and continuously replenished bowls with Chinese delicacies. Pretty service girls dressed in silken "cheongsams" take care that nothing is missing. At the end lychees are served and "kaoliang" rice brandy is offered to support digestion.

I am a lover of art and have seen a great deal of galleries and private collections all over the world. Secretly I had wished to own some of those overwhelmingly paintings at least as fine copies of famous masters to adorn my later dream house to give them a dignified place. In Hong Kong's district Stanley existed a market for fashion of surplus articles. In the first floor of an inconspicuous building was the atelier of Master Wu. On shelves he had catalogues of auctions by Southebies and Christies as well as from museums from all over the world from where he selected paintings to copy. I acquired some in the following years and also gave him commissions for me and friends. Wu kiu-wai was a gifted artist and I spent hours in his atelier studying his catalogues and his ready painted pictures. Sometimes he spent months finishing one picture. He saw my real interest in art and we became good friends. With the investment of some thousand US$ one could enjoy paintings whose originals were traded for sometimes millions of US$.

Finally I found my long time searched home, where my treasured paintings got a dignified place in fitting Italian frames. Some less impressive pictures from my own hand are hanging in the cellar and garage. An old acquaintance of mine H.G. Zach had found a solution by transforming a former industrial hall to a private museum where rare furniture, statues, oil pictures, oriental carpets and Rolls Royce limousines found a pleasant ambience. The single exhibition pieces are witnesses of the incredible phantasies and ability of artists when tools were very simple. To end the day in a stimulating environment the crews met at "Jimmys" a pub where we could play darts and where a Chinese jazz band gave its best to entertain also crews of other airlines.

Like the hurricanes in the gulf of Mexico the typhoons of South and East Asia are a catastrophe with destruction and human lifes to deplore. A typhoon with the name "Hope" hit Hong Kong I will never forget. It left a chaos of sunken ships, destroyed scaffolding, turned over cars, buses, cranes and up-rooted trees. A deluge like rainfall inundated the Crown colony. Suddenly a deadly silence set in and the pale sun could be seen through the centre of the typhoon and suddenly it raged from the other side. Slowly it moved on and a strong rain set in again. I could watch the drama from one of the upper floors of the Sheraton Hotel. The water was ankle high in the room despite the sealed windows and the rolled towels I had placed at the gap of the door. I had stored my shoes on the upper shelf of my wardrobe. Finally it eased to rain and the people animated the streets like ants to clean up the damages the typhoon had caused. Next day the airport Kai Tak opened and LH Boeing 747 landed again. Business as usual.

Some time later I had a layover in Manila/Philippines. The Hilton Hotel was situated directly at the bay. A strange view of an upside down cargo ship that had been stranded in front of the Hotel. It was a victim of the typhoon "Hope" before it had hit Hong Kong. On top of the ship a clever Filipino had erected a hut. The international sea law rules that a ship that had been abandoned by its crew belongs to that person that occupies it later on. Starting in the early morning he was hammering in the wreck to gain material for sale. It sounded like a woodpecker in action.

Thanks to my knowledge of exotic languages I could arrange my flights to the Far East according to my wishes. The political détente concerned China. Once a week LH started to fly to Beijing. That signified that the crews had 6 days time to explore the city. That was only possible by bike that could be cheaply rented at certain places. To stay unobtrusive I bought two working class outfits in green and blue with a fitting cap. At this time the whole population was under obligation to wear it before the rules were loosened. On one occasion I took my mother with me. It was still difficult to get a visa for her. Clad in Mao look we drove by rented bike through the fields passing some duck breeding places to the summer palace. The greatest attraction was a ship made of white marble. When back in the city we were invited to listen to one lesson in an elementary school. After the lesson we engaged in a small talk that the teacher and the pupils liked very much. Foreigners were still a rarity at this time in China.

I was able to convince our station chief to arrange a permit for us to visit the autonom region of Inner Mongolia. Because I spoke some Mandarin we could go without a guide to the capital of the region Hohhot by steam train.

Our reserved sleeping bunks were taken by some Party bigwigs. We made us as comfortable as possible sitting on the floor and playing cards to pass the time. For me it became a little bit boring. At the next stop equipped with a couple of Marlboro packets I went to the locomotive and asked the driver if I could accompany them. The team enjoyed the distraction especially when I took the shovel and helped feed the oven with coal. The driver explained the use of the different handles and wheels that supplied the machine with steam. We passed Datung the greatest coal mine and Buddhist ceremonial place in Northern China. It was amazing to experience the locomotive in full action. In Hohhot we were expected by a guide with a truck and drove us into the great plain that was green because it was the rainy season. It was not far from the edge of the Gobi desert where the small village of jurtes was located. There were the pasture grounds for the horses, yaks and double humped camels. The round yurts were rather comfortable and could be taken apart when new pasture grounds were chosen. I had been told that the Mongolian kitchen was very frugal. I had an idea how to enrich the menu. I was able to convince our guide with some packets of Marlboro to organize a shotgun for hunting wild fowl I had seen some temporary lakes with wild ducklings. We were successful and brought home a couple of ducks. I had to take a bath to collect them. The village women were busy plugging the feathers of the birds after a treatment in boiling water. After the intestines were taken out they were filled with herbs, onions and garlic and put on the grill. The rice brandy "Kaoliang" was again helpful to digest. The next day was dry and we spent it riding in the plain. Those who were not used to horses took a patient camel. The following day we made a sightseeing tour in Hohhot and took the train back to Beijing. This time we had bunks to take a nap. Mongolia is a divided country.

In the time of weakness after the abrogation of the Qing dynasty the Northern part of Mongolia was taken away by Russia.

At Perestroika this part became independent with the capital of Ulan Bator. The Inner Mongolia is a treasure box of rare earth that is used for computers, mobile phones and TV sets. China exports rare earth only in processed form. Like I could ascertain during a later visit of Inner Mongolia one could find everywhere memorials of the greatest hero Genghis Khan who extended his short lived empire up to Europe. His grandson Kublai Khan created a new dynasty and became Chinese emperor. From him originates the expression: "To defeat a nation with a disciplined army is an easy matter, but to govern it later on is a very difficult task". Secretly Inner Mongolia supported the Japanese in the war who promised them to reunite them with Outer Mongolia. Mao tze-tung took offence in this attitude and treated them badly. That is past, now the Mongolians and Manchurians have adapted well. Not so the Tibetans and Uiguriens in the Muslim Xinjiang. All participants were inspired by our short excursion. At that time our accommodation was the worthy Peking Hotel near the forbidden city and the "Tian An Men" and "Palace of Heavenly Peace". The members of the nearby Peoples Congress came here to dine because it was good and cheap.

Every year in spring time came storms that brought life to a stand still. They carried masses of dust with it and formed loess dunes in the streets. Those people who dared to move outside wore face masks. The reason was the long time of exhausting the soil and the ruthless exploitation of the forests. A government's initiative "The Green Wall" is taking care of this problem and has already achieved surprising successes. With some of my crew members we had found protection at the entrance of a government tenement house from the sudden storm. To our surprise the left hand door of the ground level door opened and a friendly gentleman asked us to come in. Like I heard in the following conversation that our host was one of the editors of the "Social Security Newspaper" that every Chinese receives once per month. We were lucky to be invited inside, because of the storm he had stayed at home. His wife was a teacher and was locked in the school. His daughter Ying also came back home. The bank where she worked had closed for the day. She spoke fairly good English despite of the fact that she had never been abroad. Her father Liu, Jian Lun spoke no English but with the help of Ying we had a lively conversation. For my colleagues it was an unusual opportunity to see how Chinese families were living. As editor our host had the privilege of a simple government owned apartment. With his wives mother they had 3 rooms, kitchen, WC with shower and floor. The tenement house was near the government offices and the ancient city. They had to pay only for gas and electricity. When the storm quieted down we left the hospitable home and I promised to come again. At one of my next visits I happened to meet a relative of Mr. Liu who was a scroll painter whom I could watch at his work.

For hygienic reasons the government had forbidden the keeping of birds and other animals in the houses. This rule had been loosened a bit to allow old people to keep small animals for fun. It was a nice experience to see the elderly outside in small places with their bird cages and boxes with crickets to exchange views and experiences. In the early morning others met for shadow boxing that was considered as healthy gymnastics.

When I met Mr. Liu again he surprised me with the news that his daughter had met a Swiss and had been betrothed to him. I was amazed and was invited to the marriage party in Bern. Later they came to see us in Germany with their first daughter.

For visits in China one needs an official letter of invitation and a guarantor. Fortunately that was handled for me by the Chinese assistant of my brother Amy Chen in Beijing, who had organized all the film tours of my brother. She was desperate when covid19 spread and my brother could not continue with his documentary film projects. My Chinese friend Chang, di was trapped in China for two years.

Before the epidemic disease I had travelled China extensively and took my mother to the wall "Wan li chang jiang", the Ming Tomb and the Temple of Heaven. We booked a ballet show and saw the palaces of the forbidden city. On another occasion I took my wife for a round trip and flew from Beijing to Xian with the best maintained city wall in China. Xian was originally the start of the silk road to the West. The main attraction was of course the exhibition of the terracotta army of the emperor Qin Shi Hung Di. It had been discovered accidentally by a farmer when digging for a well. The government had assured him a little pension and since that time he sat with his pipe in front of his hut to be photographed with tourists from all over the world. Our next destiny was Chongqing, the provisory capital of China during the war. It was the starting point of the cargo ships down the Jang -Tsekiang river to Shanghai. After the completion of the giant dam the level of the water had been lifted for 16 meters. The dangerous three gorges could be handled much easier now. Several cities with millions of inhabitants had to be demolished. The rubble served to prevent erosion. New cities were created for the dislodged people up in the mountains. Smaller tributaries became navigable. In one of those were hanging coffins up in the rocks of deceased fishermen who did not want to leave their beloved valley. Behind the three gorges we passed with our ship a giant open-cast work for coal. Cargo ships delivered it to the power works in Shanghai. According to the mythos exists further down the entrance gate to the underworld. The imposing Lord ruling over the empire of the death holds a voluminous book in which the good and the bad deeds of every single Chinese are listed. I still got some banknotes from the underworld.

When someone dies they are burned and serve as currency to lead a comfortable life in the other world. I suppose that the Jang Tze Kiang dam is still the greatest one in the world. The turbines producing electricity have been delivered from the West. The mighty locks offer enough space for smaller seagoing ships, but it takes quiet a time to fill the lock chambers after the flood-gates have been closed. When the river leaves the mountains it extends enormously and reaches near Shanghai a width of several km.

We left our ship much earlier to visit a silk processing company. After that, we took a plane to Shanghai. There we took a walk at the "Bund" where in the 30s the most powerful banks and companies had their seat in the International Concession. Opposite of the "Bund" in the "Pu dong" district is the Shanghai tower with 128 floors, the highest building in China. Not far away from the mega city Shanghai is the Venice of Far East Suchow. Countless bow bridges crossing canals which are all connected with the 1800 km longest and also oldest commercial canal In the world. The Imperial Canal connects Hangzhou in the South with Beijing in the North. It provided the imperial capital and its surroundings with rice, wood, building materials, silk, tea and other important goods. When the railway system foremost built by the Belgian-Congo company, the Imperial Canal lost its importance and serves nowadays for irrigation.

China gives us always the impression to be an overpopulated country, but that is only true for the central Han region. The other

4 autonomous regions are Manchuria, Inner Mongolia. Tibet and Xinjiang are underpopulated and consist partly of desert-like areas. The province Qinghai for example has endless forests and beautiful lakes but few people. The mountainous Szechuan district has areas where are no people living at all and where one can easily get lost because streets are not existing. China has probably the greatest variations of climates in the world. There is the Himalaya with its eternal snow and ice and the tropics in Hainan island. This big country can only be governed with severe hands. At this moment I cannot imagine a democracy with many parties and greater liberties as now that could only end in chaos. The present mixture of socialism with capitalism allows enough freedom for the people to develop their personality.

The Monarex Hollywood Corporation gave me the opportunity to accompany the film team on a shooting trip for a documentary movie ordered by the Chinese Ministry of Culture. Its title was: "Burma Road and Flying Tigers". The story was the following: 1937 the Japanese had without declaring war suddenly attacked China at the Marco Polo bridge near Beijing and had occupied with superior forces the whole Pacific coast. China was cut off of its supply for its Kuomintang army. Under highest priority the governor of the Yunnan province had organized to build with primitive means and assistance of the whole population a supply road over inaccessible mountain spurs of the Himalayas. Following the completion after the incredible short period of one year convoys brought supplies from Mandalay/British Burma. When the Japanese army occupied Burma, the Chinese government, thanks to contributions of Chinese business companies all over the world, could buy cargo air planes to fly supplies from British India to Yunnan. 16 runways and hangars were built with the army and the population. In default of motorized road- rollers one had created them of concrete. They had to be pulled by 20 or more workers to grade the landing strips. To resist attacks of the Japanese air force with its "Zero fighters" a secret squadron was created that was called " Flying Tigers" and existed until the armistice in August 1945. The adventurous pilots managed to shoot down over 300 Japanese fighters. The valley of the Salveen river is still called "Aluminium Valley" because of the many planes that had crashed there.

A clever Chinese had started to collect the remains of the equipment of all combatants. In the city of Tengchong exists his museum and is a great tourist attraction. The film work led us to the loneliest places in the mountains where once fierce battles had been fought. We inspected the air direction center of the Flying Tigers that was hidden in a mountain cave. Fascinating were the interviews with farmers, citizens and soldiers who have been involved in this history. An interesting story I have to tell about a former optician whose job it had been to provide soldiers and civilians with spectacles. The international fighter and cargo pilots could not dispense of coca cola. It was delivered in those attractive pressed glass bottles. Glass for spectacles was an article that could not be found in this war shaken country. The optician had a clever idea to grind and abrade the bottoms of the coca cola bottles in a form to make lenses for spectacles of it. I am sure that one also found a use for the rest of the bottles. In remote villages I have seen youngsters that wore sandals made of used tires and hinges of doors of the same material. Chinese people are quite inventive when it comes to using wasted material. Bottles of a certain plastic material are used now to make a fibre to create pullovers and jackets. Remarkable is that many Kuomintang units left China and settled down in British Bengal/ India and mixed with the local population.

In the West of Yunnan is one of the most beautiful middle age cities of China Dali. Further North is another pearl, Li Jiang. Here is also a former runway that serves now as a horse racing track. In the impressive old city we met an art painter specialized in historical themes of the war. A Chinese Lady friend of mine from Shanghai was invited to accompany us while pictures were taken. She had never before been in Yunnan.

The whole film tour was organized by the government. A pleasant young Chinese who spoke good English accompanied us and took care of matters that make travelling sometimes so annoying.

Like in China Lufthansa started to fly before the Olympic Games once the week to Seoul/South Korea. At this time only Government employees and business people could leave the country to prevent that too much money was leaving the country. After the devastating three years of war that ended with the establishment of the provisory 38° degree latitude border, all the provisions had been exhausted and in the famine the population was even cooking the bark of the pine trees to survive, the forests were decimated in such a degree, that President Pak forbade its further destruction and started a national reforesting campaign. Nurses and miners were sent to Germany as contract workers and part of their income was sent to the treasury of the South Korean Government to help improving the run down infrastructure and to construct new highways, bridges and tunnels. High rises and schools were built for the refugees from the communist North

Korea. When LH started to fly to South Korea I had already contacts there and could enjoy my long layover and travelled extensively often accompanied by my later wife. At one occasion much later my wife, her two sisters and I went for a trip to the exotic subtropical island of Cheju in the South and opposite of Hondo/Japan. This island has about 300 extinct volcanoes. The highest is the Halasan with 1956 m. I climbed it all alone after my companions had given up half way. One of the underground lava tunnels had a length of over one km. At the time of Kublai Khan most of his cavallery was based on this island. Nowadays Cheju island is very attractive for Korean and Chinese "Honey Moon" couples.

In 2018 the South Korean government accepted 500 refugees from the war in Jemen. They were settled in Cheju island. After a short period there was an upheaval. The reason was that the authorities did not separate the different Muslim religious groups like Shiites and Sunnites and that they could not adapt to the local customs. At the Northern coast we could observe professional women groups in action diving for sponges and mussels. When driving home to Seoul we stayed at relatives at the coast of the Yellow Sea. They were professional fishermen and took us out to the sea to watch them at their work. They had a charcoal stove on board and we enjoyed fresh caught grilled seafood. On another occasion we collected wild berries, mushroom and edible chestnuts in the mountains, while my brother-in-law went hunting wild boars, a plague for the farmers.

Often we went to enjoy an "onzen" a volcanic spring that reminded me of the similar basins with different temperature in the Roman bathes.

I miss especially the huge fish markets were the seafood could be prepared on the spot at the adjacent restaurant where I could enjoy my favorite sashimi (raw salmon) with wasabi horse radish.

My younger sister-in-law was employed at an extended Botanical Garden outside of Seoul where in all seasons was something to admire. Another highlight was an original village from the 19th century.

My brother-in-law was a typical Korean workaholic who managed together with his elder brother a company that produced different kinds of ready cements that were delivered for example for the construction of the Inchon International Airport and the Rapid Railway Line from Seoul to Pusan. I convinced him to forget his business for some days and accompany us for a visit of the famous strange mountain district in central China. Before I had lured him and his clan to Germany and showed them with a rented transport the most important highlights and landscapes in central Europe. We two planned to fly to Utan Bator/Outer Mongolia, but had to forget it because of the Corona epidemic.

On the other side of the Pacific is a country however small worth to be mentioned. A student I met in Germany invited me to Nicaragua situated between Costa Rica and Honduras on the Central American landbridge. Her father was the president of the Nicaraguan Red Cross and was just rather busy with the recent problems after a mega earthquake that had destroyed the greatest part of the capital and surrounding and caused many victims. I accompanied him on his inspection tours through the ruined city and assisted when medical cases had to be taken care of.

Just a few modern buildings and some villas including his own one had survived the catastrophe unharmed. The reason was that they had been not damaged was that the architects had provided them with a conical shaped foundation. The mass of the owners of building had renounced that measure because it was very expensive. At this time the dictator President Somoza tried to keep law and order and finally went to exile in Paraguay where he was killed by the US supported contras. Originally the now operating Panama Canal going from Colon to Panama city from North to South was planned to go through the Managua inland lake from East to West but was for financial and political reasons never realized. The infrastructure was deplorable. There existed for example no street from Managua to the settlements Bluefield and Goldfield at the Caribbean side of the country. The impenetrable jungle in-between is a treasure chest for scientists. One of those happened to have lived in a tree house for several years to study the unmolested flora and fauna of this oldest tropical wilderness in the world.

Coffée is the greatest export good of the country and was cultivated first by catholic missionaries since 1790 especially on the volcanic slopes in the foggy altitudes of 1.200 – 1.500 Meters of the mountain chain Isabelia. It has a sligt taste of chocolate. Because of natural catastrophes and the civil war 1980 its cultivation came to an absolute standstill. It also exports cotton, textiles. bananas and tobacco. Despite of that it is the second poorest country in America after Haiti.

On one occasion my Lady friend took me to a voodoo happening practised by the black minority originating from West Africa. It was tolerated by the authority. I have heard that a majority of black citizens where living along the misquito coast in Bluefields and Goldfields. They all spoke an old Victorian kind of English and were descendants of slaves working on English predominant banana plantations of the United Fruit Company. I decided to visit Bluefield because of a rumour. The famous US-American Billionaire Howard Huges, producer of oil drilling heads, living as tax evader in exile on a lonely Caribbean island was an excentric. Besides other interests like movie production and chasing film stars he developed different kind of aircrafts. His biggest one the "Spruce Goose H-4 Hercules" with 8 engines and mostly produced of wood to escape being tracked by radar units. Shortly before the end of the WWII this biggest aircraft and troop transporter of the world was ready but could not be put into service.

His friend, Somoza the dictator, offered him to construct a private runway opposite of the bay of Bluefield where he could unmolested test his airplanes. The only way to reach that strange places Bluefield and Goldfield was by means of a battered run down DC3 that landed on a simple grass runway when the weather was good. Bluefield had no streets but consisted of pedestrian ways and houses on stilts. The only primitive guest house was directly at the pier where most of the boats where anchored. I convinced one of the boat owners a Misquito Indian to take me for a tour including the Huges air piste. It was rather long and could have used by a DC10. The Indian warned me not to explore the installation to avoid trouble. I decided to return because there was no activity anyway. My guide invited me to his home, where his wife prepared a tasty meal with seafood, bamboo shoots, maniok/cassava, tomatoes and after papaya with lemon. The tomatoes from the garden of my host were delicious. I experienced it nowhere else. I forgot to ask for some seeds. I am sure the result of growing them at home would have been disappointing because the right climate is very important. Next day it was raining cats and dogs and the DC3 did not land in Bluefield because the grass piste was not ready to receive the heavy plane what happened often. I had seen a one engine Cessna air plane of the Air Force parked besides a storage and a sergeant smoking a cigarette. I approached him and asked him if he was looking for some action and flying me for a "financial support" to Managua? After some hesitation he agreed and it was no problem to take off with the light weight of the Cessna. It had stopped raining and we had a marvellous flight close to the treetops of the jungle. At Managua Airport my pilot dropped me near the side gate and returned to Bluefield.

In the meantime the damages of the earth wake have been eliminated but it can happen again like the history shows. A family clan governs the nation, promised much and realized little. That seems to be a worldwide disease.

I had presented the idea of an international Rover Club meeting. It was decided that I should organize it in Weilburg/Lahn.

I booked a hotel and a villa with a park for this event in spring time. Our club president took care of the invitations. On a Friday evening when everyone had arrived and found his room we sat together in the villa for an aperitif to get acquainted with each other. Later we went to a restaurant in the medieval city for dinner. I had booked a bagpipers band that appeared and played when coffee was served. The next morning after having distributed bags with some goodies to every driver we moved with our cars to display our vintage Rovers at the hunting castle. Originally it should have happened on the market place near the castle, but for restoring reasons it was closed. A Chinese student had translated my information into Chinese for the other Chinese students who were studying at the technical school in Weilburg and living in the student home besides the hunting castle. When the journalists had taken pictures we continued our tour to the mine "Fortuna". On the way we passed a mineral water company. I knew the owner and he gave every participant a bottle of his mineral water. I had booked a visit to the mine and we took, protected with helmets, the elevator down into the mountain and then used an electric open narrow gauge train to the working area. All its appliances and devices were still working and its usage was demonstrated. The veins underneath ours were filled with water and served as drinking water supply for the city of Wetzlar. The iron content of the ore is 44%. Despite this fact the costs of hauling pit-iron and the wages were so high that the mine belonging to Krupp had to be closed. In Wetzlar existed Buderus where the smelting was done and iron pipelines, ovens, ducts, sever lids, pumps, decorative water basins, fountain enclosures, small track rails, railroad wheels were casted. Wherever you go in Germany you will find evidence of the creativity of this company.

Through well maintained forests we continued the trip with our exotic cars to Tiefenbach where the owner of the rustic restaurant was waiting for the hungry pack of drivers. The speciality of Oscar Sehrt, the owner of the restaurant "Lime tree" were delicious veal cutlets. I was an old customer who often brought guests from all over the world to his restaurant. At our arrival the windows and doors opened and the curious people admired our vintage cars. For any case I had asked my mechanic to drive with us. Something really unique: a "Hanomag recovery service truck" from 1936 that belonged to a truck driver of my village accompanied us. After having seen the only vineyard in the region we waved "goodbye" and crossed the Taunus mountain with destination "Hessenpark" with its assembly of medieval farm buildings and all kinds of animals, a smithery, maker of cartwheels, a pottery, bakery and a cabinet maker. All were in working condition. The buildings had been rescued from demolition. After the five o'clock tea time we returned through the Weil valley, where we stopped at the ship's tunnel constructed 1849 for the freight boats carrying iron ore. After we had relaxed we went to the "Castle Hotel" for the candle light dinner. The mayor of the city made a speech and enlightened us about some historical facts concerning Weilburg.

The next morning we left for Braunfels. I got the permission that our cars could be displayed on the market place. To reach the castle we had to climb up passing the pillory, the extremely deep main well, the short term prison and three trap-gates and fortified watch towers. We arrived short of breath at the appointed time and entered the older part of the castle with a large, pillared knights hall where some knight arming's, weapons, horse armours were displayed. In that medieval times the men must have been muscled but much smaller by size. Especially in winter it must have been a torture to wear such an armament.

To protect the wood-tiled floor all visitors were provided with felt slippers as usual in such historical buildings. Big oil paintings were displayed in the drawing-rooms, that could be heated by cast iron or tiled ovens and some others could be fed with firewood from the floors. Most of the paintings displayed ancestors and relatives and in the hunting room were antlers and oil paintings with scenes of game or fox huntings. In the weapon rooms one occasionally saw paintings of gentlemen in magnificent uniforms. The counts and princes of Solms had often married noble partners of other European countries. One had for example been from England and had begged her husband to change the appearance of the castle to Tudor style. The old furniture was pompous and could not fit in any modern home. From the aspect of workmanship they were unique. Outside on the terrace were placed a couple of cannons with impressive castings. From up there one had a wonderful view over the Lahn valley. In a side tract of the castle one had access through a turnstile where valuable artifacts were displayed under glass like old helmets, decorations, sabres, handguns, tin articles like pewter pots and jugs, fine China wear, crystal wine glasses and sealed documents. After we had also seen the chapel we went down to the market again. This time we took a closer look at the main well shaft with a depth of over 250 meters. It was of course sealed to avoid accidents. A big shield warned the medieval users to obey the rules listed when getting water. We took a walk through the park with some exotic trees. In summertime a life band was entertaining the visitors from a pavilion. Often overseen is a bust of the short time emperor Frederic III. who was the father of William II. This beautiful monument was dedicated to him by the faithful citizens of Braunfels. After having taken a coffee in one of the cozy establishments we drove down to the valley where every participant received a farewell gift before we separated.

This first international meeting was so successful that every year it was organized by one of the European Rover Clubs. Next was the Austrian club who invited us to Salzburg and the nearby Salzkammergut (Lake district) followed by the Swiss to Bern and surrounding and the Italians at the Lago Maggiore.

The by chance meeting of the the Chinese student Chang, di developed to a good friendship. He was born a month earlier than my daughter and came often to visit us. When he was going to be expelled from Germany because his permission to stay could not be extended I stepped in and offered bail. It was accepted by the authorities. He could finish the technical high school and his practical time in the office of the mayor of Weilburg who had offered it. Then he switched to the high school in Giessen to study informatics. Besides he had a regular income working for a Chinese tourist company in Frankfurt that handled group tourists from the "Land of the Middle" which came by Jumbo Jet of China Airline to Germany. For those bus transport, provision, accommodation and guided tours must be organized and that became his job. The travel restrictions for foreigners to China had also been facilitated.

At the "Techno Classica Fair" in Essen 2004 the high minded-ness was still prevailing because two renowned producers of first class cars could celebrate their 100th birthday. First was Rolls Royce that from the start became famous for its superior quality with its "Silver Ghost". The Rover Company however had be-fore started to build the first usable bicycles and continued with motorcycles until their first reliable car the Spartan Rover 8 HP came 1904 on the market. At this exhibition the German indus-trialist H.J. Zach was also present. Besides his private collection of 23 Rolls Royce's he got a real showpiece, the "Star of India", the former hunting car of the Maharadja of Raycot. Zach had acquired and restored the technical jewel unique in the world. He displayed this car that was in silver and saffran yellow and it was the magnet of the show. I presented myself as a member of the Rover Club and told him that we also celebrated the 100 years of Rover. We emptied a bottle of Bordeaux together while engaged in "petrol talks". I was of course curious to see his collection and was happy when he invited me to see It. His private museum had a very special ambiente because it displayed also rare furniture, paintings, statues, oriental carpets, wood carvings, candelabras, church clocks and ship bells. I was lost in amazement about his unique and precious exhibition in such a splendid surrounding. Originally it had been a production hall for machines. When H.J. Zach suffered two heart attacks he decided to liquidate a part of his collection at an auction by Christies in Monaco. The remaining few Rolls Royces he kept still in his treasure box. Recently he added some mini- cars to give all a real contrast.

Now something amusing concerning the fabulous RR figure the "Spirit of Ecstasy" with the more popular name "Emily". The rumor insists on the fact that the secretary and lover of Sir Henry Royce was sitting as a model for this figure. What a visible compliment could be more charming than such a lasting monument. The double RR brand had since 1904 been purple red. When Sir Henry died it was changed to black may be as a sign of affliction of the whole staff.

What a shock it was when 2005 the bomb exploded with the news for all Rover fans, that the Rover company belonged to the past. The gates of the works in Solihull near Birmingham and in Oxford were closed forever. The assembly lines were dismantled and sold to a successful Chinese truck manufacturer near Shanghai. He continued to build the last Rover from the drawing board under the Chinese name of Roewe (mighty) that was a rather good middle class car. Land and Range Rover belong now to the Indian Tata group and are still produced in England.

My brother a film producer in Los Angeles was asked by the Chinese TV sender in Kunming to counsel them on a Western system of broad- casting. When he had accomplished this job to their full satisfaction he was asked to produce a documentary film about Yunnan province.

He and his team got from this point on a permanent visa for China that facilitated travelling from the USA enormously. He was able to continue his work in China through recommendations of the different governors and called his following series of documentary films the "Mysterious China Series". One of the governors told the former Chinese president about the work of my brother. The president had once been governor of Tibet and had shot a couple of film-strips there. He asked my brother if he could make a documentary film with all this existing material to impress his party colleagues and friends with it. My brother did a perfect job and was from that time on respected by the president and the government and was kept busy with movies for his series.

Chang di, my Chinese protégé, had finished his informatics studies but stayed in the tourist branch in Frankfurt. In that time the interest rates were near to zero to support the staggering economy. Chang di was clever and acquired some run down apartments and restored them with the help of some practical Chinese friends. Until now it provided him with a regular income. He rented them exclusively to reliable Chinese tenants. He wanted to avoid the so called "tenant nomad's" which could not be simply put on the street when they did not pay the rent. Chang di had married a clever and charming Lady from Manchuria who had studied economics at Frankfurt university. She was able to support him with his business. After a long time, I nearly had forgotten this matter, I got a message from my trader in noble limousines, that he had finally found that I was looking for so long, a "Bentley S1" from 1959 for a reasonable price. Especially the chassis needed a general overhaul, but the moderate price would compensate for that. I sold some of my shares and placed the bundle of money into the usual brown envelope and took the train to Bavaria. At the station I was picked up with a snobbish "Rolls Royce Silver Cloud", the twin brother of my "Bentley BS1". In the workshop I inspected the precious piece. The car displayed the usual signs of patina. I was dressed in my mechanic outfit and crept underneath the car to check the chassis thoroughly. Some work was waiting for me and my mechanician. The engine was however in excellent condition with correct compression. The starter had however to be exchanged. The tyres had 8 mm grip but were extremely old and had to be exchanged too. It was a sign that the car had been driven only on rare occasions. According to the English car documents the car had been owned by the CEO of the metal import company that was notorious for its scrupulous practices especially in the Congo, Zaire and Central Africa, where the people excavated with bare hands and under inhuman conditions rare metal and jewels. The prices were kept low and the local profits were used to buy weapons and ammunition and helped to keep going the endless civil wars. After some years the beautiful Bentley, after having changed hands a couple of times, was acquired by an electronic engineer who kept it for nearly 40 years until he became too old to drive it. With me it came again in good caring hands and gave me a lot of pleasure. What my German spare part supplier Erbrecht could not deliver I got from "Flying Spares" in England or from Los Angeles where my brother was living. Not far away from his company Tony Handler has the greatest Rolls Royce & Bentley recycling company in the world. His ancestors came from Bavaria and he could supply about everything. Smaller items my brother could bring in his suitcase when he came to Germany, bigger parts like a front grill had of course to be sent by airfreight. That was with customs quite an expensive matter.

I became a member of the "TOC – The other Club" for Bentley and Rolls Royce owners. By coincidence it has the same name as the famous debating club that was founded by Sir Winston Churchill right after World War I. for an elite group of politicians.

Besides writing some articles for the club magazine "Continental Express" I did not engage in club matters, my activities in the Rover Club were enough. Just one time I suggested a meeting that I could organize in Breslau/Wroclaw in Poland together with the Polish Rolls Royce Enthusiasts Club. We would have been lodged in the former castle of the Prussian Marshal Prince Blucher. Tourist sights were countless and the mayor of Wroclaw would have supported us and my mechanic could have accompanied us. My proposal was rejected because of the long distance. But I think that prejudices against the Poles were the real reason and made the reconciliation so difficult.

A funny story happened during a vintage car meeting in 2019 in Baden-Baden, where the TOC celebrated the 100th birthday of Bentley. At the gala dinner in the Casino of the health resort I had not reserved any special place and came to be seated besides the French couple Monier who came from the Normandy and represented the French "Bentley & Rolls Royce Enthusiast Club" with a RR Corniche. After the excellent menu and wine, we started a pleasant conversation in which we talked about our life. They were often in England to take part at happenings. I told them that I became an author with a pseudonym of my French Huguenot ancestor de Mons. Hearing this Madame Monier rummaged in her bag and showed me her carte d'identité where I read: "née Monique de Mons". I was speechless. I had found a far removed relative. We celebrated this with a bottle of champagne. My ancestor mothers side had been a French Huguenot Comtesse M. de

Mons. This religious group was persecuted by the catholic church and the king who were interested in the property of this citizens. Her parents left France and were welcomed by the Prussian king who granted them twenty years of tax exemption to help them to build up a new existence. My ancestor L. Count v.d. Schulenburg married this Huguenot Lady. Another French Huguenot adherents in my family are the d'Orville producers of drapery who also married into the v.d. Schulenburg family of my grandmother. They became successful business people and were honoured by the German emperor with the title Barons von Löwenklau.

My daughter Unjee-Francoise finished her studies in economics with "summa cum laude" but married right away. Three years later my grandson Theodor was born. Despite his premature birth he grew up perfectly. From the start he showed an unusual interest in technical matters. He visibly had inherited the mathematical abilities of both of his parents. Then I underwent my first orthopaedic operation and got an artificial hip-joint. A walking stick adorned with a dog head handle gave me a safe feeling while walking.

I often visited my Italian friend Grazia-Maria in Magenta near Milano. Magenta was famous for a ferocious battle between Austria and France that was won by Napoleon III. The conditions of the victims and the primitive medical facilities led to the foundation of the International Red Cross by Henry Dunant in Switzerland. Near the Lago Maggiore in Tichino is the Lago de Orta where a school friend of M.Grazia had his boat that we often used to sail on this beautiful lake. When my wife could manage we went to the mountains where we explored the alpine areas around St. Moritz, Davos and more to the West where the population still speaks Retro Roman, a kind of Latin. The yearly International Rover meetings always contained trips to touristic and technical sights.

Something dreadful happened on an excursion to the North together with my friend Claus. On the way we visited my cousin Elizabeth, who with the help of Polish and Russian craftsmen restored the manor of the brother of my grandmother that was once expropriated by the communists. She was living in London and could only come in summer.

We continued our trip accompanied by our dogs and met a former darling of Claus who managed an alternative farm. While we were sitting in the courtyard enjoying coffee and cake her dogs were romping around. I had taken my little dachshund "Aisha" on my lap. Suddenly the English fighting dog appeared from nowhere and dragged Aisha from my lap and shredded her throat and would have killed her when the host would not have beaten the beast with a club and locked it away. The clever beast had opened the door by itself. I pressed my thumb and a towel on the throat artery and drove with the daughter of the host to the veterinarian who operated on my tiny dachshund right away. When driving to the veterinarian I did not care about speed limits and flash guns. As a result I had to pay a high fine, lost my driver license for one month and had to join a course for traffic delinquents. Claus had a greyhound that took care of Aisha by continuously licking her. After we met another friend of Claus who was a veterinarian. She treated Aisha professionally. Later we went to a friend of Claus who had like Claus been a motorbike racer, who had participated at many motor-cross events to become later the owner of the successful German Oil Company specialized in high performance racing oils in Wittenburg. He owned a trucker hotel where we could stay as his guests. At perestroika he had acquired a lovely castle and restored it. It served for marriage parties and other festivities. In his company's area was one big hall where he stored his own and friends' vintage cars. Another building was reserved for refugees from Syria. A special event was the 90th birthday of the owner of some night clubs and Eros Center's in the red-light district of Hamburg, the "Reeperbahn". In former horse stables he had some vintage cars. We were invited to join the party, where prominence of the show business were also present to show their reference for the sturdy jubilant. Girls from the Eros clubs were also present to animate the guests.

When I returned home I suffered despite of my innocence a lot of criticism because of Aisha's accident. The medical costs were taken over by the liability insurance of the owner of the aggressive dog. It took an endless time until my dog regained its old lovely spirit. My argument that my breaking the speed limits only because I was rescuing a life was ignored by the authorities.

At times when my friend from New Zealand came to Poland to see how matters went on in his castle he invited me to join him. I enjoyed performing little restoration works. One of my disused 2500 Litre oil tanks I had transformed into a working boat to trim the reed covering the lakes and ponds surrounding the castle. Then I established a cosy library in one of the corner rooms with international literature.

To the castle belongs a golf course, the problem was however that the wild boars turned the lawn regularly upside down in search of tasty roots.

The Polish authorities never gave him a shooting license to solve the problem and provide the kitchen with tasty meat.

An architecturally beautiful former cattle and horse stable from the 19th century could have been transformed into a marvellous technical museum, but the restoration was always delayed because of more urgent matters like the repair of the heating system and the restoration of the former manager house. At one time "Amazon Poland" organized a big festival on the grounds of the castle. The beautiful castle was financially a barrel without a bottom, but my friend Christopher never gave up, because he enjoyed the challenge so much to give it into strange hands was not imaginable. One big room in the ground floor was chosen as a private museum. In glass cases, vitrines and at the wall were displayed items that had somehow relation to the former owner the Prussian Marshal Prince Blucher who had vanquished 1815 Napoleon Bonaparte together with the English General Duke Wellington in Waterloo. In the wardrobe were some decorative uniforms, but few fit me. There were also some weapons and guns on display. When it was raining we were sitting at a large table cleaning and polishing the decorations of several nations. From me he got a colt revolver from the end of the 19th century and some tin soldiers to revive the battle of Waterloo in a glass case.

At the start the castle had not yet been furnished. Everything had been stolen when the castle was abandoned. The search covered Poland, Czech Republic and Slovakia and was an adventure. It took a long time to furnish all the rooms. All had a different style, but that did not damage the overall atmosphere. With maps 1:25000 from pre war times we explored the surrounding and discovered many overgrown ruins of former castles, manors and military installations. This maps I got from the institute of geodesy in Berlin in the former ministry of air defence where some members of the resistance against Hitler had been executed. Often we went to Breslau/Wroclaw to buy provisions for the hotel and enjoy the cultural aspects of this city. His partner Grazina took care of the hotel business but was living in Wroclaw. Their daughter had been adopted by Christopher. We visited the Dom and the student district with all its pubs and jazz-clubs. Here my father had spent some time when he was a student. Later when he became a lecturer of philosophy and theology at the university he met his colleagues often in the wine cellar of the gothic style city's town hall at the "Rinek" that is now a fashionable restaurant. The war damaged facade had been restored to its former beauty.

Occasionally we made a trip to Morava/Murau castle near Stregom where an enterprising aunt of mine resided. The imposing castle in neo- classical style had once belonged to her father. After the war it had been a Polish agricultural school and kept in good condition. Later it had been empty waiting for another use. That was the moment when my aunt Melitta stepped in. Not telling the authorities that she was the daughter of the former owner and nobleman she asked them if she could establish a kindergarten and school for social neglected and orphan children there. The government was delighted and gave permission to establish a Polish-German Foundation called "Jadwiga". With the international financial support of private sponsors the kindergarten was a success. The upper floor was transformed into a hostel where refugees from Silesia could stay and show their grandchildren where the roots of the family were before the war. When she was young my adventurous aunt worked as a stewardess for an exotic airline. Later she was an au pair girl for a French noble family at the Côte d'Azur. In Monaco she met the Hungarian coffee planter from Portuguese Angola. When her husband died she managed the farm alone until the civil war started and she was expropriated by the communist government of Eduardo dos Santos. She could not take her savings with her when she left Angola. Empty handed she first earned some money by taking care of disabled old Ladies until she got the idea with the foundation. She spoke Polish, which she had learned in her youth in Silesia. Besides the kindergarten she convinced the German Goethe institute to hold summer courses in German for interested Polish students and music courses by German schools. The meals reminded me of those in the "refectoriums" of monasteries. My aunt was honored by the government with the Polish citizenship.

She was always happy when I brought her suitcases full of good dresses, shirts and shoes I had collected for her to give them to needy people. Everythings I had formerly taken to Pakistan and Ethiopia went now to fill the stores of aunt Melitta. Just for fun I restored a neglected cast iron fence at the side of the castle.

Aunt Melitta and my friend Christopher got on very well. She had a fable for Englishmen. No wonder, her mother was from the Scottish clan of the Johnstones. Melitta is very old now but lively like quicksilver. Her 16 years younger sister Thesi is taking over the management. As winner of many international equestrian sport goblets she is still rather fit.

On a private trip I met Dr. Margaret Krohn a paediatrician living near Capetown in Noordhoek on the way to the Cape of good Hope. She was the widow of Hugo "Bush" Krohn an interesting relative of mine. I invited her for a trip through the Cape province. His life story is rather interesting. He grew up on the Krohn property in Madeira. His educational time he spent however in London-Hampstead where the Krohn clan owned a big villa. Because of the difficult situation after the First World War his parents emigrated to Transvaal/South Africa where they started farming. Near Johannesburg he worked first as miner in a gold mine, later as overseer and finally in the drawing and planning department.

Then he was eximinated and drafted by the government and sent for military training to Kenia. Mussolini had invaded Abyssinia and England had taken action to get the Italians out and to reinstall the Emperor Haile Selassi on his throne. After this campaign was successful accomplished the Commonwealth troops of New Zealanders, Australiens, Indians and South Africans were sent to North Afrika to support the British Royal Army in their struggle in the desert with the German-Italian forces. Bush was taken prisoner by the Italiens and was first sent with others to Bengazi.

It took some time until a freighter took them to Italy. There they were put to work draining a swamp. Then they were sent by train to a large POW camp near Trieste. There "Bush" started to prepare with some courages chaps an escape through Yugoslavia. It worked and they survived thanks the help of the civilians and the partisans who were trained, informed and equipped by British parashooters. After some adventures they managed to reach an island from where they crossed by boat to Brindisi that had become free after the Italiens had declared armistice. From there they were lucky to get a flight to Cairo and another one to London. The rest of the war they spent in a repatriation camp for POW's near Brighton. For South Africans it took however some time after the end of the war until they got a ship home. "Bush" was happy to find his parents in good shape and to get a job at his former mining company.

I just mentioned "Bush" because there have been countless POW's on both sides who experienced similar situations.

I can't describe all my travels and excursions which I have done after my retirement. Some were very adventurous and daring and I can only shake my head that I have handled them well without coming to harm. Friends and acquaintances asked me which corner of the world I still like to know.

I told them the Antarctic because of its strange underwater world. I also was asked which country on our globe I considered the most interesting and best to live in. I could not answer this question honestly because even the most infamous country has incredibly bright sides. The most important are however the people and good species of them you find everywhere. After our frequent flights to our relatives in South Korea, my last longer trip was going to Sri Lanka. 50 years ago while working on a ship I have been in Colombo, but the stay was so short that I had no time to know the country. We booked a 3 weeks tour with a small group and tour guide. We had the opportunity to use the biggest airplane Airbus 380 with Emirates Airline to Dubai but a smaller aircraft brought us to Colombo. At immigration the officer had problems with my documents, because on the passenger list only one christian name was mentioned instead of my seven ones. I also showed my ID card and driver license where all names were mentioned. Finally the officer decided that I must be a high ranking VIP and called another officer to help me with my luggage. He excused himself for the inconvenience caused. Outside our driver was already waiting for us. We were lodged in an individual bungalow situated with others around a main building in a beautiful park. When we went there in the evening to meet the tour guide and for dinner we nearly stumbled over one of the rare warans that seemed to belong to the hotel's inventory. When we later returned to our bungalow a second subtropical wonder expected us. At the ceiling a gecko that belongs to the lizard family was hunting for flies and mosquitoes. They have special feet that enable them to walk upside down at the ceiling. They took care, that insects did not spread inside the rooms. They are considered as domestic animals and could get attached to the inhabitants. On account of the high humidity of the air the moon looks much bigger and clearer than in Europe. The starry sky looks also much brighter. Sri Lanka is considered as a subtropical paradise but was not spared from local unrest. In the North Thamiles from India had immigrated and contested the ownership of agricultural lands with the local Singaleses. That had several times ended in a civil war with terroristic activities from the side of the Thamiles. That caused many victims especially after the British colonial power had released the country into independence. Another muslim minority descended from the Arab merchants. One of the main export goods is tea. Originally it came from the Chinese province Yunnan. Despite of the strict ban of the emperor of taking tea plants out of China English ship captains had circumvented this law by bribing farmers and had tested the plants in Ceylon successfully. Later the growing of tea spread to India's summer resort Darjeeling and further East to Assam. The fresh leaves are collected by diligent young women in big cotton bags. Women who had the mens or were expecting aftergrowth were temporarily excluded from this job.

The sweat of those females diminished the taste of the tea. The most expensive tea consists of the fermented ground leaf buds of the tea. It is called gunpowder tea and is especially exported to Japan. Further trade goods are spices, coconuts, copra, semi precious and precious stones and textiles. The tourism branch had expanded considerably.

Accessible forests are still freed from trunks by working elephants where tractors cannot move any more. Sri Lanka is a paradise for birds which have disappeared elsewhere. There are caves with giant Buddha figures up in the North that have been sponsored by Buddhists all over the world. Precious stones are still excavated in primitive manual ways. After the location has been decided on, two partners dig a pit of maximal 8 meters depth. Baskets with soil are lifted to be sorted out. When they are lucky they find precious stones that are clear and big enough to be accepted by the trader or jeweller. To search for such you need a permission from the district authorities. The deep pits happened to bury people alive. Finding the right prospecting place was a secret. The hardest stones like diamonds and smaragd's when not used for jewellery called industrial diamonds were used for cutting and polishing metals. Drilling heads when searching for oil are trimmed with diamonds. Diamonds for jewelry are polished with diamond dust. In spite of the fact that it is the hardest stone it burns because it is a form of carbon. Semi precious stones were taken to decorate the palaces of the Mogul rulers in India, like the Hawa Mahal in Jaipur, the Red Fort in New Delhi and the memorial Taj Mahal in Agra. In the centre of Sri Lanka exists a giant monolith "Sigiriya" Lion's Rock. There was once the residence of a king up there that was nearly unapproachable. Now everything is dilapidated.

Iron stairs have been at one side of the rock installed to climb it with some exertion. From its top you have a breathtaking view over the landscape. Up in the cool mountains exists a small city that served as summer residence for English administrators like Simla in India. All public places like the market hall, post office, town hall, police office and even some private homes were built in English style.

The Singhalese kitchen is excellent and appetizing. Like in India much curry, cardamom, kurkuma, pepper and other spices together with coconut oil are used. As a side dish diverse kinds of rice are offered. As dessert, tropical fruits were served.

Back in rainy Germany we met our deeply grieved looking dachshund "Aisha". She had attracted cancer with incontinence. The veterinarian could not help. She had stayed with friends who also had two dachshunds. She passed away in my arms. We lost a faithful comrade and buried her near our goldfish pond where she had enjoyed playing with her ball. Long before I had already set her a literary monument in one of my satire books.

It was the first time we were invited to an international Rover Club meeting in Salzburg/Austria. On our way home we stayed in the guesthouse of an aunt of mine near Berchtesgaden. In the morning we enjoyed the breathtaking landscape and took a walk along the brook that passed my aunt's place and discovered a lot of edible snails an collected a bag full of this creatures that are considered as delicacy in France and Switzerland. We fed them with macaroni that cleans their intestines. On our way home we took the opportunity to visit the Langenburg castle in Franconia. The prince of Hohenlohe owns a private car museum with English and French classic cars. We enjoyed the visit to the castle and the museum. When we returned to the parking place where a tourist bus was parked, a group of Japanese were standing around our Rover taking pictures. Not my vintage Rover was the reason for their interest but the snails that thought it more comfortable to leave the bag. They were everywhere, on the steering wheel, the instruments, the gear lever, windows, seats etc. We collected the snails and cleaned the car. We were feeling sorry for the creatures and released them into liberty at the next brook.

An aggravating incident with my Rover P6V8 happened on the way to Aachen where I had been invited to take part at an event at the Technical University with the TOC club. Instead of my Bentley S1 I had taken my Rover with me to check the efficiency of its brakes. On the highway there was a lot of traffic when I noticed a big piece of metal, probably a part of an exhaust system in my centre lane. Because of the dense traffic I could not leave my track and hit the piece. As a consequence my oil pan was damaged and I lost all my motor oil and my motor was destroyed by lack of lubrication. With switched on warning lights I managed to reach the next exit of the highway. There I parked the Rover and disconnected the battery for any case and called the recovery service. The starter had also been torn off its fixings and the motor was in a deplorable condition. Just the cylinder head and the carburettor could be used again. The search for another motor block took a couple months to be accomplished. Our club mechanic heard about my problem and offered me his just generally overhauled motor block he had prepared for his own Rover P6. He was retired and had much time to overhaul another block for himself. My P6 had escaped the scrapyard and had like a phoenix risen from the ashes. I could not enjoy that long because the Covid epidemic heralded its coming.

My brother was just busy shooting a documentary in the Western Pamir region of China when a snowstorm forced him and his team to leave China for the time being. Two days later when they were already in Los Angeles the corona disease started to spread from Wuhan all over the world. China's borders were closed for years.

He had promised me to try to fulfil a hearts desire of mine and to realize a film idea of mine in the Muslim part of Western China. The political situation in the Near- and Middle East excluded it to realize the project there. On account of corona no financial reserves were left and the project was forgotten when my brother died.

I like to present here the shortened version of the "Silk street and oasis story": Somewhere in the extended desert of the Middle East the French archaeologist and ethnologist Jerôme d'Orville was searching for the origins of a lost religious sect. He had again travelled from France to the Middle East to continue his search in a far away desert region where he had never been before. In a caravanserai he buys a sturdy horse and well equipped he leaves the place in the direction of the rising sun. After an endless eventless ride a first soft and continuous sandstorm blew that developed to a mighty hurricane. In a wide spread tract of a cave in the mountain range he and his horse find a shelter and try to sleep. He feels very cold and suffers from a shivering fit. After endless feverish dreams he wakes up and realizes to his horror that his horse with all his provisions had disappeared. Fortunately he was left with a canteen of water and some dried dates. After he

had invigorated himself he ascertained that his fever had disappeared. At the wall of the cave he discovers marvellous paintings and mosaics. They originate from the religious sect whose traces he had already searched for many years.

He steps in front of the cave. The sandstorm had subsided and bright sunshine ruled over the desert. Far away down in the valley he discovered to his immense surprise an extended oasis with an impressive fortified city. From the distance it looked as if this place had just been laid open by the sandstorm. When he started to march out of curiosity down to the valley suddenly a "Fata Morgana" like the date palms got green, caravans approached the oasis from different directions while others left the city heavily loaded with diverse trading goods. Farmers were working outside

tilling the fields and caring for the orchards. He also heard the noise of the camels, donkeys, goats, sheeps, cocks and peacocks. All this pandemonium was drowned by the call from the minarets where the muezzin reminded the Muslims to pray five times the day to honour Allah and his prophet Muhammed. When he entered the animated city the people viewed him curiously because of his unusual dress and look. In addition his strange Arab attracted attention. Besides a mixture of different languages one spoke in an old fashioned Arab and Farsi the language of the Persians. In his leather bag he was wearing at his belt he still had some Syrian and French coins and bills. He went to one of the money changers who had no use for the bills he seemed to have never seen before, but the strange coins found his immediate interest and showed them to some of his customers. Finally he offered him a pile of local currency for its rarity that filled his leather pouch again. Instead of banknotes, silver and gold coins circulated for higher denominations. He began to explore the maze of lanes of the strange city and reached finally an extended place where the most magnificent mosque of the city was situated. He pulls off his dusty leather boots, cleans his feet and enters the imposing building. While he admires the splendid interior architecture with its impressive arabesques one of the present imams watches him and addresses him in Greek. As a scientist he had also studied Greek and Latin, so both of them were in the position to converse easily with each other about God and the world. "Azis" the imam related from a stay in a far away empire where the people spoke Greek and its impressive residence Constantinople, where a mighty Khan governed over a nation whose people believed in a prophet Allah's Isa Ibn Maryam.

The stranger concealed his sandstorm adventure not to be considered as phantast. The imam and he separated as friends. At the water salesman "Ali" he refreshed himself with lime juice and water. On a palm tree shaded place he joined an attentive group of listeners to the fairy tale teller "Abdulla". When this one mentioned the name of "Scheherazade" he comprehends that the story dealt with the Persian fairy tale "Thousand and one night". When Abdulla has finished, the stranger tells him about his sandstorm adventure. Abdulla relates this with some literary embellishments to his audience that receives it with enthusiasm. In the bazaar he admires the skilful copper and iron smith's that produced richly decorated plates, kettles, household articles, crooked swords, daggers and helmets. Others were busy with wood carving instruments to decorate furniture and sandal wood chests. A long time he stayed in a shop selling good smelling oils of flowers.

Spellbound he suddenly stops in front of the emporium of a carpet dealer. There only one Persian silk carpet is exhibited to attract the attention of the customers. The selection of colours and elegance surpasses everything he had ever seen. The owner "Hassan" had discovered right away that the stranger was a pronounced connoisseur and expert on carpets. He invites him inside where they conversed while drinking tea and eating fresh dates only occasionally interrupted by customers. Thanks to his acquaintance with Hassan, he met him frequently and used that occasion to admire the rare carpet he could probably never afford. He continued his walk and got at a food stand a flatbread, still warm from the bakery filled with scraped roasted mutton meat and fried egg plant. Finally he started the search for a cheap accommodation. The severe smell of camel and donkey manure led him to the portal of a caravanserai. After the usual haggling he got a cheap sleeping place underneath stone stairs. After some days he discerns the necessity to find a job, not to end as a beggar man in front of the mosque. On his search for a job he meets an appreciative jeweller "Hadji Suleiman" who recognizes immediately his potential and agrees to help. He leaves his emporium to his assistant and accompanies him to his best friend. What a stroke of luck, it is the carpet dealer Hassan.

After a thorough introduction he was charged with the manual task to repairing damaged old carpets until he spoke the current Arab fluently and could handle all kinds of customers easily. His beloved Persian carpet was never sold. Hassan intentionally did not want to sell his treasure. One day the stranger got heavily sick with shivering fits. Hassan and Haji Suleiman missed him and finally sent out a tracing party to search for him. When they finally found him a tabib/doctor was called and he wrapped him up in several blankets and gave him some natural medicine. He was carried to the private dwelling of the jeweller. There he was cared for by the charming and competent daughter Aishe. While the recuperation both developed a strong affection for each other. When he was healthy again he continued his work with Hassan, who made him his business partner. Once a week on Friday, the Muslim holiday, the close group of friends of Hadji Suleiman came together after the morning prayers. The meeting point was the old spacy watch tower at a small lake in the middle of a magnificent park outside the city that belonged to the jeweller. On the top layers of the tower resided the impressive fortune teller

and soothsayer "Fathima" watching over the property. Besides the stranger "Abdullah" the fairy tale teller belonged to the group of friends. When the heat got too much they retreated to the shady top floor of the tower where delicious tidbits and fresh fruit juices were offered by a servant. From there one had a marvellous view on the old city, the mountain range and the endless desert.

One came together to discuss the latest important happenings, philosophy, poetry, agriculture, breeding of animals, training of hunting falcons and camel racing. Most exciting however were the reports of the jeweller Haji Suleiman who is often away for a long time with heavily protected caravans that were often targets by gangs of robbers on the way to China, Transoxania and India. There he offered his unique jewellery and acquired precious stones and jade. He related his adventures in foreign Sultanates and Kingdoms and fights with robbers that were attracted by the silk road. He describes a giant many thousand lee long wall that protects the Chinese empire from the Mongolian riding hordes and from a canal that connects Southern China with the imperial residence. In India he had seen palaces where whole facades were decorated with semiprecious stones. Beautiful women dressed in silken garments wore necklaces, arm laces and earrings made of filigree gold- and silver wire. They used flower oils to smell agreeably. The local rulers used to consume fine sweets and fancy bakeries covered with gold dust. Unusual for Muslims were the lively representation by artists of nature, animals and human beings. Their means of decorations were the arabesques.

Suleiman was one of the few dignitaries of the city who had the right to add to his name the title Hadji because he had as pilgrim already been twice in the far away Mekka in the West. His listeners were extremely impressed about the many rituals related of his sojourn there. At the start the holy black covered meteorite "Kaaba" had to be surrounded seven times in the direction of the rising sun and calls like "Allah-ul- akbar!" accompanied the crowd. Near the Kaaba exists a bridge whose pillars represent devilish temptation. During the Muslim sacrifice festival pilgrims surround the pillars which represent the sheitan (devil) and stone them. What is concerning the Quran, the mass of the believers could not read and write. They knew his contents only from the preachings of the Imams. Muhammed the prophet was an analphabet. His teachings were selected by his scribes and gathered in the Quran.

Finally Hadji Suleiman, who had no son, accepted the stranger as son-in law. Jerôme had in the meantime converted to the Islamic faith and accepted his new Muslim name "Al Kismet" and had taken him over as a business partner from Hassan and had introduced him to the fine art of creating beautiful jewellery. For the marriage ceremony with his daughter "Aishe" that was arranged by the Imam Aziz the jeweller presented his daughter and him with identical carved Lapis Lazuli gold rings.

After this happy event the gold merchant Hadji Suleiman left with a caravan towards Transoxania but returned surprisingly soon. At the usual Friday meeting on the watchtower he related about rumours that had induced him to return immediately. The rumours were based on reports about great, wild and heavily armed riding hordes from Mongolia that on their way to the South had ravaged whole provinces and cities. The fortune teller "Fathima" warned also about a great danger. The friends discussed the problem thoroughly and decided to act immediately.

They convinced the city's elders that in times of peace neglected fortifications had to be repaired. They agreed and the whole population participated in this exertion. Young defenders were trained and the black-smith's were busy producing spearheads, arrows, helmets, scimitars and daggers. When everything was ready for the defence the "Dschihad"/Holy war was pronounced.

Sometimes later Fathimas call from the watchtower rang, that far away in the East a giant dust cloud announced the coming of the enemy. Fast all prepared for the battle. At the Eastern city gate provisions for the enemy warriors and their horses were displayed and all gates were hermetically closed. When the Mongols finally arrived they were surprised not to experience any resistance. When they had taken food, beverages and the horses had been taken care of, a representative of the Mongols was asked to enter the city to inspect the fortifications and the fighting force and report everything he had seen to his Lord Barbur Khan. A delegation of the city's elders then offered an appropriate tribute to Barbur Khan. After some hesitation he agreed but asked for some extra provisions for his men and horses. All agreed to this proposition. After the Mongol warriors had been provided with everything they left in Western direction to continue their raids. After this critical incident that had spared the old city from fire and destruction, there was a surprise in the home of Hadji Suleiman. His daughter Aishe had given birth to a magnificent boy that was named "Karim" by the Imam Aziz. He was treated like a little prince and learned even some French when he got older.

Like usual all the close friends met in the old watchtower to discuss about Allah and the known world. Thanks to many new ideas of "Al Kismet" the jewellers emporium prospered. Finally Hassan had also married a charming Persian Lady. They met often outside the city walls absorbed in their pass time of falconry and riding. The women were trading news and were busy with lovely embroidery. In one of their Friday meetings Fathima had predicted a catastrophe. She warned the citizens to leave the city to search for a new dwelling in the West. Only a few listened to her advice and left the city. Some weeks later a light not offensive sandstorm started to blow but developed into a hurricane. Many

courageous citizens still tried to escape, but in vain. The sources, wells and the lake in the park dried up. The cholera spread. The stranger was alone. His wife, son and friends had perished and were buried in the catacombs. In his despair he tries to reach the mountains where he once had come from. When he had finally reached the top, radiating sunshine welcomed him. When looked down he sees just a giant brown cloud covering the valley where the oasis must be. He finds the entrance of the cave and meets a group of monks clad in yellow who have taken rest there. They offer him water and provide him with a sleeping place and he lapses into a deep sleep with heavy dreams. When he wakes up next morning he steps outside and discovers that the city and oasis have disappeared completely covered by sand.

Despite the monk's hospitality he decides to proceed further to the West. Good provisioned by them he started his trip along the mountain range.

After some difficult walking days he discovers down in the valley a heavy loaded caravan moving slowly to the West. With all his efforts he manages to reach it. The surprised leader accepts him as member of his group and offers him a young dromedary as a means of transport. He got some gold and silver coins in his poach which fetched enormous prices at the money changers on the route because of their rarity. After an endless trip the caravan reaches the Syrian Harbor city Latakia. As stroke of luck Jerôme d'Orville managed to catch a mixed cargo freighter to Genoa and Marseille. Finally the scientist could use his real name again. After a long time of abstinence he enjoyed a bottle of Bordeaux from the ship's store. At Marseille he took the train to Paris and found his apartment untouched like he had left it. At the Sorbonne he was received like a hero by his colleagues and students. All had considered him dead and lost in the desert. Asked what had happened to him he told them all that he had become terribly sick and that respectable Bedouin's had nursed him to health. On the question if he had found the remains of the lost sect, he denied it. Had he told the true story the people would have thought he had attracted a sun stroke while staying too long in the desert. One day he and a friend of his, a professor at the Sorbonne, sat in the café "Fouquet" at the Champs Elysées to enjoy coffee and cognac. While they were conversing his friend became curious about the whereabouts of the precious engraved lapis lazuli ring his father in law had once presented to him at his marriage. He simply answers: "I found it in the sand !"

The condition of the Corona epidemic travelling to New Zealand to see my friend Chistopher was out of the question. I thought of an idea to keep my mind and body busy without having infectious contact with masses of people. There existed an abandoned railway property of the government where nobody had ever shown interest in because of its inaccessibility since its shutdown in 1969. The object belonged to the railway line that had been inaugurated by the last German emperor William II. in his first year of reign 1889. I acquired the whole object well knowing that I could never use it economically. It was just fun for me to eliminate the jungle that had spread since the shutdown over 50 years ago. From the railway junction at the main railway line along the Lahn river the embankment leads over a now missing bridge to a 300 m long tunnel with a beautiful portal and a warden's storage that were subject to preserve older monuments. The tunnel was a habitat of bats and also protected by the authorities of conservation of natural beauty and wildlife as well as the biotope at the Southern end of it. The embankment continued to a Krupp steel bridge over the Weil river that was blocked at both ends by sturdy lattice railings. The rails were still intact, but the enormous oak sleepers were after 130 years completely rotten. The line was once used for cargo trains transporting iron ore, manganese, copper, basalt, wood and agricultural products. It came the time when maintenance, mining and wages became too expensive, so the line had to be closed down. The iron ore contained 44% of iron, but it became cheaper to import it from Brazil, Mauritania and Australia. In the biotope I hung up a couple of nesting boxes to attract birds, but they were soon occupied by dormouse's. After the jungle had been cleared I created a place where open air movies could be shown and jazz concerts could play for a selected audience. Underneath the waste branches I had stored inside the dry tunnel where I hid my tools, benches, boards, rolled film screen and generator. At one side of the tunnel I created a small path where one could easily walk. There were 17 protection gates besides the path where maintenance workers could stand while a train was passing. There have been reflectors that had been destroyed by vandals that I replaced with modern ones that are used on the streets. The hinges of the missing door of the warden's storage were still existing, so I constructed a wooden door fish bone style. To reach the terrace of the storage I got an extendable aluminium ladder and locked it to an iron bar at the entrance of the tunnel. From the terrace I had a wonderful view on the Lahn river, on the castle and the main railway line. After having done all my restorations I turned my interest onto the railway bridge. I left the sleepers because I had no means to take them and the heavy rails away but eliminated the moss and trees growing out of them.

With some boards I constructed at one side a passage over the bridge.

The steel girders were in surprisingly good condition. They were rust proof by menninge a red lead paint that is very effective but forbidden today. By means of wire brushes I took away the old paint where it was necessary and used modern rust proof at some places. The search for a perfect cover colour was difficult. Unfortunately the paint used by the the railway company and armed forces were not available. Finally I found a good paint from the USA. On the other side of the bridge was no foot passage. My working platform was an aluminum ladder with two boards that could be moved easily. There were only 10 m to finish the job when destiny played me an ugly trick. Stepping further sidewards holding a brush and paint container I missed the board on the ladder and fell 6 m deep on stones in the river. I was pulled down by the stream in the ice cold water but could hold to a tree that helped me not to drown. It was April 27th, 2021 that my life was changed completely. Finally somebody living near the bridge found me when feeding the fish. He informed the Red Cross and a helicopter that brought me to the University Hospital in Giessen where the surgeons sorted out first the puzzle of my broken backbones and stabilized it with a metal tube. Two OP's were accomplished to handle the problem. All the 31 double nerves had been shredded and I was paraplegic. I was lucky so far that I could move my hands and my arms and my brain was functioning perfectly. Because of Covid 19 I was isolated and was forbidden to receive visitors. Because there were no means for training at disposition I asked the nurses to fill double latex gloves with water and knotted tight. That were from now on my improvised dumb bells for training my arms. Now the search for a suitable rehabilitation hospital specialized in paraplegic cases started. It was rather troublesome, but finally with the help of a friend of my wife we found a REHAB-clinic in Greifswald near the Baltic Sea. After the endless time in bed I was looking forward to some action, but was disappointed when the doctor found a decubitus at my backside that needed immediate treatment.

The long transport to Greifswald was handled by two pretty young ladies from the "St. John's order". Despite listening all the time to the radio advertisements I proposed an author's reading. They accepted cheeringly. While one was driving the other girl was sitting beside me listening with interest. At midway they were changing their position. At the end in Greifswald they re-jected a tip from me telling me, that the management had made it a rule. To my pleasure they told me that listening to my texts had been so far the most interesting trip they had ever experienced. My operation and skin transplantation happened next working day and sent me to bed for another couple of weeks.

During that time I got an urgent message from Los Angeles that my brother had died suddenly and that I as next of kin was responsible or handling the matter personally, because he had not been in the state to leave a testament or a power of attorney for his vice president. I was lucky and could use the telex of the hospital to contact Los Angeles. I rejected the inheritance because my brother had some debts. I informed the vice president how to handle everything. To get the "declaration of death" I had to present myself at an authorized US attorney of law. Because I could not do so I deferred it to a time when I had left the hospital. Finally after I was at home again I could get an appointment with the US general consulates notary in Frankfurt. The matter took just a minute and I sent the application by telex to the indicated department In Los Angeles. When I did not get the certificate after waiting some weeks I sent a complaint and got an immediate answer. The indicated telex number had been for American citizens dying in the USA. My brother was a foreigner and another department was in charge. To make it short I finally received the "Certificate of Death" and could provide some authorities with its copy.

Now I want to mention a "tabu" theme concerning especially paraplegic affected patients. To name it decently it is "losing the capability of begetting". The Osman description of an eunuch warden in the serail whose exclusive job it is to protect the Ladies from unwanted strange visitors of the harem is: "He knows how to do it, but is incapable of doing so!" For many especially young people, victims of grave accidents with paraplegic as result it is a physical and psychical catastrophe. For ages above 80 sex does not play a certain role any more. But it is in any case depressing to refrain from it. Level headed and unemotional considered the whole sex circus is ridiculous. Nature has arranged it like this and serves only to preserve the "homo sapiens" and all other creatures.

A Jew at a marriage broker: One customer expresses the wish for a woman with a hump. Asked why? He explains that a wife with a hump will certainly never cheat him with other men.

Now there is an enhancement from the animal world that concerns camels and dromedaries. The marriage broker tries to present a pretty camel-mare to the interested camel-stallion. The broker praises her good character, her household talents, her intelligence, education, extraction from a respected family and last not least not least her considerable dowry. He finally had to concede however that she had a minor drawback, she had no hump!

In spite of being chained to my bed after the decubitus operation it was not completely wasted time because I trained systematically with my thera-stretch-band. I refrained from watching TV and left that to my room-mate under the condition that he used earphones. I was happy with my laptop, mobile phone and books. While outside there was marvellous sunshine, I felt like a galley slave chained to the oars. Finally I convinced my station doctor to grant me the privilege of some sunshine. An auxiliary aid pushed me in my bed to one elevator at the far side of the building and deposed me at the goldfish pond. I loved this illusion of freedom and watched the other patients training with their wheelchairs. In the smokers pavilion others were enjoying the taste of their vitamin-rich cigarettes. I thanked the doctor for his initiative and proposed jokingly to drive me next time with my bed into the centre of the city. He stated that such an action would certainly fail at the high curbstones.

Greifswald is situated in the Northeastern federal state of Germany Mecklenburg-Vorpommern. It has the thinnest population of all states.

Equivalent low were the governments investments in the infrastructure of telephone and internet. Phone conversations and the internet were suddenly interrupted. The many spams we were flooded with were of Polish and Russian origin. Many foreigners were employed in the hospital coming from Poland, Russia, Ukrainia and the Balkan states. Vietnam workers had preferred to stay in Germany after reunification. My cleaning woman was from Thailand and very happy when I greeted her in the morning with some Thai expressions. The assistant nurse who trained me with dressing told me that her husband originated from Senegal. He had studied medicine in Greifswald. An assistant doctor from Serbia made the patient visits in the wheelchair. Another nurse from the Balkan was responsible for taking blood for tests. She was so badly equipped for this job that she used up to seven needles to find the correct taking spot. When I was fed up with this vexation

I asked for a skin marker to indicate the right spot. The marking also helped other nurses to set the drainage correctly. Those served mainly to prevent blood clot. A signal sounded when the liquid provider was empty and the bottle had to be changed. Sometimes the tube had been creased and blocked or the drainage at the arm was not working any more and had to be changed. In those cases the call button had to be pressed. Often it took an eternity until a nurse appeared, a typical disadvantage of scanty staff. To prevent misuse there was no signal system for emergency cases. There was only one way to attract immediate attention by yelling. Outside of the patients rooms was an optical and audible signal system that indicated where assistance was needed. The night nurse had to be confronted with the following proceedings: catheter and stoma changes, alleviation of pain, changing of dressings, changing of bedspread, emptying the catheter bag, changing of the sleeping position, eliminating excretions and giving consolation and changing the infusion bottle. All has to be documented. It happens of course that a patient suffers a sudden heart attack or dies. Not to rattle and intimidate others, such occurrences are handled discreetly and fast. From other stations enforcement is ordered and the doctor on duty is called to take care of the patient. In the extreme case of death it will be certified by a doctor.

I always had problems with the timely exchange of my catheter. To relieve the staff I took over the regular exchange of the one way catheter 7 times a day. That went on like this until my release when I got a permanent one that had to be changed all 4 weeks. Day and night I had to change my sleeping position, but I could do it only with assistance. Under these circumstances my sleep was always interrupted. At this time I got the message of the death of my brother. With all this stress I could finally leave the bed and start my delayed training to be transferred to the wheelchair by means of a lifter and later with a sliding board. After followed training with special appliances and group exercises. Finally I had won my relative freedom. The auxiliary who was in charge of dexterity aptitude games proposed to me to make an excursion into the arboretum of the university that boarded the REHAB hospital. After a long round trip on gravel ways I found a cosy corner and read to her from one of my books that amused her enormously. The weather was fine and I learned a lot about exotic trees from all over the world that survived even in our climate. I was fed up of the neon & led light in my room and was thankful to my caretaker to repeat the excursions in the arboretum as long as the fine weather lasted. I also was interested to learn how to swim again even only with arms, but the swimming hall was closed.

The job of the psychologist is to test the mental and physical ability of the patients to adapt to this new difficult situation. After having passed all the written and oral tests she asked me If I suffered from depressions I answered that I did not know what depression were. After this reply she understood what kind of solid wood I was cut of and did not molest me with questions any more. Instead she also offered me some trips to the arboretum. Then new trouble arose. My bladder system was blocked and I was taken again to the neighbouring university hospital to rinse it. After this unfortunate surprise I got problems with my stomach. It was an infection of a higher degree. I changed my diet completely and refrained from all kinds of meat products. In the evening I just ordered a bowl of mixed salad. I think my stomach had simply rejected the masses of pills and infusions I got.

A new problem arose when MRSA, a serious infection spread over the whole hospital. At the end all patients had to be isolated and visitors were not allowed any more. In this annoying situation my caretaker let me into a secret. The REHAB had been sponsored by the city and from private parts with books for a patient's library. My caretaker was responsible for it and even had positioned a shelf on wheels with a selection of books besides an elevator. Because of lack of interest from the patients she had ended this initiative and locked all books in a room where only she had access to. She handed me over the key begging me not to tell anyone about my privilege. The room was full of ordinary, world literature and theatre plays in precious bindings. From now on I was fully occupied selecting and reading books.

In the meantime my poor wife was burdened with matters concerning daily life like taking care of doctors bills and tax matters. The most difficult job was to prepare our home for my needs with an electronic bed, patient lift, wheel chairs, compatible shower room, hygienical floor, transport system to reach the cellar and our double garage. I had to discuss all matters with my wife and the craftsmen by phone to avoid misunderstandings. For my wife it was a burden. Before she had never taken interest in matters concerning correspondence with authorities, insurance companies and hospitals. I had taken care of that all my life.

Her life was turned suddenly upside down. Half a year later she retired from her job as operation nurse, but helped the Red Cross to handle the injection procedure of corona for the population in our district.

In my time in several hospitals I have met a lot of excellent nurses who with many years of experience could after an additional education easily have become a doctor. Unfortunately our inflexible system does not allow this.

Finally the time came to release me. It was winter and my wife had to take over the troublesome job as nurse. Until I got rid of my MRSA it still took some month's. I got an appliance to train passively my legs to help the blood circulation and actively to train my overburdened arms. My right leg started to swell and a hernia operation was booked for March. My physician decided to operate my hip joint to solve the problem with the protuberances. I felt like a guinea pig.

At home I got bored and thought about taking action again. For a long time I have not seen my colleagues from my Rover club. Some were present at the Retro Classica Fair at Stuttgart airport together with other clubs for English vintage cars. I wanted to participate and asked the Red Cross being an old sponsor if they could offer me an ambulance with an interested crew to get me to the fair. I could convince them and I appeared with my wheelchair in the garb of a Scotchman at the "English Corner" to the absolute perplexity of my club team. My black friend from Togo pushed me through the six halls where auto mobile treasures of the past were displayed. Dominant was Daimler Benz. A special attraction was of course the first motor carriage which the first female driver Berta Daimler used for shopping and longer excursions all alone.

The excursion was a beneficial change to my present situation where I have been locked up like a galley slave. After my planned OP was accomplished I was transferred to a REHAB. I had attracted MRSA again and bladder stone was ascertained and was successfully eliminated by endoscopic means. Again I had to stay some weeks in bed before I could use my wheelchair.

At home again I enjoyed the visits of people I have not seen for a long time and sitting outside on my rear terrace in bright sunshine. When I had an appointment I had to call a wheelchair taxi, a rather expensive matter. My wife had not the strength to bring me to my car where I could only with help getting on the passenger seat. Realistically considered I was in a much better condition than most of the other paraplegic patients I had met. There had been some famous people who had achieved something in their life while being chained to the wheelchair. The foremost was the US president Franklin D. Roosevelt, who governed four legislation periods. I must admit that he had all medical and financial resources at his disposal, but without his discipline he could not have handled the situation.

It makes me furious when I think how much money is spent on the development of nuclear and other weapons and on space programs instead to concentrate on solving medical, famine and overpopulation problems first. In my life I have met many reasonable and extraordinary people. Many of those I have not mentioned in this book, it would have been beyond the scope. Some have been killed in action in the Gulf, the Afghanistan or civil war in Mozambique. As long as I am granted to live

I will try to go on writing. Unfortunately less people take a book into their hands. How to deal with the electronic media is a paramount issue. Reading a good book gives one time to reflect, the media just creates restlessness and superficiality.

Carpe diem!

Jean Christian de Mons
Autumn 2024

Other books by the author

DIE FLUCHT ... Kindheitserinnerungen 1944-55, ISBN
9783749437900

EIIN PAPAGEI TRIFFT JESUS ISBN 9783748106982

ESTHETIQUE ... Proportio Divina ISBN 9783749437894

ON THE RUN ...Childhood memories 1944-55 ISBN
9783752874785

*DER FREQUENT TRAVELLER ... EINE MODERNE
ODYSSEE* ISBN 9783758341908

THE JOY OF LIFE ... A MODERN ODYSSEY ISBN
9783769374605